BOUN

A volume in the series

American Popular Music

Edited by Rachel Rubin and Jeffrey Melnick

BOUNCE

RAP MUSIC

AND

LOCAL IDENTITY

IN NEW ORLEANS

MATT MILLER

University of Massachusetts Press
Amherst & Boston

LC 2012003648
ISBN 978-1-55849-936-2 (paper); 935-5 (library cloth)

Designed by Jack Harrison
Set in Adobe Garamond Pro with Boycott display
Printed and bound by Thomson-Shore, Inc.

Library of Congress Cataloging-in-Publication Data
Miller, Matt, 1969–
Bounce : rap music and local identity in New Orleans / Matt Miller.
p. cm. — (American popular music)
Includes bibliographical references and index.
ISBN 978-1-55849-936-2 (pbk. : alk. paper) —
ISBN 978-1-55849-935-5 (library cloth : alk. paper)
1. Bounce (Music)—History and criticism.
2. Rap (Music)—Louisiana—New Orleans—History and criticism.
I. Title.
ML3531.M46 2012
782.42164909763'35—dc23
                              2012003648

British Library Cataloguing in Publication data are available.

To Holly, Lila, and Mia.

Contents

Illustrations

Acknowledgments

First of all, I thank my parents, James and Martha LaFollette Miller, for their support and encouragement of all of my creative endeavors, including this book. I am indebted to Allen Tullos, Tim Dowd, and Anna Grimshaw at Emory University for their help in the early stages of the project. I am also grateful to my colleagues Steve Bransford, Leah Rosenberg, and Nate Hofer for their help with the research.

My heartfelt appreciation goes out to all of my collaborators on the *Ya Heard Me* documentary film project: Stephen Thomas, Karen Thomas, Jon Spano, Sue Lamond, John and Glenda Robert, Jason Gillis, and Cristina Hernandez. I also benefited greatly from the insights and experiences of all of the individuals associated with the New Orleans rap scene who took time to talk with me or other members of the Ya Heard Me project: Jerome "DJ Jubilee" Temple, Earl Mackie, Henry Holden, Willie Puckett, Katey Red, Leroy "Cooly" Paige (R.I.P.), Big Freedia, DJ Ron, Henry "DJ Redneck" Adams (R.I.P.), DJ Silver, Cheeky Blakk, Joe Blakk, Mia X, Tim Smooth (R.I.P.), Isaac Bolden (R.I.P.), Dartanian "MC Dart" Stovall, Abdul Malik (J' Ro' J), "Captain" Charles Leach, "Slick Leo" Coakley, Darwin "Choppa" Turner, Baby Boy, Sean "Boss Hogg," Melvin Foley, "King" George & family, Big Slack, Chev off the Ave, Sissy Nobby, Vockah Redu & tha Crew, Kevin "T. Tucker" Ventry, John "Bustdown" Bickham, Ice Mike, Kilo, Shine Baby, Gotti Boi Chris, Déjà Vu, Dime Girl Drell, Ha Sizzle, Nake Niggedy, Sthaddeus "Polo Silk" Terrell, Lil Ya and Tec 9 from U.N.L.V., George "DJ Duck" Thomas, Jimi "DJ Jimi" Payton and family, "Wild" Wayne Benjamin, Roland "DJ Ro" Watson, Gregory "D" Duvernay, Lucky, 10th Ward Buck, DJ Blaq 'N' Mild, Big Al, Lil Tee, Gary Holzenfeld, Rusty Lien, Sharoni Rhea, and DJ Money Fresh.

I would also like to express my gratitude to Alison Fensterstock for her help with research and contacts and for her valuable work in the Where They At project; Aubrey Edwards, Eric Kiesewetter, and D. Lefty Parker all deserve mention for their contributions documenting rap music in New Orleans and their willingness to share their materials with me. I'm grateful to the staff and owners of *OffBeat* for allowing me access to their archives. I am indebted to Colin Meneghini, Andrew "Noz" Nosnitsky, Sean Schuster-Craig, Andy Hopkins, Daniel Green, and Ben Lawless, for their willingness to share recordings with me over the last ten years. Thanks also to Richard Campanella, Stephen Thomas, Abdul Malik, Doug Parker, and Edwin Curry for their help in the process of acquiring illustrations. I greatly appreciate the efforts of series editors Jeffrey Melnick and Rachel Rubin, and the team at University of Massachusetts Press, including Brian Halley, Mary Bellino, and Carol Betsch, for their thoughtful and diligent work on my project.

Of course, I owe a great deal of thanks to my wife, Holly, and my daughters, Mia and Lila, for their patience and support over the course of this project. Finally, I thank all who have expressed interest in and encouraged my research on bounce, and acknowledge the inspiration that I have derived from everyone involved with the New Orleans music scene, past and present.

BOUNCE

Introduction

In late July 2005 I was in New Orleans, working on the documentary film project *Ya Heard Me?* I walked in the sweltering midday heat through the French Quarter to Odyssey Records on Canal Street, where I paid $9.98 for a self-produced CD by DJ Chicken (Kenneth Williams Jr.). The compilation featured popular songs by mainstream R&B and rap artists (along with a couple of oldies) "remixxed with Dat Beat." As rapper Marvin "Dolemite" Skinner put it, "When people say that beat, they're talking about bounce music. That's what the new generation call it, that beat."[1] "That beat" is the New Orleans beat, a particular mid-tempo rhythmic feel created by a propulsive, syncopated bass drum pattern in combination with layered, continuous percussive elements such as handclaps or simple melodic lines and often featuring particular sounds sampled from other recordings. Even after the devastating hurricane that struck the city a few weeks after my visit, "dat beat" remained a touchstone of local musical identity and a beacon calling the city's dispersed population back.

The persistence of "that beat" poses questions about the role of the local in rap and other highly mediated forms of cultural production. Where does it come from, and what does it do for people? Cultural critics like Bakari Kitwana—who wrote in 2002 that "Black youth in New Orleans, Louisiana, and Champaign, Illinois . . . share similar dress styles, colloquialisms, and body language with urban kids from Los Angeles, Chicago, and New York City"—argue that the "commercialization of rap music" is simply another avenue through which the corporate-controlled media promotes its own homogenizing and commodifying agenda.[2] But this representation of mass conformity and homogeneous, national-level African American popular culture does not explain the persistence of "that beat" in New Orleans. Alongside efforts to conform to rap's aesthetic mainstream and capitalize on its potential for mass appeal, a stubbornly and self-consciously local approach runs throughout the history of rap in the city. This suggests that, in New Orleans and elsewhere, the local context—including its ethno-cultural, economic, historical, and even climatic dimensions—still exercises a considerable amount of influence on the experiences of the people who inhabit a particular locale and the cultural products that they create.

DJ Chicken's CD was only one in an ongoing series of interventions in the chain of consumption linking New Orleans audiences and the mainstream of the national music industry and market. "That beat," whether behind a local rapper or mixed in with mainstream radio hits, connects with the experiences of local audiences in the context of everyday life in the city in ways that nationally popular music usually does not. While some aspects of the New Orleans rap scene resemble their national counterparts, bounce, the participatory, dance-oriented "project music" that has been an enduring local staple since it emerged in the early 1990s, expresses a musical and lyrical perspective that is highly localized and, in many ways, continuous with earlier eras of New Orleans's musical history and culture.[3] In a city where a collective musical sensibility has been fostered through active, embodied participation in parades, parties, and nightclubs, perhaps it should come as no surprise that local musical identity can be reduced to a near-ubiquitous "beat"—after all, the city's "golden age of R&B" in the 1950s was itself defined by a driving beat that contributed important rhythmic elements to rock 'n' roll and funk.[4]

As Ned Sublette writes, "New Orleans hip-hop . . .[is] the youngest part of the New Orleans music family, but it's family," the latest manifestation of a "New Orleans sound" that lies at the heart of many of the city's best-known contributions to earlier popular music genres.[5] It is globally connected and constantly evolving and yet remains the site of an enduring cultural continuity that seems to exist on an almost unconscious level. It is neither accidental nor intentional that female rapper Cheeky Blakk's moniker echoes the name of Cheeky Black, a 1920s New Orleans pimp mentioned in Louis Armstrong's 1954 memoir.[6] Other anecdotal evidence suggests a similar level of continuity with earlier eras of popular music in New Orleans and with the local African American vernacular in general, such as the prevalence of descriptive nicknames (based on size or skin color) like "Baby," "Slim," "Lil," "Big," "Red," and "Black" in the world of New Orleans rap. The word *bounce*, which came to represent the idiosyncratic local style of rap that emerged in the early 1990s, has prior associations with New Orleans music, and it speaks to the historical prevalence of dance music in the city. A 1970 release in the Urban Blues series on Imperial Records bears the subtitle "New Orleans Bounce."

Operating within this remarkably consistent cultural particularity, African Americans in New Orleans took the idea of rap and made it their own—a syncretic process of creolization and experimentation led to the emergence of distinctive musical style and forms of identification. This local style and voice emerged from a highly contested and competitive New Orleans scene, which, while often isolated and self-referential, was also attuned to the wider world of rap music, absorbing changes in its technical and stylistic evolution and its ways of imagining the relationships between place, identity, musical style, and lyrical content. In a process that has been under way for nearly thirty years, New Orleans–based rap artists and audiences participated in the collective creation and imagination of sociocultural identity in the realms of musical style, lyrical content, and public discourse.

This study encompasses a wide-ranging exploration of the rich and complex results of the adaptation of the rap form in New Orleans. I examine the connections between rap and other forms of popular music and vernacular expressive culture in the city, both earlier and contemporaneous, as well as the relationship (in both its material and imagined aspects) between New Orleans–based artists and audiences and the rap genre and industry at the wider, national level. These investigations allow us to understand more fully the dynamic evolution of rap as a genre and cultural practice in a particular local setting. The story of New Orleans rap speaks to the transformative power of music and provides a perspective into the mentalities, values, and concerns of young African Americans in a very specific place, who were often excluded from more mainstream media venues.

In the pages that follow, I have conducted an in-depth investigation of New Orleans's rap scene, trying to remain sensitive to both its internal, ground-level politics and its intersections with national companies and markets. As Ingrid Monson writes, "detailed knowledge of musical processes is crucial in situating music within larger ideological and political contexts," and for this reason I provide a thorough, periodized analysis of the contributions of many successive waves of rappers, producers, record label owners, club and radio DJs, and audiences, all of whom helped challenge and define prevailing stylistic conventions on the local, regional, and (in a few cases) national levels.[7] I look at the idea of local musical identity from multiple perspectives, tracking shifting understandings and attempts to represent, exploit, or escape the local in rap music in New Orleans over several decades. I hope that my efforts will contribute to our understanding of popular music's relationship to place and collective memory and experience, and the complex and often contradictory processes through which it changes and evolves. The relationship between the local context and nationally or globally mediated culture industries is not only multi-directional but also sporadic, selective, and subject to change based on a multiplicity of factors.

The case of New Orleans shows that we should operate with extreme caution before assuming that conclusions about rap at the national level—concerning its musical practices and values, its stages of technological, stylistic, and thematic evolution, its relationship to wider cultural phenomena, the nature of its engagement with established music corporations, the ways in which it reflects or effects changes in mentalities and ideologies—can be scaled down and applied to a particular local context. It also shows that, at certain moments, ideas or practices drawn from the local environment can exercise a substantial influence on the genre at the national level. The local rap music culture of New Orleans has, to an important extent, penetrated into the national consciousness, contributing to the evolution of rap and showing how the local, regional, and national are intertwined in the process of creating change in popular music. The analysis and conclusions will, I hope, be useful to readers interested specifically in the history and future directions of New Orleans's cultural and musical traditions, as well as those who seek to understand the transformative and dynamic intersections of place, popular music, and identity on a more general level.

Sources and Methods

My work in this book draws on a wide range of primary and secondary sources. It builds on previous efforts in the history and criticism of rap music and in the analysis and description of New Orleans's culture and history, as well as scholarship on the relationship of music and place. Primary sources, including oral history interviews, sound recordings, and journalistic articles from inside and outside of New Orleans, have helped focus a fine-grained perspective on New Orleans rap, drawing on the experience and wisdom of rappers, producers, label owners, and rap listeners in New Orleans. Up until the mid-1990s this coverage was limited to local publications. As the local record labels No Limit and Cash Money rose to national prominence after 1996, articles about New Orleans–based artists and companies also proliferated in nationally distributed rap-oriented publications as well as in mainstream news outlets. While the presence of artists from New Orleans in the national spotlight has been reduced considerably since its peak in the late 1990s (with the important exception of

Dwayne "Lil Wayne" Carter), in the years since Hurricane Katrina local rap has been the subject of many articles in the city's leading newspaper, the *Times-Picayune,* and New Orleans rap has continued to intrigue music journalists from outside the city.

With such a wealth of material to work with, it has been important to use these sources strategically and comparatively. In each chapter, I examine cases selected for their potential to contribute to a more developed understanding of the intersection of rap music and local identity in New Orleans. When necessary, I have used general, overarching historical narrative to contextualize my "thick description" of the careers or biographies of participants, the musical and lyrical dimensions of sound recordings, and other aspects of the local scene. While my broader perspective is informed in important ways by the work of other scholars and critics, I challenge several aspects of the dominant narrative of New Orleans rap, including specific assertions about musical style and lyrical content as well as more general shortcomings related to periodization and contextualization.

The origin and perpetuation of the distinctive qualities that mark popular music in New Orleans cannot be separated from the city's historically rooted social and material realities. New Orleans's existence is itself a product of its strategic but troublesome geography, and its residents continue to be challenged by a semitropical, swampy environment. In chapter 1, I provide a basic overview of some of the events, phenomena, individuals, and groups of people that shaped the cultural and political-economic history of New Orleans, based on the understanding that the city's past informs its present in important ways. New Orleans's advantageous location, its challenging natural environment, and its nodal role in trade for a variety of commodities (including enslaved blacks) all shaped the city's economy and social geography, and, by extension, the everyday experiences of its inhabitants. The city's supremely complex demography contributed to a chaotic and dynamic process of creolization; its rich musical history unfolded within this larger synergistic process.

The perspectives and horizons of young African American New Orleanians in the rap era were influenced by the social realities of the preceding decades, many of which—segregation, for example, and, later, suburbanization, the construction of public housing on a massive scale, the "war on drugs," a declining urban industrial base and move to a service economy—perpetuated the socioeconomic and spatial marginalization of the city's black poor. But expressive cultural forms and collective celebrations have helped to mediate the psychic effects of oppression and deprivation, and the vibrant and highly musical vernacular culture of New Orleans has thrived during some of the hardest economic times. The number of "social and pleasure" clubs—parading mutual-aid societies rooted in the city's black neighborhoods—began to expand in the 1970s, a process linked to the increasing proliferation of brass bands.[8] These phenomena, along with other distinctive forms of grassroots expressive culture, influenced local rap in direct and indirect ways, contributing specific musical ideas and providing a model of self-determined cultural organization and enjoyment.

In the early years of rap, aspiring performers, producers, and entrepreneurs outside of the genre's centers of production frequently looked to New York–based pioneers for inspiration and leadership. Over time, local rap scenes and distinctive stylistic interpretations emerged as the cumulative result of these initially derivative efforts. The extent to which they were able to connect to national audiences depended in large part on their distance from the centers of rap music production. In chapter 2 I examine the formative period of rap in New Orleans, a time when it was heavily dependent on biographical, thematic, and stylistic connections with the genre's New York origins. Efforts to create rap at a local level involved the cultivation of basic competence and a slow and halting process of experimentation with musical style and content. Producers and record label owners who had established themselves in earlier genres of black popular music like soul and funk were behind the earliest rap releases in the city, but as the 1980s progressed they were joined (and, eventually, superseded) by younger participants whose careers developed and expanded along with rap generally over the next two decades. The chapter documents and analyzes the emergence of local groups, venues, and record labels during the decade of the 1980s. Their contributions set the stage for the dramatic and relatively sudden rise to dominance of a highly localized interpretation of the rap form.

In late 1991, Kevin "MC T. Tucker" Ventry (backed by Irvin "DJ Irv" Phillips) was the first artist to capture the attention of local audiences with this compelling new style of rap performance, defined by a preference for chanted refrains rather than extended lyrical narratives and the use of several core samples to form the backing music. Chapter 3 details the rise of this style, which became known as "bounce" and which achieved enormous local popularity in the early 1990s. The most promising rappers from the years preceding the emergence of bounce faded into the background, eclipsed by the runaway popularity of a new generation of artists catering to an ultra-local focus in lyrics, musical style, and artistic personae. Established producers and record label owners had less trouble changing with the times, and they generally profited from the expansion of local rap that bounce entailed, producing sales that often surpassed those of national artists. Nevertheless, the style was heavily contained within New Orleans and was seen as unlikely to spread beyond the city and its hinterlands.

Local music critics dismissed bounce as apolitical "rap-lite" with crude "sex and violence"–based lyrics meant to entertain an underclass in pursuit of pleasure and escape. But this evaluation depended on a narrow definition of politics and underestimated the extent to which bounce served as a forum for the critique of prevailing attitudes and practices both within and outside of poor and working-class black communities. The bounce heyday of 1991–1994 was marked by the decline of narrative and the rise of an exhortative, dance-focused lyrical voice, but the latter shared space with critiques of white racism (dramatically represented by David Duke's candidacy) and a repressive justice system generally. Indictments of the racism and brutality that marked local police–community relations were often framed within a broader consideration of the war on drugs and the associated militarization of law enforcement. In contrast to the explicitly political nature of these expressions, however, local rap was more often a forum for the resolution or exploration of more local or personal micropolitics, such as male–female sexual relationships or the rivalries between different neighborhoods, wards, or parts of town.

The rise of bounce energized the local rap scene in the early 1990s, but the city remained an uncharted backwater as far as national companies and audiences were concerned. The emergence of a distinctive and (on the local level, at least) profitable subgenre of rap actually seemed to increase the insularity of the New Orleans scene, although its participants stayed abreast of emerging trends and talents in the national music industry. This state of affairs conforms to a more general trend in New Orleans; as the architect and critic Stephen Verderber observed, "The civic pride based on being 'different' has unfortunately been the city's undoing, for it cuts both ways—cultural uniqueness too often impedes economic advancement."[9] But the disconnect is also attributable to other factors, including the city's remoteness from the centers of industry concentration and the shortsighted conservatism of the national record labels, which only belatedly realized that New Orleans could be a source of profit in wider markets.

Circumstances changed dramatically in the late 1990s, when New Orleans's thriving and distinctive local music subculture gave rise to a generation of more successful artists and entrepreneurs, who helped catalyze a shift in the conceptual geography of rap music on the national level. Beginning around 1995, artists and labels from southern cities, including Atlanta, Memphis, and New Orleans, rose to the level of mainstream success that had once been the exclusive province of their peers in New York or Los Angeles. Chapter 4 covers the years 1995–2000, when No Limit Records and Cash Money Records emerged from obscurity to lead the "Dirty South" takeover of rap. In ways that were distinctive to each company, they synthesized gangsta rap and the New Orleans musical style and cultural identity, becoming the two most successful independent rap labels of the late '90s.

While significant differences existed between No Limit and Cash Money with regard to musical dimensions as well as conceptual underpinnings and marketing and growth strategies, the two labels shared important features. Both secured lucrative and advantageous "pressing and distribution" deals with national companies based on their impressive sales in regional and "underground" markets. Their subsequent transition from regional to global dominance provided a highly selective infusion of wealth and fame into the local New Orleans scene, which in turn provoked changes in musical style and the imagination of wider career possibilities. Access to national companies and audiences was to a large extent monopolized by these powerful local independents. Their early success depended heavily on local artists and producers, but their connections to the New Orleans scene became progressively more tenuous as their national exposure and wealth increased.

In light of the elevated expectations created during the boom years of the late 1990s, the half-decade leading up to Katrina was marked by a series of failures, disappointments, and foreshortened possibilities with regard to the wider commercial viability of New Orleans–based artists and labels. As I show in chapter 5, the half-decade of record-breaking success represented by No Limit and Cash Money did little to change the ultimately marginal position of New Orleans rap within the national mainstream. As in previous eras and genres of popular music, the presence of abundant talent and experience was not enough to draw more than passing interest from national companies. Instead, the influence of heavy-handed intermediaries like Percy "Master P" Miller or Cash Money's Bryan and Ronald Williams declined, and the city's rap scene returned to a state of relative isolation, invisibility, and disorganization.

Few of the artists who enjoyed national exposure in the late 1990s—including Juvenile, B.G., Mystikal, and Master P—retained their position in the post-millennial period. Second-tier local record labels, their efforts hindered by an overly local sensibility and the saturation of the national market with New Orleans–based artists, were unable to recreate the success that No Limit and Cash Money had enjoyed. James "Soulja Slim"

Tapp, considered to be a promising prospect for a transition to a national career, was shot to death in the front yard of his mother's house in 2003, just as his career was taking off thanks to a high-profile collaboration with fellow New Orleanian Terius "Juvenile" Gray in the song "Slow Motion."

While New Orleans faded once more into the background of the wider rap industry, a new wave of rappers and record labels emerged to supply local audiences with the distinctive call-and-response-oriented dance music that had been a local favorite for more than a decade. Though largely ignored by local music critics and national audiences, a cohort of openly gay men labeled "sissy rappers" played an important role in the resurgence of locally oriented rap music in the years 2000–2005, and achieved wide popularity with New Orleans audiences. As with the bounce artists of the early 1990s, however, the careers of these rappers were tightly constrained within the local market.

In late August 2005, Hurricane Katrina overwhelmed New Orleans's inadequate flood control infrastructure and disaster planning in one of the most traumatic and destructive events in the city's history. Enabled by decades of neglect and a racially inflected urban geography, Katrina's devastation exposed the economic stagnation and poverty experienced by inner-city New Orleanians and drew attention to broader implications in the areas of human and civil rights. Many citizens lost property and family members, but those who were already on the margins—poor and working-class African Americans who lived in some of the lowest-lying areas of the city—bore a disproportionate share of the suffering and displacement. New Orleans's local rap scene was rooted in some of the most heavily inundated areas, and its participants experienced the full spectrum of displacement, destruction, and disruption. In my final chapter, I examine the ways in which the rap scene has been affected by the disaster, looking at how local rappers and producers in New Orleans or in the Katrina diaspora have responded to this life-changing event. In the years after the storm, many have returned to New Orleans, some dedicating themselves to political activism and others to entrepreneurial projects, while others succumbed to the pathological aspects of New Orleans life, which in many ways remain as influential as ever.

Locally oriented rap has retained its importance in New Orleans in the post-Katrina period. It continues to play an important role as an outlet for a grassroots New Orleans musical sensibility, helping to create a sense of place and belonging for young African Americans in the city and providing, to some extent, a set of modest possibilities for economic gain. New Orleans native Lil Wayne has risen to become one of the most prominent stars in hip-hop, although he is the only New Orleans–based performer to retain any success in the national market. But the disruption and loss associated with the Katrina disaster have been accompanied by an increased level of interest in documenting and promoting New Orleans rap, especially the so-called sissy rappers who gained a local following in the years before Katrina.

Music, Place, and Identity

Since the 1980s, rap music has come to play an important role in the expression of a sense of place on the part of young people, especially African Americans. While its particularities have shifted over time, the relationship between place and identity has remained an important feature of both marketability and authenticity in rap. Over its thirty years of history, the rap form has seen an expansion of the number of places accepted as authentic sites for the music's production. Decades of experimentation and local adaptation in previously marginal places like New Orleans, Memphis, and Atlanta helped fuel the emergence of these cities as dynamic and profitable nodes in the rap industry and within its regional imaginary.

While some of the most mainstream rap aspires to a sense of placelessness, in other ways the genre has increasingly depended on the proliferation of and incorporation of local music scenes for its creative sustenance. To an important extent, this diversification is the function of changing strategies within the dominant economic system; Adam Krims observes that "the present-day musical kaleidoscope [is] a phenomenon of capital," which works by "simultaneously diversifying culturally, and segregating economically and spatially."[10] Still, it would be premature to therefore dismiss or ignore the particularity and creativity of the many local hip-hop and rap scenes that have emerged in various cities in the United States and have produced enduring and influential music despite their participants' often modest means.

My discussion of New Orleans rap in this book is guided by an understanding of the relationship between music and a sense of place as dynamic and characterized by mutual influence. Sara Cohen writes that music not only "reflects social, economic, political, and material aspects of the particular place in which it is created . . . but also produces place." Music, Cohen argues, has the power "to establish, maintain, and transform social relations," and for this reason it plays an important and active role in the process of forging a sense of place.[11] On an individual and a collective level, people use live or recorded music as a "technology of identity, emotion, and memory," interacting with it in ways that involve their bodies and their emotions as well as their eardrums and rational mind.[12] Part of music's transformative power is rooted in its ability to bridge the distance between audience and performer. Charles Keil argues that "music is our last and best source of participatory consciousness," endowed with a "capacity not just to model but maybe to enact some ideal communities."[13]

In this sense, rap music in New Orleans (both before and after the Katrina disaster) has been a crucial tool of psychic survival during experiences of poverty, deprivation, and displacement, an example of what the folklorist Roger Abraham called the "ultimate and fascinating relationship between social and psychological adversity and the black cultural mechanisms that promote emotional flexibility and creativity."[14] Further, as Martin Stokes writes, "Music does not then simply provide a marker in a prestructured social space, but the means by which this space can be transformed," a power that African Americans in New Orleans have repeatedly summoned in order to transcend, at least temporarily, experiences of poverty, violence, spatial concentration, and foreshortened opportunity.[15] The phenomenon of block parties—large, outdoor gatherings in housing projects or poor neighborhoods—represents an important expression of this transformative power of music and collective, participatory, embodied experience to shape consciousness. Former college basketball star Perry McDonald, who grew up in the Desire housing project, recalled, "Those days, man, when the DJ was out in the court [the open courtyard between project buildings], it was something—today I still really don't believe it happened that way. With the camaraderie between the people in the Desire, we always figured out a way to come together to have fun. The DJ in the court was one of the ways."[16]

The type of social harmony McDonald describes represents a utopian ideal of the intersection between music, place, and identity in New Orleans, which usually produced more nuanced results. In her study of music's role in imagining community in Tanzania, the anthropologist Kelly Askew concluded that "the nation they brought into being was disjunctive, fragmented and internally contradictory," and the same adjectives could be applied to the New Orleans imaginary that rap has helped to construct over the past three decades.[17] Rap music has been a venue for challenging racism and white supremacy, but, like jazz and R&B, it has also served to focus tensions within the African American community related to music, respectability, and public space. Local rap asserts and challenges distinctions of gender, sexuality, and social class (based on income, education, heritage, or an allegiance to what Curtis Jerde labeled the city's "pervasive street and saloon ambience").[18] Within the orbit of a dynamic and fractious local cultural scene, a diverse assortment of groups, companies, individuals, and neighborhoods have vied with each other in intense and ruthless competition; their efforts contributed to a shared cultural and social perspective that is distinct within the national context.

The understanding of genres of music or local music scenes (or, for that matter, places and "imagined communities" in general) as natural, harmonious unities has constraining and limiting effects. The relationship between place, identity (on a collective or individual level), and musical style is not only constructed but also fluid, multiple, fragmentary, inconsistent, and subject to rapid change based on developments within the local context and beyond. Like other vernacular forms of expressive culture in the city, the richness and complexity of New Orleans rap emerge from processes of conflict and contestation as much as from cooperation and collaboration. The rap scene is a site of tension between the local and the extralocal with regard to lyrical themes and musical aesthetics, but it is also a site of intense competition in itself, as various actors and constituencies struggle for dominance in the local market and the possibilities of national exposure and expansion that it entails. Bounce and New Orleans rap derive much of their creative energy from the negotiation of tension between an inclusive New Orleans–based collective identity and exclusive allegiances on the neighborhood or ward level that promote divisions in the local scene and sometimes escalate into interpersonal violence.

The richness and diversity of rap in New Orleans depends on the intersection and negotiation of mass-mediated expressions with highly localized styles and perspectives. In important respects, this relationship has unfolded episodically, in ways that speak to the cultural and geographic particularity of New Orleans. The idiosyncratic and locally oriented nature of rap in the city has often frustrated the efforts of locals and outsiders alike to gain exposure in wider markets, a state of affairs that led several prominent rappers and producers to look beyond New Orleans for opportunities to expand their careers. While local audiences could provide a relatively predictable level of support, they also imposed stylistic and thematic preferences that were often understood as constraining in the wider national context. The enthusiasm of New Orleans audiences for the distinctive, dance-oriented interpretation labeled "bounce" was often framed as a provincial outlook that held back more serious rappers with mainstream potential.

The tastes and preferences of New Orleans rap audiences overlapped substantially with those of their national counterparts, and the local scene and its music were often imagined in relation to other contemporaneous rap scenes within a mediated and commercialized national/global youth subculture.[19] But New Orleanians also drew substantial inspiration from elements present in the local environment and from earlier forms of historically grounded local cultural identity. Local social geographies and expressive cultural forms provided inspiration and content; in turn, their use in rap had the potential to reinforce, elaborate, and bring up to date a sense of local cultural and social distinctiveness. The qualities that distinguished New Orleans rap as it evolved over time were not predetermined, but they were also far from random. They emerged from the dynamic relationship between a deeply rooted Afro-Caribbean sensibility and contemporary, commodified developments in musical style, practice, and technology.

Geographically and culturally, New Orleans is a liminal space connecting the U.S. mainland with the Caribbean and South America. While this has been the basis of the city's economy and development, it has also helped to perpetuate a long-standing divide between New Orleans and the U.S. mainstream; behind the benign exoticism that draws tourist trade and at times helps New Orleans musicians market themselves lies an imagined moral dystopia marked as "third world" by squalid poverty, corrupt politics, violence, and blackness. To an important extent, New Orleans's geographic distance and cultural difference from the U.S. mainstream structured the consistently problematic relationship between the local popular music economy and national companies and audiences. Like the oil industry, New Orleans's rap scene has operated in a boom-and-bust cycle driven by the combination of an abundance of raw material, an isolated location, dependence on unstable and unpredictable wider markets, and the unwillingness of outsiders to invest in lasting local infrastructure.

New Orleans's outsider status and distinctive musical practices have also enabled it to make key contributions to the wider musical culture and industry of the United States. Artists from the city have periodically infused our popular music with participatory, collective energy, creating innovations that achieved exposure and commercial success in the genres of jazz, rhythm and blues, rock 'n' roll, and funk. Similarly, bounce and New Orleans–based rap emerges from a contact zone between commercial, mainstream, centralized rap music industry and grassroots local preferences, which remain rooted in West Indian and West African values. Participants in the New Orleans rap scene have collectively established, contested, and revised a sense of place that exists at the intersection of deeply rooted vernacular music traditions and the modern, globalized economy of commercial popular music.

As home to the nation's oldest African American neighborhood (Tremé) and a number of seminal contributions to the nation's popular music culture, New Orleans seems, in many ways, to embody continuity and rootedness. Vernacular traditions like gumbo, brass bands, social and pleasure clubs, and Mardi Gras Indians can be traced back a century or more. The city's black Creole community retains a high degree of cultural pride of place and ancestry. West African and Afro-Caribbean sensibilities and ideas have remained at the heart of the city's African American expressive cultural forms, from the impromptu "second line" dancers who follow parades, to the fierce spectacle of the Mardi Gras Indians, to the practices and beliefs in small spiritualist churches. But the persistence of these African-derived cultural values in New Orleans cannot be attributed to the kind of isolation that prevailed in places like the Georgia Sea Islands; they are perpetuated and adapted within a cosmopolitan and dynamic urban environment.

Rap music in the city engaged with, responded to, and challenged the social, political, and economic realities faced by young African Americans. As in other places, themes such as relationships and sex, drugs, crime, and police–community relations were frequently aired through the medium of rap and were given their own contextual particularity. Other, more locally specific themes included the city's parade and carnival culture and the rivalries between different parts of town, as well as aspects of the local rap scene itself—its evolution and associated dances, places, and events. Explicit references to the city's carnival and parade traditions have served to construct a self-consciously historical sense of the local in rap, but the influence of New Orleans's expressive cultural forms and historically rooted traditions is not limited to the use of specific musical devices or lyrical themes; it also resonates along more general levels of conceptualization and experience.

Like other local popular and vernacular music forms, New Orleans rap draws on and contributes to the collective memory of the city's black residents. The approach to making and consuming rap music in New Orleans was informed by prior ideas about collective enjoyment, expressive culture, and public space in the local context. The continuity that exists between rap and earlier genres of African American popular music rests on more than a common reliance on certain core musical ideas. It also depends on the persistence of geospatial and economic realities that contributed to a distant and intermittent relationship between artists and companies in New Orleans and audiences in the centers of music industry power. Like jazz, R&B, and funk, the business of New Orleans rap was hindered by the city's geographic remoteness, which has continued to discourage national music companies from establishing branch offices in the city.

The evolution of rap in New Orleans was also shaped by the city's particular political-economic realities. The intensive, small-scale entrepreneurial activity around rap since the 1980s speaks to the economic realities of contemporary black New Orleanians, who have often depended on such endeavors to survive in a local economy in which steady, well-compensated employment is increasingly a rare commodity. Rap music played an important role in defining place-based identity on the level of neighborhood or housing project within New Orleans, forms of identification that often fueled intensely felt rivalries. In its content and in the biographies of its participants, it also engaged with the lethal interpersonal violence that has flourished in the city's housing projects and poor neighborhoods.

Katrina

Hurricane Katrina and its aftermath changed every aspect of life in New Orleans, including the city's rap music scene. Rap music, as an established but still evolving contemporary genre that served as the primary musical frame of reference for African American youth in the city, was one of the most important arenas for the development of distinctive and influential New Orleans–based innovations in popular music.

For civic leaders, the fact that Katrina flushed out the city's poverty-stricken underclass was cause for celebration, but along with the problematic aspects of concentrated urban poverty in New Orleans, the storm also laid waste to a highly productive social nucleus that animated New Orleans popular music from jazz to rap. What was most critically endangered by Katrina was not the rich musical and cultural history of New Orleans but rather the future possibilities that it represents. Framing the destruction of New Orleans as the loss of a place particularly rich in cultural and musical *history* was more easily achieved than an understanding of the city as a vital, self-renewing, and ongoing site of innovation. The endangered New Orleans culture and population was represented by iconic individuals and couched in the familiar terms of jazz music, Creole cuisine, and picturesque architecture. Few observers recognized that the city's highly esteemed contributions to older genres like jazz and R&B were products of an ongoing cultural process that continues into the present day, in which New Orleans's poor neighborhoods and housing projects have continued their role as, in the words of the photojournalist Michael Smith, a "cultural 'wetlands' for much of the traditional music and folklife which has made

New Orleans famous the world over."[20] Like New Orleans jazz or R&B, the genius of local rap relates to its contagious enthusiasm, expressed through collective and participatory structures. Local audiences supported the emergence of a rapidly changing array of artists and companies, in which women and gay rappers were represented in greater numbers than in the national rap industry.

The storm's effects were complex and continue to unfold, but it seems increasingly unlikely that rap in New Orleans will die out or become less distinctive and self-consciously local. Bounce or similarly distinctive locally oriented rap will play a central role in this process. Bounce is one of the channels through which community is forged "on the ground" in New Orleans, a site for the imagination of collective identity that is more real and complex than (and yet in dialogue with) mass-marketed music and the forms of identification that comes with it. An awareness of the potential role that rap music and culture can play in the reconstruction of damaged communities in New Orleans requires an understanding of the ways in which these forces operated in the city pre-Katrina and their intersection with other vernacular cultural forms. Based on this model, we can infer that rap's contributions will be multivalent, complex, incremental, and contradictory rather than unified, organized, and coherent. We should recognize the importance of everyday practices and experiences in restoring the sense of place in New Orleans's black communities. To a greater extent than Lil Wayne or Juvenile, the teenagers and young adults who make up the audiences at nightclubs and community centers and dance at outdoor block parties hold the future of New Orleans rap—and by extension its future within the field of popular music—in their hands.

1

African American Life and Culture in New Orleans

From Congo Square to Katrina and Beyond

As a European colony, New Orleans was always liminal and problematic. The city's geographic position, connecting the vast North American interior to the Gulf of Mexico and the Caribbean, held out tantalizing possibilities with regard to the dominance of trade and territory, but its remoteness, semitropical climate, and the related difficulty of social control presented daunting challenges. Slavery and colonization had devastating results for Africans and Native Americans, but members of these groups also exploited the weaknesses of colonial powers and the fluidity of boundaries that was possible under French and Spanish rule, by rebelling and escaping, by attempting to secure their freedom legally through military service or self-purchase, or by forging or acceding to various kinds of relationships (including sexual ones) with whites.

Though structured by the prevailing power relations, contact and exchange within the wider Caribbean sphere informed a process of "cultural creolization," which the folklorist Nicholas Spitzer describes as "the development of new traditions, aesthetics, and group identities out of combinations of formerly separate peoples and cultures—usually where at least one has been deterritorialized by emigration, enslavement, or exile."[1] Cultural practices—syncretic, creolized forms based on the dynamic reorganization (according to stylistic sensibilities rooted in West Africa and the Caribbean) of ideas and technologies present in the local environment—were central to African Americans' ability to create independent psychic and social spaces within the New Orleans context. Musical expression existed in a mutually influential relationship with black efforts in the political and economic realms, communicating autonomy, inviting participation, claiming public space, and ultimately challenging the dominant ideology of white supremacy.

Nevertheless, the political transfer of Louisiana to the United States introduced profound and disruptive changes to the society, culture, and urban geography of New Orleans. With the Louisiana Purchase, New Orleans began its transition from a far-flung outpost of the French and Spanish empires to the United States' most important southern port and the critical nexus point enabling the spread of African slavery westward into newly acquired territories. In the nineteenth century, New Orleans embodied a paradoxical mixture. Its political and cultural heritage, its economic and geographical identity as a port city, and the presence of large numbers of Irish and Italian immigrants all served to differentiate the city from the rest of the U.S. South. But New Orleans was a central hub of the slave trade, tied in to the sugar and cotton industries as well as to the westward expansion of slavery, and the city's social and economic life was structured by the "peculiar institution" and the system of racial classification on which it rested. The end of slavery marked the dawn of a new era of white resistance, in which legal means and extralegal terrorism were employed to enforce segregation and the subordinate status of blacks.

Before the Civil War, New Orleans became a hub of the slave system; after abolition, it was a magnet for English-speaking blacks from surrounding rural areas, who brought religious, linguistic, and cultural values that were distinct from the city's "creole," urban, Franco-African counterparts. "American" blacks and black Creoles were respectively concentrated above and below Canal Street. Despite their differences, both groups resisted the oppressive efforts of whites, using legal means (such as those that resulted in the landmark *Plessy v. Ferguson* case, which established "separate but equal" as the law of the land) or expressing their anger through violent outbursts, as in the case of the black militant Robert Charles. But even as New Orleans seemed to be coming apart at the seams, a dynamic and compelling new form of music-making (eventually labeled "jazz") arose from the city's vernacular spaces in response to the demands of working-class black audiences and habitués of the "sporting life."

Jazz embodied all the complexity and contradictions of New Orleans during this period. Home to both expressions of refined sophistication and gut-bucket rural blues, the city enabled the fusion of several distinct strains of black musical experience into what was identified early on as one of the most important American contributions to the world of music. The particular conditions that allowed jazz to emerge from New Orleans—the mixture of urban and rural, West African, French, Anglo-American, and West Indian, the celebration of carnival and the related importance of public and participatory musical events rooted in a lively street and saloon culture and its "ratty" preferences—remained vibrant and contributed to important developments in the city's musical culture and history in the twentieth century.

The blending of rural Protestant African American culture and traditions with those of the city's black Creoles was a key feature of the "uniquely fertile social climate" that enabled the emergence of jazz.[2] As this synthesis was coming to fruition in the decades between 1890 and 1910, however, segregation was solidifying its hold in New Orleans and across the South. During this period, black New Orleanians lost the right to vote and were slowly deprived of almost all access to public education. As they relegated blacks to second-class citizenship and inferior "Jim Crow" accommodations and services, whites attempted (with some success) to erase prior divisions of class and status among African Americans. Even after the abandonment of de jure segregation, New Orleans remained a city of stark racial and social divisions, as poor and working-class blacks were increasingly isolated within low-lying areas made up of reclaimed swampland.

Expressive culture, including music, was a crucial dimension of African Americans' psychic survival under these conditions. The city supported a rich array of grassroots musical practices, which included religious and secular forms and reflected the diversity of backgrounds, social class, and musical taste of the city's growing African American population. The city's African American parade and carnival traditions drew on and helped to perpetuate a collective musical sensibility as well as a more general sense of cultural autonomy and enjoyment. These features allowed New Orleans to make essential contributions to the development of several important commercial genres within U.S. popular music, including jazz, R&B, rock 'n' roll, soul, and funk. The city's distance from the centers of music industry power, however, along with its cultural and social distinctiveness, worked against the establishment of any lasting presence of national music companies in the city.

New Orleans–based artists and companies were not only challenged by their geo-cultural marginality, but they also grappled with a variety of local or regional social and political problems. Even after the dismantling of legally sanctioned segregation, blacks in New Orleans faced racism and neglect in the areas of education, employment, housing, and the judicial system. As the analysis in this chapter shows, these wider social forces influenced the local musical and cultural environment in complex and contradictory ways. While New Orleans remained a "cultural wetlands" of music and expressive culture, the experience of many African Americans in the city in the years leading up to Hurricane Katrina was defined by poverty, reduced opportunity, and high levels of violence.[3]

The evolution of a local rap scene and style is a process that has interacted dynamically with the wider social and cultural forces detailed above, the roots of which extend back to the city's colonial period. While rap represented, in many ways, a dramatic break with earlier genres of popular music along the lines of instrumentation, composition, production, narrative voice, and imagery, it also embodied strong continuities with prior commercial and vernacular music styles within the African American tradition. This laid the groundwork for an early, enthusiastic, and participatory embrace of rap on the part of young blacks (and a few older folks) in New Orleans.

If these elements added some sense of stability, or at least inevitability, to the processes at work in the local rap music scene, other factors—including technologically enabled suburbanization, the concentration of black poverty in the city, and a declining industrial base—had the opposite effect. While the local economy, civic institutions, and spatial organization of the city's population had undergone radical shifts in the second half of the twentieth century, one thing had not changed: black New Orleanians were at the bottom of the heap, even as the cultural forms that originated in poor and working-class black neighborhoods were increasingly celebrated and globally disseminated. In important ways, this contradiction structured the ways that participants imagined the possibilities and limitations of the rap era.

As the twentieth century came to a close, New Orleans saw the growth of concentrated black poverty, especially in the city's numerous public housing complexes. Many of these "projects" suffered from a combination of remote location, inhuman scale, crime, and neglect. Along with decreased educational and economic opportunities, these conditions helped usher in an era of spiraling homicide rates in the city, which, toward the end of the century, gained notoriety as the nation's "murder capital." New Orleans's rap scene emerged within a context of mounting challenges that strained the fabric of family and community life. When Hurricane Katrina hit the Gulf Coast in 2005, the city's preexisting social and economic problems set the stage for devastating consequences, as New Orleans's poorest residents bore the brunt of the storm's effects.

Colonial New Orleans

The contemporary African American culture of New Orleans bears a strong imprint from the city's colonial past, when lower Louisiana was the site of what the historian Gwendolyn Midlo Hall labels "the most Africanized slave culture in the United States."[4] White colonists depended on enslaved Africans to grow crops, clear land, and build urban infrastructure, and the early groups of slaves brought to the colony often shared a common cultural and linguistic background.[5] Colonial Louisiana represents a prime example of the ways in which, for Africans, the oppression and violence of slavery could exist simultaneously with a high degree of cultural cohesion, mutual intelligibility, and mutual aid.

While French authorities sometimes used armed blacks to fight hostile Native Americans, a shared opposition to white dominance and forced labor regimes often spurred resistance, cooperation, and solidarity between the two groups. The 1729 Natchez Rebellion, in which Native Americans and their black allies killed over two hundred French settlers, dampened the enthusiasm of the colonizers. The importation of slaves slowed to a trickle, and the French retreated from their strategy of growth and expansion to one of basic and limited occupation. This isolation of the colony further contributed to the development of a relatively stable Afro-Creole culture, which organized diverse influences according to a West African grammar.

Music was a central dimension of the expression and evolution of this Afro-Creole sensibility. New Orleans, Curtis Jerde writes, "served as the site of some of the earliest and most extensive Afro-American music development of any urban community in the nation."[6] This was a complex and multilayered process that occurred at various levels of formal organization. It drew on the world of antebellum African American folk music, which included secular forms such as work songs, field hollers, and street criers, as well as sacred music, including spirituals and "ring-shout" religious services in which collective movement and call-and-response fostered a participatory, communal ethos.

The establishment and perpetuation of a localized African American folk musical culture relied on highly diffused and small-scale practices as well as larger and more organized events. One of the best known of these venues was Congo Square, a large open field at the edge of town (located off of what would become Rampart Street) where slaves and free blacks would congregate on Sundays. Congo Square (known under French rule as Place Congo) was one of several public markets in the city where slaves were allowed to sell their own produce, socialize, and engage in a variety of cultural practices, including music and dance. These markets served as a gathering place for slaves and free blacks from within New Orleans as well as those who had come from more remote areas of the city's rural hinterland.[7]

One of the most striking features of Congo Square—to both modern researchers and contemporaneous observers—is the regular presence of "neo-African drumming" and dancing performed by blacks (grouped according to their tribal affiliation and including recently arrived Africans and West Indians alongside the native-born) until the mid-1800s, despite such practices having been "effectively outlawed" in other parts of the United States.[8] With regard to music and dance, Congo Square and similar spaces served as important venues for the perpetuation and transmission of African-derived cultural values and practices. Ben Sandmel provides an inventory:

> Polyrhythm: the simultaneous use of several different, yet related rhythms, unified by a dominant rhythm known as the time line; syncopation; improvisation: the spontaneous creation of lyrics and/or instrumental parts; call-and-response: an interactive dialogue between a leader and a group of vocalists and/or instrumentalists; emotional intensity; the use of the human voice as a solo instrument, rather than to simply tell a story with lyrics; and the use of bent, slurred, or deliberately-distorted notes.[9]

Slaves and free people of color maintained familiarity with African-originated instruments, such as the banjo and a vast range of percussion instruments, examples of which were sketched and described by the architect Benjamin Latrobe after a visit to Congo Square in the early nineteenth century. Instruments derived from the European tradition included guitar, harmonica, and fiddle, among others.[10]

As a symbol of the continuation of African-derived cultural practices in the United States, Congo Square has accrued a level of significance that may be out of proportion to its actual historical role (to the extent that this can be quantified) within the diverse and multilayered evolution of African American vernacular music in New Orleans. Nevertheless, scholars generally agree on the historical importance of the Sunday gatherings off of Rampart Street and other analogous events, where collective, autonomous practices perpetuated a West African–derived sensibility and contributed to the formation of a distinctive local culture. In Congo Square and places like it, blacks perpetuated expressive cultural forms and styles with clear West African roots, but over time they also absorbed or adapted ideas and technologies from European and other cultures. The cross-cultural contact and exchange in early New Orleans went in multiple directions; Congo Square gave fascinated white observers a window into a world of distinct cultural values and practices.

Louisiana passed to Spanish governance during the last three decades of the eighteenth century, before briefly returning to the French prior to its purchase by the United States. The numbers of Louisiana-born blacks who achieved their freedom under the Spanish were augmented by Caribbean immigrants who arrived before, during, and after the assumption of control by the United States in 1803. They included those fleeing the turmoil of the revolution in Saint-Domingue (later Haiti), which began in the 1790s, as well as Cuban émigrés.[11] Cultural affinity and a more liberal policy than in the Anglo-American seaboard states regarding free black immigration made Louisiana a frequent destination for these refugees.

Under French and Spanish political control and cultural influence, the colony had developed a "three-tiered, multiracial social [structure] in which a class of marginal status and frequently mixed origin was inserted between blacks and whites."[12] In French Louisiana, this took the form of the "creole," which, Hall writes, "referred to locally born people of at least partial African descent, slave and free, and was used to distinguish American-born slaves from African-born slaves when they were listed on slave inventories."[13] As Spitzer observes, the term is currently used "in a variety of ways as an ethnic designation in many Caribbean societies where cultural elements of mostly African and Mediterranean origins persist in new arrangements and densities." The term also took on a more general meaning "associated with populations of mixed ancestry in the slave trade and plantation sphere of West Africa and the New World."[14]

The Louisiana Purchase and Americanization

During the years of French and Spanish rule, New Orleans had evolved from a remote and sparsely populated colonial outpost to a large and prosperous port. This transformation was replete with economic, political, and environmental challenges. But the city "never had to deal with anything like the numbers, assertiveness, determination, or sheer foreignness represented by the American invasion" initiated in the early years of the nineteenth century, when the Louisiana Purchase (1803) brought New Orleans into an expanding United States.[15] The change involved much more than a mere administrative transfer; basic linguistic and religious differences were tied into a wider clash of ideologies regarding the regulation of social, cultural, spatial, and sexual/biological contact between different groups of people.

A defining element of the "sheer foreignness" of the new American regime was the Anglo-Protestant racial ideology, which was much narrower and less nuanced than its analogue in colonial endeavors initiated by the French, Spanish, or Portuguese. When white Americans began their political takeover of New Orleans in the first decades of the nineteenth century, they were made to feel "extremely nervous" by the presence of "large numbers of free people of color, some bearing arms and most consorting intimately with slaves, who themselves appeared to enjoy a freedom of movement and action unprecedented in the rest of the South."[16] The treaty ceding Louisiana to the United States had guaranteed the political and civil rights of free blacks, but American authorities soon took steps to curb the latitude they enjoyed under French and Spanish rule.

With a comparatively high level of education and economic achievement, free blacks in eighteenth-century Louisiana nurtured higher expectations of civic inclusion than their Anglo-American equivalents. Further, Louisiana was the only state in which blacks were not barred from militia duty.[17] The new American authorities, like their French predecessors, could not entirely eliminate the need for black soldiers in military endeavors such as the War of 1812.[18] For these reasons, among others, the process of bringing New Orleans into line with the prevailing American racial ideology was a slow and tortuous one lasting more than a century.

As a result of cultural and political tensions between French-speaking Creoles, both black and white, and newly arriving Americans, the city was divided into three municipalities, creating separate political and civic control structures for "American" and "French" sections, which were separated by the boundary of Canal Street. The so-called American side, known as "Uptown," was located southwest of Canal Street and included neighborhoods such as the Garden District, the rough "Irish Channel" near the river (named for the large numbers of Irish immigrants who arrived in the 1830s), and the Audubon Park area, among others. Blacks, whites, and people of mixed race who had a predominantly Franco-American cultural orientation congregated in "Downtown," to the northeast of Canal, which included the French Quarter as well as historic Creole neighborhoods like Faubourg Tremé and the Seventh Ward.[19]

The wider cultural differences that structured the city's politics and ethnic geography after Americanization extended to all levels of society in New Orleans, and resulted in the emergence and persistence of two distinct African American social groupings.[20] On one hand, descendents of pre-1803 black inhabitants, along with most of the newer West Indian arrivals, formed a group "commonly called Creoles, or black Creoles, but more accurately called Franco-African, a French-speaking Catholic group who lived mostly in downtown New Orleans, i.e. the area of the city down-river from Canal Street."[21] Built in the 1830s, the Faubourg Tremé (now called simply Tremé) neighborhood was adjacent to Congo Square

and formed a hub of Afro-Creole culture and progressive social organization. For the most part, blacks from an English-speaking, Protestant background—Anglo-Africans or "American" blacks—lived across Canal Street,
in the less desirable "back-of-town" parts of the Uptown area. Each of
these communities had their own cultural traditions, including distinctive
musical practices, and the catalytic nature of their interaction is central to
the emergence and development of jazz in the late nineteenth and early
twentieth centuries.

Miscegenation was "pervasive" in nineteenth-century New Orleans, and
both black and white populations were crosscut by fluid and proliferating
divisions of status and social classification.[22] By the time of the Civil War,
the number of free people of color in New Orleans "had grown to nearly
19,000, far and away the largest concentration in the Deep South."[23] The
situation was complicated by changes in both black and white populations. English-speaking black migrants from the surrounding Mississippi
Delta region, French-speaking refugees fleeing the Haitian Revolution,
substantial Irish immigration in the 1830s, and Sicilian immigration in
the 1870s all added layers of complexity to the mixture of race, class, reli-
gion, language, and national origin in New Orleans. With the expansion
of the United States into new territories after the 1848 Mexican War, the
city became the "gateway to the West" through which the slave system
expanded into the newly conquered territory.[24] Sectional tensions and the
ever-present fear of slave rebellion contributed to a worsening racial situation in the city as the Civil War loomed on the horizon.

New Orleans and the Civil War

Louisiana seceded from the United States in 1861, and the majority of
the state's white residents (and even a few free blacks) enthusiastically embraced the Confederate cause.[25] Rebel naval forces failed to adequately
defend New Orleans, however, and in the first year of the war the city
surrendered peacefully to the federal fleet under the command of Admiral
David Farragut, remaining occupied by federal forces under Major General Benjamin Butler until 1865. After the war, whites used every means
at their disposal to resist changes in the racial order. A deadly attack by a
white mob on black and white participants in and supporters of a constitutional convention at the Mechanics' Institute in 1866 put New Orleans at
the center of the national debate around postwar policy in the South. The
riot was the subject of congressional hearings and spurred legislative action
in the form of the Reconstruction Acts and the Fifteenth Amendment.

New Orleans again became a city occupied by federal troops; whether this was perceived as an intrusive or necessary intervention depended largely on one's position in the racial hierarchy.

With the political power of the former Confederates temporarily restrained by the Federal occupation, New Orleans settled into a period of relative calm. Whites and blacks came to terms with the new political reality with varying degrees of resentment, resistance, resignation, apathy, or enthusiasm. Inconsistency was the order of the day as far as race relations were concerned.[26] The "redemption" of the city by former Confederates after 1877 was still limited in its success at reducing blacks to a uniformly abject position.[27] The rights that free people of color had enjoyed in previous eras and the city's diverse mixture of cultural, ethnic, and class backgrounds contributed to "the inherent indeterminacy of racial classifications" in New Orleans and worked against its assimilation to the rigidly dichotomous American racial order, which the city's black residents often resisted in sophisticated and strategic ways.[28]

Even after the Civil War, important cultural and religious differences persisted between the downtown Franco-Africans and the uptown Anglo-Africans, although contact between the two groups was pervasive. As the nineteenth century came to a close, the two groups were increasingly united in their opposition to attempts to segregate the population on the basis of skin color. Black Creoles' traditions of education, civic and military participation, and cultural autonomy put them at the forefront of efforts to resist segregation and second-class citizenship. Despite their efforts, the last decade of the nineteenth century and the first decade of the twentieth saw the disenfranchisement of blacks and their almost complete exclusion from access to public education, as European Americans set aside sectional differences and embraced the cause of white supremacy.

In spite of its problems, New Orleans retained its status as the South's largest urban center and remained a beacon for blacks from all over the Mississippi River valley. Emancipated slaves flowed into the city from the rural hinterland of the Mississippi Delta, contributing to the city's growing population and, for the most part, joining the ranks of English-speaking American blacks living in the Uptown section.[29] The cultural and social orientation of these rural migrants differed from that of the more cosmopolitan black Creoles, as did their musical sensibility, although both groups were equally diverse in terms of their inclusion of a wide range of social class and occupational status.[30]

The Emergence of Jazz

In the last decades of the nineteenth century, New Orleans was the site of a wide variety of musical practices and styles. Educated, middle-class blacks and members of the city's white elite often shared an appreciation for high culture in the European mold. The evolving forms of band music—drawing on both the rural string band tradition as well as military marches—were more widely popular, and formed the kernel from which jazz developed.[31] Creole musicians were often able to read music, but the recent arrivals from Delta plantations brought with them an ear-playing style based on the ability to "rag" a tune—that is, to embellish a familiar melody.[32]

The emergence of jazz as a distinct genre was a self-reinforcing process that involved the transformation of playing style and repertoire through the use of African-derived "rhythmic and tonal alterations," including "'dirty' blues sounds—bent notes, growls, and smears—and a 'hoarse and crying' tone." As the new style took hold, new ways of organizing musical performance evolved, with written scores replaced by a reliance on "improvisation, called 'head music' or 'ratty' music, with the first cornetist playing the melody straight and the second, the 'hot man,' polyphonically adding embellishments or harmony parts."[33] The change in style both depended on and encouraged the formation of "new kinds of brass bands—'ratty' or 'barrelhouse' bands—that played entirely by ear."[34]

Not only did jazz bring together several distinct but essentially compatible and complementary cultural traditions, it also evolved in diverse contexts and at many different levels of scale. The "street and saloon" culture of the city included bars, brothels, and dance halls that flourished in Storyville, the legally sanctioned "sporting district" between the years 1897 and 1917.[35] While Storyville had its share of high-end establishments where patrons were entertained by accomplished "professors" such as Tony Jackson or Jelly Roll Morton, the district was also home to many smaller and rougher venues, which provided work for musicians of various levels of skill and sophistication.[36] Other opportunities came in the form of more respectable events such as weddings, formal dances, and the like. Street parades and concerts at large outdoor spaces like Lincoln Park (a privately owned enterprise where black crowds could enjoy a variety of amusements, ranging from musical performances to hot air balloon launchings) enabled the exposure of these bands' music to wide segments of the city's population.[37]

In the jazz era, the common practice of hauling wagon-based bands through the city to advertise upcoming appearances or other events created an opportunity for celebratory, rowdy public expression. The fiercely competitive nature of the New Orleans vernacular music scene found one of its most charged and confrontational expressions when two of these outfits met in the street.[38] In these settings, musicians not only played out their own sense of professional and stylistic competition but also mediated and focused the rivalries between different neighborhoods or parts of town, especially when they moved through urban space in the context of public, mobile performances.

It was in circumstances like these that Buddy Bolden, a black working-class cornetist and bandleader from the Uptown area, developed the composition and performance techniques that would earn him the sobriquet "the first man of jazz." Many of the concrete details of Bolden's biography remain unclear, and his historical legacy is colored by speculation and mythmaking. The specific features of his musical contributions are also unknown, as he never recorded his seminal strain of "hot," improvisation-oriented cornet playing. From the recollections of his contemporaries, however, Bolden was obviously a central figure in the New Orleans music world of the time, an artist who embodied the revolutionary creativity and exuberance of jazz by tailoring his compositions to the tastes of New Orleans's black working-class audiences.

The particular circumstances under which jazz emerged in New Orleans involved a volatile cultural politics that often played out across racial and class lines, as well as the Uptown/Downtown division of the city. While record sales and concert tours spoke to the music's widespread popularity, jazz was also seen as a potent cultural threat in these early years, precisely because its boundary-breaking experiments threatened the dominant social and aesthetic order.[39] As Bruce Boyd Raeburn writes, New Orleans's newspaper of record, the *Times-Picayune*, "did not reverse its [negative] editorial attitude towards jazz until 1961, making it truly the very last to recognize what has since come to be widely regarded as the city's most important contribution to world culture."[40] Whites were not the only ones to express distaste for the rowdy music and the demographic it served; many black Creole musicians also reacted negatively to the increasingly popular jazz style.[41] Tensions around musical style and practice tied in to a more generalized prejudice (with prominent racial overtones) against the poorer, English-speaking blacks.[42]

Buddy Bolden's importance is indisputable, but other early bandleaders like Chris Kelly and John Robichaux also contributed to the new art form that was taking shape. And, while Bolden's music was principally oriented to the tastes of working-class, "American" blacks, this was not the only demographic sector that was involved in the creation of early jazz. As

Raeburn observes, "the prevalence of music in the streets . . . meant that musical innovations coming out of the African American community were available to everyone within earshot," regardless of their race or ethnicity.[43] The first few decades of the twentieth century saw participation by artists from the city's black Creole community, including Sidney Bechet and Jelly Roll Morton, as well as white players such as Nick La Rocca and his Original Dixieland Jass Band, who in 1917 were the first group to record the style. New Orleans's location at the end of a vast river network helped jazz spread to other parts of the country. Steamboats carried musicians and musical style to river towns like St. Louis, Kansas City, and Chicago. New York and Los Angeles, already central in the emerging national popular music industry, were also natural destinations for these traveling groups.[44]

Early on, there were many opportunities for the music to spread beyond the limits of the uptown black milieu in which it had taken shape. The music was adopted by different groups in order of their proximity to the uptown blacks on the social hierarchy; black Creoles and whites from marginal groups such as Italians and Jews contributed greatly to the early generations of musicians who developed the style in New Orleans. In ways that resembled the city generally, jazz represented a tense intersection of the cosmopolitan and the rural, the sacred and the secular, the West African and western European, the "creole" and the "American."[45] The emerging musical sensibility relied on the relatively fluid and complex nature of the city's social culture in terms of race, space, and class.[46]

The city's most famous jazz player, cornetist Louis Armstrong, was the product of a marriage that crossed the Creole–American divide.[47] Born in the rough back-of-town area of uptown New Orleans, Armstrong grew up surrounded by a variety of vernacular musical influences, from rag-and-bone men who advertised their services by playing on tin novelty horns to the many established brass bands—among them the Onward, the Excelsior, and Frankie Dusen's Eagle Band—that performed around the city.[48] Armstrong soon began his career as a professional musician by playing the blues for prostitutes, gamblers, and other habitués of the dives and honky-tonks (illegal gambling establishments) that incubated the city's lowdown culture.[49] The ideas and techniques learned during these experiences served Armstrong well as he graduated to playing aboard touring riverboats that plied the waters of the Mississippi. His mentor Joe Oliver convinced him to relocate to Chicago, setting the stage for Armstrong's rise to the status of a nationally beloved musical celebrity.

While the individual soloist would become the norm in later decades, in its New Orleans period jazz was largely defined by collective improvisation and polyphony. This style reflected more than a simple lack of discipline or unbridled enthusiasm; it articulated a particular philosophy regarding the importance of spontaneity and the bridging of the artist/audience divide.[50] Recording technology and the growth of the commercial music industry facilitated the adoption and transformation of the genre by musicians from other places, and this fact in combination with the steady exodus of African American musicians from New Orleans contributed to the increasing marginalization of the city as jazz moved into a more commercialized form in the late 1920s and '30s. While New Orleans's prominence in the jazz world had plummeted by the '30s, the cultural resources that inspired and informed many of the musical ideas and performance practices of jazz—street parades, carnival societies, brass bands, "saloon culture" and the "sporting life," street vendors' cries and music, blues and other plantation-based musical traditions brought to the city by rural migrants, and a tradition of musical instruction amongst the Creoles—persisted, serving as a self-renewing resource for future generations of audiences and music makers.

New Orleans's Black Carnival Culture

As in other places in the circum-Caribbean, such as Cuba, Brazil, and Trinidad, West Africans and their descendants enthusiastically embraced the pre-Lenten carnival in New Orleans. Despite a variety of efforts by white elites to maintain control over the celebration, its appropriation by blacks was inevitable; their efforts expressed and perpetuated the pervasive influence of West African–based cultural practices and attitudes in the city. Not only did blacks take advantage of the "world upside-down" spirit of carnival to engage in symbolic acts of resistance and rebellion against the dominant order, they also adapted the celebration to their own pleasurable ends, using the European holiday as a starting point for creative expression and the claiming of public space. Music—public, loud, and enthusiastically supported by a lively, participating audience—was a crucial component of both of these impulses.

In 1910 working-class blacks formed the Zulus, now New Orleans's oldest formal black carnival organization. The group appropriated imagery of African primitivism (minstrel-style makeup, grass skirts, coconuts, characters such as "Witch Doctor" and "King") to mock white notions of black "savagery" and inferiority and also to provide ironic commentary on the spectacles presented by elite white "krewes" such as Comus and Rex.[51] But these veiled messages were usually lost on white observers, for whom the Zulus comically confirmed the otherness of both African Americans and

Africans. White civic leaders came to see the Zulu parade as an important part of the tourist-friendly spectacle of Mardi Gras; their support for its continuation often caused consternation among middle-class and educated blacks who considered the parades to be an exercise in self-degradation.

African Americans in New Orleans have initiated a variety of other kinds of carnival societies and practices that further testify to the creative dynamism of diasporic culture as it has historically existed in the city. A prime example of this grassroots activity around carnival is the emergence of the so-called Mardi Gras Indians in the late nineteenth century, probably inspired by the touring Wild West shows of the period. The Indian maskers are working-class blacks organized along neighborhood and family lines who parade during carnival season dressed in riotously colorful feathered costumes with intricately beaded elements, including panels that frequently depict the vanquishing of whites by Native American warriors. While the costumes have evolved over the years, becoming larger and more elaborate, they have consistently represented a stereotyped "Plains Indian" look seen through the prism of an Afro-diasporic visual sensibility. During carnival and also on St. Joseph's Day (March 19—a holiday appropriated from the city's Italian immigrants) and Super Sunday (the Sunday closest to St. Joseph's Day), groups of Indians gather at sites within the city's black neighborhoods, walk the streets, and engage in confrontational encounters with one another.[52]

In addition to spectacular visual displays, the Mardi Gras Indians' practices include important musical dimensions, which draw heavily on African-derived concepts and techniques.[53] Their music, typically rehearsed in neighborhood taverns, consists of group-based call-and-response accompanied primarily by tambourines or improvised percussion instruments such as glass bottles, cookware, or scrap metal. Their music received wide exposure in the 1970s, when several individuals and groups involved with the Mardi Gras Indians released albums documenting the distinctive music of this subculture, and the appreciation and documentation of "Indian" culture in general has increased dramatically since that time.

The percussive music of the Mardi Gras Indians, with its privileging of chanted call-and-response phrases in distinct melodic patterns, has exercised a significant influence in popular music from New Orleans since at least the 1960s.[54] Direct musical appropriation of lyrics, instrumentation, or rhythmic approaches is the most obvious testament to the Indians' importance. They also wield a more general and diffused influence as one of the primary local models of spectacular expression, the integration of audience and performer though collective musical practices such as call-and-response and the use of expressive culture as an arena for competition between social groups.

In addition to carnival societies like the Zulu or Mardi Gras Indians, so-called second line parades and the brass band music that accompanies them form a central axis around which the African American expressive culture of New Orleans turns. "Second line" encompasses a range of meanings in the city, referring in its most general sense to a large, inclusive musical parade that features a brass band. Though they have been strongly linked to funerals in the wider popular imagination, these parades are also staged for other reasons, including the anniversaries of the African American "social and pleasure" clubs that sponsor them.[55]

Second line parades are defined by spontaneous participation by individuals who are neither paid musicians nor members of the sponsoring organization: "the raggedy guys who follow parades and funerals to hear the music."[56] These informal participants engage in highly expressive dance, which has engendered the verb "to second line," and they can also add musical contributions by singing, clapping, or playing extemporaneous percussion parts. The music of brass bands and the vibrant costumes and choreographed parading of club members both fuel and feed off of the crowd's participation. The spirit of the second line, which revolves around participation, spontaneity, and the claiming of public space, has exercised broad influence over the expressive culture of New Orleans. Similarly, the music associated with second line parades—and "the seductive, propulsive rhythmic device called the 'second line beat'" at its core—has shaped the vernacular music culture of the city.[57]

Second line parades and other events on the grassroots level are central to the persistence of a distinctive and widely shared musical and aesthetic sensibility, but they also draw some of their creative energy from the expression, provocation, and transgression of a "fierce neighborhood territoriality" that has existed in the city for several centuries.[58] The exuberant and celebratory tone of these events should not be misunderstood to construe an absence of tension or conflict. For much of the twentieth century, participating in second lines required a willingness to scrap, and these events were dominated by aggressive young men, "street people of a lower socioeconomic class."[59] While the parades became less volatile toward the close of the twentieth century, they are still sometimes marked by violence, as they form a community gathering place where enemies can be located and scores settled, a dimension of second line events that has figured in lyrics by New Orleans–based rappers, including 2 Blakk in "Second Line Jump" (1995) and Juvenile in "That's How It Be Happenin'" (1997).[60] In this way, vernacular musical traditions like second line parades not only contribute to the collectively held musical values in the city, but they also help to structure the ways in which successive generations of black New Orleanians understand and experience place and local identity.

Since the 1970s, so-called social and pleasure clubs have proliferated, taking to the streets regularly during the "season" (roughly May through November), a spectacle that has provided many a Sunday afternoon's entertainment for the city's residents. The 1970s and 1980s also saw an exciting revival of the brass band tradition, in which new generations of musicians infused the form with a dynamic funkiness that connected it more directly with contemporary trends in African American popular music. The Dirty Dozen Brass Band was at the forefront of this movement, and the seeds they sowed gave rise to a proliferation of new bands in the 1980s, led by the teenaged Rebirth Brass Band, who mixed old standards with material drawn from or inspired by R&B, soul, funk, and rap.[61] This revival of interest in vernacular musical traditions in New Orleans coincided with worsening economic and social conditions, providing a psychological lifeline through the transformative power of music, dance, and collective creativity.

For many years, the organization of New Orleans's Mardi Gras celebrations was dominated by the white elite, with black carnival groups playing only a supporting role, a disparity that began to change only in the last decades of the twentieth century. Rex, Comus, and other groups still parade and put on a variety of events during carnival season, and the French Quarter still teems with mostly white crowds of drunken college revelers, but New Orleans's African American carnival organizations, institutions, and traditions—long celebrated by scholars and aficionados—are becoming a more central part of the city's self-promotion as a tourist destination. The performances of Mardi Gras Indians, second line clubs, and brass bands also contribute to a general sense of distinctiveness that now spans across race and class lines among the city's residents. But this acceptance of—and attempt to exploit—some established institutions of New Orleans black carnival culture overlies a deep history of indifference and outright intolerance on the part of white civic leaders and planners for the expressive cultural forms and venues developed by working-class African Americans in the city over the years.[62]

History and Political Economy in the Prewar Era

By the mid-1920s whites had succeeded in imposing a starkly dualistic racial apartheid in New Orleans. The city retained its distinctive and complex mixture of cultures, religions, and skin tones, but in terms of legal rights and social treatment, the first few decades of the twentieth century saw the city move toward fulfilling the segregationist goals pursued by white supremacists since the end of the Civil War.[63] New Orleans's highly creolized society was never fully reconciled with the polarizing demands of segregation, which were vigorously contested by African Americans in Louisiana. Many joined Marcus Garvey's Universal Negro Improvement Association (UNIA), which used militaristic spectacle and discipline to promote an ideology of black nationalism and economic empowerment, and which found enthusiastic support in New Orleans and in Louisiana generally.[64]

In terms of residential patterns, the early part of the twentieth century also saw the introduction of dramatic changes in New Orleans. During the eighteenth and nineteenth centuries, the natural barrier formed by the so-called backswamp area had contributed to a comparatively lower level of residential segregation than in most other southern cities.[65] This situation changed in the 1920s with the introduction of the Wood pump, which allowed for brackish areas to be drained and developed, extending the possibilities for settlement well beyond the natural levees for the first time in the city's history.[66] The amount of available residential land increased dramatically, although the newly drained areas were less stable and more prone to flooding than the natural high grounds. African Americans were concentrated within the geographically undesirable low ground of the former swamps, including most prominently the mid-city neighborhood, which prior to draining had been known as "back of town." Whites spread out into newly created suburbs such as Gentilly and Lakeview.[67]

African American enclaves like South Rampart Street anchored a wide range of cultural and musical activities, and Tremé and the Sixth Ward remained strongholds of the city's deeply rooted Creole culture. Still, the strictures of segregation and the lack of opportunity in New Orleans and the wider South provided a powerful incentive to those who could afford to leave. The 1940s saw the beginning of a wave of train-based migration of black Creoles (including several prominent musicians, such as Harold Batiste and Earl Palmer) from New Orleans to greener pastures in Los Angeles.[68] Even as many middle-class blacks left New Orleans in the 1940s and '50s, the decades saw the continuing influx of black migrants from the city's hinterlands in the Delta region, which contributed a distinct set of cultural values to the mixture in the city.[69]

Rhythm and Blues

Jazz had become an established national genre by the late 1920s, and its association with New Orleans—as well as with the lower-class African

American milieu—had faded as this process moved forward. Many of the top musicians from the city left to pursue careers in New York or Chicago. While New Orleans's local music scene carried on, its prominence within the national music industry ebbed to a low point as jazz was increasingly commodified and mass-marketed, with white-owned companies and white star performers reaping a disproportionate share of the profits and prestige.[70]

On the local level, however, jazz remained a central feature of the musical landscape through the 1940s, as younger generations of New Orleans musicians began their own explorations of the possibilities held out by new styles such as bebop.[71] Older forms also persisted; the vast world of corner taverns and hole-in-the-wall clubs provided a space for piano players such as Professor Longhair (Henry Roeland "Roy" Byrd) and Archibald (Leon T. Gross) to ply their trade for dancing patrons, and in their bluesy, barrelhouse style they carried forward a large measure of the prewar musical sensibilities of New Orleans.[72] In the city's streets, the continuing presence of a vital culture of black carnival societies and parades featuring brass bands helped to energize a collective musical sensibility that, while highly contested, by its public nature cut across boundaries of neighborhood, generation, gender, social class, ethnicity, and skin color.

The spirit that had animated New Orleans jazz—rooted in the city's lowdown and street culture of brothels, barrooms, and dance halls, and drawing on the sensibilities and techniques tied to the black church and the city's parade and carnival music—retained its vitality. Enabled by new developments in recording and sound reproduction technologies, it found expression in another vibrant and innovative music scene in New Orleans in the period after World War II, based around the style known as rhythm and blues, or R&B. The new style bore many similarities to jazz, especially the dance-oriented "hot" variety that New Orleanians perfected in the 'teens and 'twenties. Its vocal style drew heavily from black gospel, and its rhythmic dimension bore a strong imprint from the boogie-woogie genre of piano music popular in the prewar period.[73] The new genre was also strongly connected to wider, historically rooted black vernacular and oral culture. But R&B introduced new themes, such as a focus on teenage subjectivity and consumerism, and exploited new technologies of amplification, recording, reproduction, and broadcasting.

R&B's growing popularity encouraged and depended on the proliferation of independent record labels and radio stations, which contributed to a revival of the national commercial music industry in the postwar years.[74] Like those of jazz, R&B lyrics usually lacked explicit political or social messages, but the genre's association with the culture, tastes, and spaces of young, working-class African Americans often provoked reactions of dismissal, distaste, or outright fear from whites and middle-class blacks (especially those of older generations). But the considerable commercial ambitions that R&B artists, producers, and independent record label owners harbored helped push their efforts in the opposite direction toward blandness and respectability.

The emerging R&B genre ushered in a fertile period for New Orleans's music industry. It contributed to a growing local economy of clubs, record labels and distributors, radio stations, and (to a lesser extent) production facilities. African American and white radio DJs helped spread the music across social and spatial barriers, even as their careers were alternately limited or enabled by racial discrimination.[75] Between the late 1940s and 1960, New Orleans experienced a musical efflorescence comparable to the early years of jazz—a period sometimes referred to as the "golden age of New Orleans R&B."[76]

National independent record companies began to flock to New Orleans to record in the late 1940s. They brought artists from other places to record with the city's session players and arrangers, and also explored the local talent pool and recorded its most promising artists.[77] Many sought the services of Dave Bartholomew, a trumpeter whose success as a bandleader led to a busy career as a talent scout, arranger, and producer for national record labels. Bartholomew produced countless records by a variety of talented New Orleans performers, but it was the work of pianist and singer Antoine "Fats" Domino, which combined bouncy, rhythmically driving music with inoffensive lyrics about fun and romance, that captured the nation's attention.[78]

The R&B era provided some level of opportunity for entrepreneurs who wished to tap into the city's thriving music scene, but the systematic and multigenerational exclusion of blacks from economic opportunities meant that almost all of the individuals who capitalized nightclubs, record labels, recording studios, and distributorships were, up until the mid-1960s, white. These entrepreneurs profited from the creative efforts of black musicians, performers, and arrangers, and often acted as middlemen between the New Orleans scene and national companies seeking to extract talent. These individuals were rarely motivated by profit alone, however; many if not all of the white label owners, studio owners, and distributors considered themselves music lovers and exercised considerable influence over musical content, mainly through the process of selecting and cultivating artists and hiring key musicians to play and arrange their sessions.

Several of the most prominent institutions of the New Orleans R&B

scene were run by Italian Americans.[79] Ace Records, "the first local record company to operate out of New Orleans," was founded in 1955 by John Vincent Imbragulio, known professionally as Johnny Vincent (a resident of Jackson, Mississippi).[80] Its roster was dominated by New Orleans–based artists, who produced scores of R&B and rock 'n' roll recordings and a string of national hits for the label. Cosimo Matassa opened a small recording studio in 1946 after becoming interested in the local music scene through his work in the jukebox business. Although his facilities were less technologically sophisticated than their analogues in New York or Los Angeles, Matassa's simple studio remained the axis of the New Orleans R&B and soul music scenes for more than two decades.[81]

To an important extent, the success of New Orleans R&B was built on the work of studio players, including drummers Earl Palmer and Charles "Hungry" Williams, who infused the energy of the city's street parade music into drumset playing. Their rhythmic sensibility helped make the city an early center of R&B and rock 'n' roll and presaged the rise of "funk" as a musical concept in the late 1960s and early 1970s, as evidenced by the central role played by drummers with New Orleans roots in James Brown's bands of the late '50 and early '60s.[82]

While hit records by Fats Domino and others kept the nation's ears attuned to New Orleans's music, much of the day-to-day activity that sustained the city's R&B scene took place in nightclubs like the Dew Drop Inn, the Caldonia, and the TiaJuana.[83] Whites were discouraged from attending these clubs by the prevailing norms of segregation, and rarely did so; as a result, these establishments were relatively insulated environments defined by African American music and culture. Cross-dressing emcees, exotic dancers, and other performers mingled with jazz musicians who came to the clubs to jam and play bebop after their paying gigs were over for the night.[84]

In spite of its wealth of creativity and talent, New Orleans's music industry infrastructure (which included record labels, recording studios, pressing plants, and distributorships) remained small and undercapitalized in comparison with the national centers. This stunted local music industry hindered New Orleans–based artists as they struggled to connect with national audiences. The momentum of any particular artist or label could easily be interrupted by changes in the supply side, which relied on a fragile cooperation of a variety of actors, including national companies, owners of "one-stop" distributorships, radio DJs, and retailers.[85]

New Orleans was at the center of the creation and popularization of R&B, as artists and companies were drawn to the city by the acumen and sensibilities of its arrangers, engineers, sidemen, and soloists, and its native talent captured a share of national attention. Unfortunately, however, this did not result in any dramatic shift in the geographic arrangement of music industry power. In addition to producing music for the local market, New Orleans–based musicians and arrangers contributed to records released by national companies like Specialty, Atlantic, Chess, and Imperial. When a hit resulted, the majority of the profits often accrued to these companies, which were based in the established hubs of the music industry, including New York, Los Angeles, and Chicago. The few local independents that did exist in New Orleans often relied on these larger companies for national distribution, and attempts to remedy this situation by creating sustainable, locally based distribution entities have largely failed.[86] When the flush years of the R&B scene ended, New Orleans had not experienced any substantial or lasting investment from the national music industry.

The lack of infrastructural investment in New Orleans on the part of national companies was not simply a result of geographic distance or corporate strategy, although these factors certainly played a role in the city's continuing marginalization in the wider music industry. Another daunting challenge existed in "the vernacular, uncontrolled context of New Orleans music" itself.[87] New Orleans's riches had to be extracted from the tangled strands of a highly competitive and dynamic music scene, in which artists and producers relied heavily on imitation and appropriation (from local or extralocal sources). At the same time, the city's distinctive, Caribbean-inflected street parade sensibility served as an underlying organizing principle even as musical styles, markets, and technologies changed over time. At certain key moments in the evolution of the popular music audience and industry at the national level, this sense of musical identity and history has been an invaluable asset for those in the local New Orleans scene. At other times, it has served to make the city seem all the more like a self-contained musical universe that only locals are capable of navigating and exploiting.

In terms of national prominence, the 1960s and 1970s saw an assortment of talented artists—including Lee Dorsey, Aaron Neville, Irma Thomas, and Allen Toussaint, among others—emerge from New Orleans, although their success fell short of the "golden age" of the 1950s. Both within and outside of New Orleans, the 1970s and '80s were characterized by a growing awareness and appreciation of the city's unique vernacular music traditions. In 1970 the first Jazz and Heritage Festival (also known as Jazz Fest) was staged, and in subsequent years has helped gain increased visibility for the vernacular and popular musical traditions of New Orleans and Louisiana, helping to revive the moribund careers of legendary New Orleans performers from previous eras like Professor Longhair and James Booker. Festival organizers have attempted to balance the demands of geographical and historical authenticity with those of mass appeal; while "roots" genres such as jazz, gospel, zydeco, R&B, brass bands, and the music of Mardi Gras Indian groups have been central "traditional" elements of the festival's offerings, it has also included a wide range of performers in contemporary genres, including pop, rock, and rap from all over the United States and the world.

The Postwar Years: Desegregation and Suburbanization

A postwar population boom, in combination with a residential market constrained by geography and structured by racism, contributed to a housing crisis in New Orleans that led to the construction of the city's public housing projects beginning in 1940; by the end of the twentieth century these facilities housed more than thirty thousand people.[88] A shortage of affordable housing drove African Americans to the newly constructed facilities. The high demand for housing also meant that apartments in the projects housed more people than they were intended to, resulting in overcrowding and disparities between real conditions and the official population count.[89] The size of these complexes varied; some, like Iberville near the French Quarter, were relatively small; others, such as the Desire or Fischer complexes, were vast, sprawling campuses of poverty and deprivation.

The conception and evolution of the city's public housing system was influenced by other social forces—racism, poverty, job loss, and suburbanization—in ways that, both immediately and over time, infused its mission of providing temporary housing with the less noble aims of racial segregation and the containment of urban poor populations. As the twenty-first century approached, the conditions at many of the projects demanded some sort of decisive action. In the early 2000s the city initiated Project HOPE, a federally funded program to replace the concentrated poverty of the projects with so-called mixed-income housing. In the years before Katrina, several complexes were razed, including Desire and St. Thomas. After the storm, civic leaders rushed to complete the demolition of nearly all of the remaining complexes before displaced residents could reestablish themselves. With Katrina's assistance, Project HOPE effectively dispersed and displaced the poverty that had been concentrated in the projects. It remains to be seen whether the program's positive effects for former residents

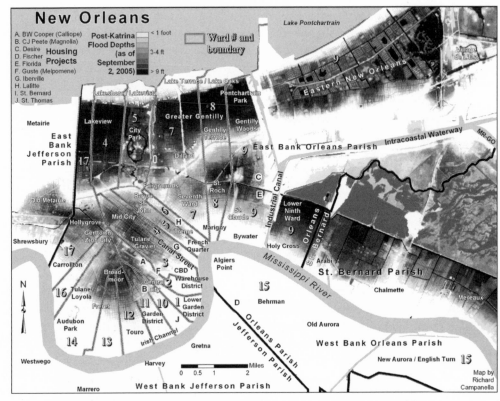

New Orleans

A. BW Cooper (Calliope)
B. CJ Peete (Magnolia)
C. Desire
D. Fischer
E. Florida
F. Guste (Melpomene)
G. Iberville
H. Lafitte
I. St. Bernard
J. St. Thomas

Housing Projects

Post-Katrina Flood Depths (as of September 2, 2005)
< 1 foot
3-4 ft
> 9 ft

Ward # and boundary

Lake Pontchartrain

Village de L'Est

Eastern New Orleans

Lake Terrace / Lake Oaks

Lakeshore / Lakevista

Pontchartrain Park

Metairie

Lakeview

City Park

Greater Gentilly

Genthilly Terrace

Gentilly Woods

East Bank Jefferson Parish

East Bank Orleans Parish

Intracoastal Waterway

MR-GO

Dillard

Fairgrounds

Bayou St. John

Old Metairie

Mid City

Seventh Ward

St. Roch

St. Claude

Lower Ninth Ward

Industrial Canal

St. Bernard

Hollygrove

Gerttown Zion City

Treme

Tulane Gravier

French Quarter

Marigny

Bywater

Holy Cross

Arabi

St. Bernard Parish

Shrewsbury

Carrollton

Broadmoor

Central City

Canal Street

CBD

Warehouse District

Algiers Point

Mississippi River

Chalmette

Mereaux

Tulane Loyola

Freret

Garden District

Lower Garden District

Behrman

Old Aurora

Orleans Parish

Audubon Park

Touro

Irish Channel

Gretna

West Bank Orleans Parish

New Aurora / English Turn

N

Westwego

Harvey

0 0.5 1 2 Miles

Jefferson Parish

Marrero

West Bank Jefferson Parish

Map by Richard Campanella

New Orleans's major neighborhoods and housing projects. Map created by Richard Campanella.

will outweighs its considerable downsides, which include the disruption of established communities and a dramatic drop in the number of housing units available to the urban poor.

The problems related to New Orleans's public housing facilities emerged over decades and were linked to other developments that altered the city's social, cultural, and economic life. Black neighborhoods were often bulldozed in the name of urban renewal; the most egregious example of this occurred when the elevated Interstate 10 freeway was built over North Claiborne Avenue, formerly a wide, tree-lined street that served as the main artery for parades and carnival processions in the predominantly African American Tremé neighborhood.[90] The hard-won victories over de jure segregation in the 1950s and 1960s opened the door for black economic and political empowerment (such as the election of Ernest N. "Dutch" Morial as the city's first black mayor in 1977); they also prompted an exodus of whites from New Orleans, who often settled in nearby Jefferson and St. Bernard parishes. In the mid-1950s middle-class blacks began to depart the inner city in droves, populating newly developed neighborhoods on the eastern side of the metropolitan area.[91] Over the last four decades of the twentieth century, census figures for New Orleans showed a shrinking and increasingly impoverished population, within which the representation of African Americans has continued to grow even as the city's total population declined.[92]

A brief experiment with integrated public schools during the Reconstruction period was the rare exception to the rule of segregation, which relegated blacks to inadequately funded, second-class facilities for most of the twentieth century.[93] As in other southern cities, the issue of school desegregation in New Orleans after the Supreme Court's 1954 *Brown* decision was highly charged and continued to reverberate into the next millennium. The battle against school desegregation in New Orleans did not capture the attention of the national mass media or wider public to the same extent as the more grotesque spectacles of white brutality in places like Birmingham or Jackson, but the issue was a major factor driving white flight from the city to suburban parishes and enrollment in private and parochial schools.[94] In the decades after school desegregation, Louisiana's citizens ranked among the lowest in the nation in terms of education, a shortcoming that had a disproportionate effect on African Americans.[95] The fortunes of younger generations in New Orleans were increasingly tied to a chronically underfunded public school system charged with educating a population in which poor and black pupils formed a steadily growing majority.

In the last decades of the twentieth century, urban residents confronted an increasingly grim economic outlook. After a brief boom in the oil industry, employment prospects narrowed, as the city's economy increasingly relied on service-industry jobs based on tourism and conventions. The city's African American population suffered disproportionately from this poverty and lack of opportunity; the 2000 census revealed a nearly two-to-one disparity in the average household incomes of whites and blacks in the city.[96] Spiraling crime rates and high levels of interpersonal violence further reduced the quality of life in the city's housing projects and working-class black neighborhoods during the late '80s and early '90s, when the city's rap scene was taking shape.[97]

Even as the economy and urban geography of the city changed, white racism remained a potent force in politics, though its strategies, rhetoric, and personalities evolved to meet the new legal and political climate of the post–civil rights era. Though hardly confined to one candidate or political party, this phenomenon was personified in the late 1980s by David Duke, a former Ku Klux Klan Grand Wizard who was elected as a Republican to the state's House of Representatives by the 81st district of Metairie, a mainly white suburban enclave on the city's northwest periphery. Duke waged two subsequent campaigns for the governor's office in 1990 and 1991; the slim margins by which he was defeated demonstrated that the 81st district was no anomaly in terms of white Louisianans' willingness to accept a radically anti-black candidate. While Duke's political career fizzled, it was a painful reminder to African Americans in Louisiana that their struggle against racism and discrimination was far from over.

The Wider Socioeconomic Context: Late Twentieth Century

A 2005 report by the Brookings Institution sums up the socioeconomic and demographic changes in New Orleans between the years 1970 and 2000. The report identifies "three especially disturbing trends" over this period: "Segregation and concentrations of poverty had sharpened; sprawl and decentralization had spread; and a low-wage economy had developed."[98] In the context of the larger metropolitan area, black poverty was increasingly concentrated within the lowest-lying and least desirable sections of Orleans Parish.

In the years leading up to Katrina, poor and working-class African Americans in New Orleans experienced worsening conditions along several key indices. The annual murder rate reached epidemic proportions in the early 1990s and surged again in the first years of the new millennium.[99] The city's rap scene was disproportionately affected by these trends, and many important contributors have died prematurely as a result of violence. Others have had their careers interrupted by incarceration, as poverty and the war on drugs churned young black men through the criminal justice system. New Orleans's beleaguered public education system remained unable to counter the forces of poverty and racially based disparity, and in the years before Katrina was but one more signal of desperate social conditions. Area politicians were largely ineffectual in their efforts to reverse these trends and often preferred to focus on relatively simplistic solutions that implicitly placed blame on antisocial attitudes and actions of urban black youth themselves. Despite clear indications that they would not pass constitutional muster, legal restrictions on sagging, low-slung pants (a style strongly associated with rap and hip-hop generally) were proposed with regularity by area politicians between 1999 and 2004.[100]

42   CHAPTER ONE

In the last decades of the twentieth century, African Americans in New Orleans's urban core suffered from mutually intertwined problems—concentration within inner city ghettoes, a narrowing of economic and educational opportunities, crime, and violence—almost all of which were getting worse. Their fragile web of survival was violently and dramatically disrupted in early September 2005, when Hurricane Katrina slammed into Louisiana and Mississippi. When the levees failed to contain a surge of water coming from the Gulf of Mexico, entire neighborhoods in the city were submerged. The effects of historically rooted neglect, impoverishment, and spatial concentration were made worse by confusion, inaction, lack of preparation, and general incompetence at various levels of government after the storm's landfall. The sad spectacle of citizens stranded on rooftop islands for days on end, broadcast around the world, was for some a ringing indictment of the failure of government and civic responsibility; for others it merely confirmed the otherness of New Orleans's black poor, as the media focus on the immediate challenges of rescue and resettlement often failed to acknowledge the deep and tangled roots of deprivation and neglect in the city.

Prior to Katrina, the population of New Orleans was already on the decline, and the storm accelerated this trend. According to the 2010 census, the official count of the city's residents dropped by 29 percent between 2000 and 2010—from 484,674 to 343,829. Though African Americans still constitute a majority of the city's residents, their representation as a percentage of the urban population has declined more sharply than that of other groups, for reasons including "shortcomings in housing programs, particularly in initiatives meant to restore the city's rentals, [which have] disproportionately affected black residents."[101] The political and cultural ramifications of these disparities have fueled debate and concern about what New Orleans will look like in future decades and whether it will retain its status as a center of black cultural and political achievement. The storm prompted a necessary and well-received intervention in the city's public school system, but other aspects of urban life in New Orleans seem to remain immune to reform; violent crime in the city has remained at epidemic levels since Katrina. With formidable challenges such as these, the psychic and economic survival of African Americans in New Orleans will likely depend on the continuation and further elaboration of music and other forms of expressive culture.

2. "The City That Is Overlooked"
Rap Beginnings, 1980–1991

The development of rap in New Orleans was strongly influenced by the genre's wider national context, including an early focus in New York and the subsequent development (in the late 1980s and early '90s) of a parallel scene in and around Los Angeles. Artists and companies from these two places (eventually labeled the "East Coast" and the "West Coast") held a near-monopoly on the production of marketable rap music, setting the standards for the genre at a wider, national level. In New Orleans, the story begins with the foundational efforts of DJs and audiences in venues such as block parties and nightclubs, where local preferences were incubated and aspiring rappers and DJs made their first forays into public performance, participating in the contentious process of defining a local "sound" and narrative voice within rap.

During the years 1980–1991, rap evolved from a marginal, subcultural phenomenon into a central feature of the national and global popular music landscape. In its most basic form, this process as it unfolded in New Orleans was similar to that taking place elsewhere—the music was shaped by the collective support of audiences, as well as the efforts of legions of aspiring producers, rappers, and DJs who, as in the English town of Milton Keynes studied by Ruth Finnegan, "engaged in and fought over and created and maintained" the local rap music scene, and "whose work both reveals them as creative and active human beings and serves to uphold the cultural traditions" of New Orleans generally.[1] Commercial ventures such as radio stations, record stores, and record labels also made essential contributions to the development of rap in the city as an ongoing cultural practice and economic enterprise.

The enthusiastic appreciation of rap music on the part of black listeners in New Orleans developed prior to the desire to refashion the form to suit local musical and thematic values; the specific questions of whether and how the genre would be adapted to the local cultural and social context were largely open and vaguely conceptualized. In the mid-1980s there was no such thing as a local New Orleans rap music sound, and little understanding existed at this time of rap's potential to accommodate and intersect with local preferences and identities. Club DJs like DJ Carriere, Leo "Slick Leo" Coakley and Charles "Captain Charles" Leach entertained local audiences with music from rap's center of creativity and production, the greater New York City area.[2]

The development of a local and particular rap sensibility began with these nightclub and block party DJs, who gauged audience response in order to identify particularly resonant or energizing songs or parts of songs. Local audiences' tastes and preferences often overlapped with those in other places, but not always; it was the DJ's challenge to identify and then exploit the exceptions. Similarly, recordings and performances that were strongly derivative of rap from other places formed the context within which a local rap sensibility began to take shape. Throughout the 1980s, New Orleans–based artists, producers, and record labels were largely concerned with replicating the styles and themes that defined rap coming from the centers of industry concentration; in the process, they also helped to build a shared repertoire of locally resonant stylistic and thematic preferences.

Within these early rap recordings and performances, participants in the local scene developed and refined key elements and concepts that would become established features of the distinctive style of New Orleans rap music that came of age in the 1990s. Some of these elements (such as the prevalence of lyrics in a call-and-response format) are organizing principles with overlapping influence within rap, African American music generally, and New Orleans's black music in particular. Often, the distinctiveness of rap in New Orleans does not rely on the introduction of completely novel elements, but rather on changes in emphasis among features that are already present in the wider context of rap.

The National Rap Music Scene

The practical or functional dimensions of New York's early dominance were intertwined with the city's notable symbolic role in the proliferation of rap music listening and practice in New Orleans and in other cities across the country. As the genre expanded and matured in the 1980s, however, a progressively wider array of musical and textual ideas, themes, place-based identities, and artistic personae were presented for consumption.

African American youth in New Orleans quickly adopted the practices and attitudes associated with hip-hop. This photograph, taken in 1985, shows Lawrence
Williams playing his portable radio on Canal Street, with Run-D.M.C.'s album
King of Rock in the tape deck. Copyright 1985, *The Times-Picayune*. All rights
reserved. Reprinted with permission.

The story of rap's birth in New York City in the late 1970s and its subsequent evolution and popularization has been ably told by many participants and scholars,[3] but a brief overview will illuminate the relationship between identity, place, musical style, and notions of authenticity that shaped the rap genre in its early years.

Rap emerged from a particular cultural, spatial, and socioeconomic context. Young people (the vast majority of them from an African American or Afro-Caribbean background) in the impoverished New York City borough of the Bronx introduced a way of making music that relied on a radical reinvention of composition, performance, and subjectivity. Drawing from diverse influences, including Caribbean forms like reggae and dub as well as such African American genres as R&B, soul, and funk, rap retained a core connection to African-derived musical values.[4] The influences of Afro-diasporic vernacular and oral culture were evident in the music's strong association with dancing, its reliance on particular narrative tropes, and its rhyming, circumlocutory vocal performance style (reminiscent of folk forms like signifying, the dozens, and black radio DJ patter).

The movement also encompassed similar innovations in the realms of dance, clothing, and graphic arts. A youth culture centered around street parties and DJ mixing coalesced into a distinct popular music genre called rap or hip-hop. Rap's status as a distinct genre was built on vocal performances that emphasized the percussive delivery of rhymed lyrics rather than singing, as well as the transformative appropriation of existing sound generation and reproduction technology.[5] DJs recombined or otherwise manipulated existing recordings to create new musical expressions tailored to the emerging preferences of rap audiences; they also explored the possibilities of electronic instruments like drum machines and sequencers, which were being continually refined by their manufacturers as part of the 1980s consumer electronics boom.

Rap gradually expanded out of the New York neighborhoods where it began, spreading through largely informal means—"house and block parties or school gymnasium dances, . . . cassette tape exchange between DJs and their burgeoning audiences"—and making early New York–based rap artists like Afrika Bambaataa and Spoonie Gee into underground legends.[6] The first record companies to show any interest in these performers were "relatively small-scale, uptown independents," including Winley Records and Enjoy Records, among others, "whose guiding lights were familiar names from the past three decades of New York black music."[7] Prior to the mid-1980s, rap remained a subcultural phenomenon disconnected from the mainstream of American taste and commerce except as a somewhat obnoxious novelty. The music had demonstrated commercial potential with the breakout success of the Sugar Hill Gang's "Rapper's Delight" in 1980, but it was not until 1984 (a year that saw the release of two popular rap-oriented movies, *Beat Street* and *Breakin'*) and afterward that the genre was transformed "from a relatively contained micromarket to a macro market of diverse and dispersed consumers."[8]

Part of this transformation involved a diversification of rap's audience along lines of race, class, and region.[9] Run-D.M.C., the trio from the Hollis neighborhood of Queens whose 1984 debut became the first rap album to achieve gold-record status (500,000 sold), was at the forefront of these developments.[10] Rapper Dartanian Stovall (a New Orleans native) recalled, "When Run-DMC came out . . . that just changed it for me. It was like, OK, this is that shit I want to do."[11] The genre's growing popularity attracted the interest of music corporations, and leading New York–based rap independents like Tommy Boy and Def Jam secured deals with major labels to distribute and market their releases. These companies in turn worked to increase the genre's exposure and expand its audience in 1986 and 1987. Rap became popular and accepted in most parts of the country, especially among African American youths, spreading through word-of-mouth, recordings (purchased, shared, or copied), and, increasingly throughout the 1980s, radio play, concerts, films, and music videos.[12]

For this far-flung appreciation and identification to develop into full-fledged creative participation would, however, be a more complex, tension-fraught, and multistaged process. On the practical side, potential participants had to learn and refine skills of rapping, DJing, dancing, event planning, and recording, efforts that ultimately contributed to the establishment or conversion of performance venues, recording studios, record labels, and retail outlets to suit the rap form. To varying degrees, explorations along these lines began in places all over the United States in the early 1980s. The cultivation of competence and local popularity, though a necessary prerequisite for entry into the expanding field of rap music at the national level in the 1980s, was far from a guarantee of transitioning to such exposure. The ability of artists from various emerging scenes across the country to connect with wider audiences was largely determined by their differential access to the distribution networks, more sophisticated marketing strategies, and more robust capitalization offered by major music corporations. This geographically based inequality in access to resources was replicated in the conceptual realm, where values related to authenticity, style, and geographic affiliation strongly favored artists associated with the earliest appearances of rap.

New York's commanding position within the organizational and imaginary dimensions of rap music lasted for nearly a decade as the genre slowly took root in other cities across the country, including Philadelphia, Houston, Los Angeles, Miami, and Seattle. Beginning around 1987, artists and producers from the greater Los Angeles area (and especially South Central L.A. and the heavily black area of Compton) rose to challenge New York's dominance.[13] By the early 1990s an idea of the division of rap into two regionally based spheres had taken hold. Although New Yorkers still dominated rap in the Northeast, they began to be grouped with artists and producers from nearby urban centers to form a cultural bloc called "the East Coast." Meanwhile, Los Angeles's status as a center of the entertainment industry helped the city become the anchor of the "West Coast." These two regional imaginaries encompassed specific artists, companies, and audiences in one or the other of the two places, as well as the distinctive musical styles and narrative viewpoints that were thought to characterize each contingent.

The contributions of West Coast rappers were explicitly or implicitly framed within attempts to establish their own geospatial surroundings (on the level of region, city, or neighborhood) as a legitimate subject for rap music texts and an authentic site for the emergence of credible, authentic artists in the genre.[14] West Coast rappers not only gave voice to the existing Southern California African American youth culture but also participated (along with record companies, journalists, and consumers) in the creation of the idea of the West Coast as a way of establishing and referencing the distinctiveness and authenticity of their expressions. Conventions linked to the local social and cultural environment quickly became incorporated into a self-conscious and strategic discourse of place-based distinctiveness, authenticity, and stylistic coherence.

The geographic expansion of rap's production was tied to the genre's growth and diversification along thematic and stylistic lines.[15] The success of West Coast artists demonstrated that rap's transition from a geographically specific to a more generalized, diversified practice relied on changes in the way participants imagined the relationship between identity, place, authenticity, and musical style. Their efforts represented an important step away from the conception of rap as inherently dependent on a New York–based imaginary and stylistic palette to one that would increasingly encourage and depend on a proliferation of distinct, musically inflected representations of place.

To some extent, the two coastal contingents could be distinguished from one another along musical lines. While New York–oriented (East

Coast) rap increasingly relied on collages of samples (excerpts of previously existing, commercially released recordings) to support lyrical themes and imagery grounded in Afrocentrism and black nationalism, the West Coast scene around L.A. became known for a style called G-funk, "whose musical tracks tend to deploy live instrumentation, heavy on bass and keyboards, with minimal (sometimes no) sampling and often highly conventional harmonic progressions and harmonies." For rap listeners, the particularities of West Coast rap, "the generally slower and more sung MCing rhythms," were linked to "representations of California as 'laid-back'"; the area's large Hispanic population and low-rider culture also contributed symbolically distinctive features.[16] While West Coast rappers did not hold a monopoly on lyrics glorifying criminal behavior and expressing an explicitly antiauthoritarian, outlaw viewpoint, the predominance of these themes in their music cemented the association of Los Angeles–based rap with gangsta rap as a subgenre.

For Murray Forman, this thematic and geographical expansion in rap was tied to shifting spatial tropes used in its lyrics: "The rise and impact of rappers on the West Coast [corresponded with] a discursive shift from the spatial abstractions framed within 'the ghetto' to the more localized and specific discursive construct of 'the hood' occurring in 1987–88." The considerable influence of West Coast-based gangsta rap along the lines of musical style, lyrical content, and imagery was paired with a general movement in rap toward an emphasis on "regional affiliations" and a keen sense of what Forman calls "the *extreme local*."[17] This "extreme local" was expressed on multiple levels—as Adam Krims writes, "A poetics of locality and authenticity can work through sound, visual images, words, and media images together."[18] But, most importantly for Forman, the emergence of a place-based concept of authenticity relates to changes in the conception of rap's narrative voice: "The tendency toward narrative self-awareness and a more clearly definable subjectivity effectively closed the distance between the story and the storyteller," rendering the relationship to place a central part of artistic personae and legitimacy within rap.[19]

The emergence of West Coast rap represented a disruption of the status quo within the rap music industry and subculture, but it also heralded the genre's growing momentum as a force in commercial music. In 1988 the mainstreaming of rap shifted into high gear with the release of popular crossover albums like Run-D.M.C.'s *Tougher than Leather;* by 1989 heavy metal and rap "dominated U.S. sales."[20] As a music industry executive observed, "Rap now has a much broader audience. The music has crossed over to new radio formats."[21] A 1991 *Billboard* article noted that "widely held assumptions about who constitutes rap music's primary audience are being shattered," as "ratings and sales" demonstrated the substantial adult audience for the music.[22] The development and marketing of stylistic niches flourished within the genre, leading to a proliferation of vaguely defined and overlapping subgenres—"reality" rap, conscious rap, gangsta rap, pop rap—based on distinct categories of lyrical content. Similarly, rap artists and producers drew on an expanding sonic or musical palette to shape the nontextual content of recordings and performances.

So-called underground or hardcore rap included recordings that were too vulgar, violent, or politically militant to be played on the radio and was often imagined as a more authentic interpretation of the genre than the pop rap of artists like MC Hammer and Vanilla Ice. Underground rap often traded in images of angry, rebellious, and dangerous blackness, which ultimately helped groups like N.W.A. and Public Enemy garner a substantial audience among white, middle-class listeners. Female performers were rare in the various subcategories of underground rap, which was strongly associated with masculine subjectivity and audiences; while gangsta rap artists often relied on demeaning or misogynist representations of women, most "conscious" or "political" rap implicitly figured politics, culture, and the public sphere in general as a patriarchal, male domain, with black men speaking for passive and marginalized women.

In addition to Los Angeles, other major cities in the United States were beginning to develop self-sustaining rap music styles and scenes. In the late 1980s two of the earliest independent labels in the South—Houston's Rap-A-Lot and Miami's Luke Skyywalker Records—"slowly tapped into the southern audiences' musical tastes, displaying aesthetic and thematic content that resonated with local and regional consumers."[23] While substantial differences existed between the two labels and the grassroots scenes to which they were tied, their rise nevertheless indicates the trajectory toward continuing geographic expansion that would characterize rap music in the 1990s.

The commercial potential inherent in rap's geographic diversification was made more readily apparent by the introduction of SoundScan retail accounting technology in 1991, which allowed unprecedented access to the specific contours and trends of thriving local and regional markets served by independent labels and distributors.[24] Major labels began to explore the possibilities for exploiting these previously obscure markets and sought out relationships with artists or companies in places outside of the established centers of production. These included previously marginal southern cities, among them Atlanta, Houston, and Miami.

New Orleans Rap Grassroots: DJs, Block Parties, and Nightclubs

In the early 1980s there were no record labels in New Orleans devoted exclusively to rap, and little in the way of established rap groups. Grassroots activities around rap music in the neighborhoods, housing projects, streets, schools, and jails of the city laid the foundations for an emergent local scene as rap quickly became the dominant frame of reference within popular music for black children and teenagers.[25] The culture of rap music consumption, performance, and production expanded with growing momentum throughout the decade of the 1980s, as artists, audiences, DJs, and club owners all participated in the gradual establishment of a local scene. In New Orleans, as in other places, club and party DJs both foreshadowed and facilitated the transition to the rap era; their efforts represent a crucial nexus between local audiences and national music companies. DJ Carriere, Slick Leo, and Captain Charles were among the many local DJs who moved the crowds in commercial establishments such as bars and clubs, as well as at neighborhood events, including "house parties," dances held at schools, churches, or community centers, and block parties—large outdoor neighborhood gatherings with a sound system and dancing—where rap music formed an increasing portion of the musical offerings.[26]

Early in the 1980s, Slick Leo became a sought-after club and party DJ who "paved the way for Captain Charles and all the famous DJs."[27] Rap fans who were not old enough to hear him spin records at the Famous Theatre Disco could hear his sets broadcast on radio station WAIL-FM.[28] Eric Barra, a Desire Projects resident and dance group member, recalled, "We used to give dances and go to dances where he used to be the DJ, cause if you don't get Slick Leo, you ain't *nothin.*"[29] While Slick Leo gained prominence for his mastery of "New York-style scratching," DJs who followed in his footsteps found their own ways to stand out, and often enhanced their mixes by adding their own vocal or musical contributions.[30] Captain Charles, rapper Joseph "Joe Blakk" Francois recalled, "did a lot of chanting and people sang along" when he DJed at Club Discovery in the late 1980s.[31] These various techniques and tricks contributed to DJs' ability to "set a party off" by establishing, building, maintaining, or interrupting the musical flow, depending on the circumstances.[32]

In addition to working at clubs, DJs built their reputations at neighborhood-based block parties, outdoor events with no cover charge or age limit, located in spaces that are accessible and familiar to all members of the surrounding community. With roots in "community dinners and courtyard barbecues," block parties have long served as a central space for the collective enjoyment and creation of rap music in New Orleans, contributing to the establishment of a collective local musical sensibility that spans across generations. As Yolanda Marrero, president of the resident council at the B. W. Cooper (formerly Calliope) housing project, remarked in 1998, "It's something that's unique to our culture . . . We use our positiveness, our looseness to celebrate."[33]

Organizing and participating in these events had the potential to contribute to a wide variety of skills, including dancing, music making, sound engineering, event planning, and food preparation. Block parties were a source of community enjoyment and also contributed to a diverse array of small-scale entrepreneurial activities, providing income for the DJ and stimulating neighborhood businesses, which often sponsored the events. Their small-scale commercial aspirations intersected with grassroots notions of social control; as Raymond Williams, who lived in the Desire Projects, recalled, "On the weekends, Ms. Erzie used to get the DJ for us. She knew a DJ out there would keep the children out of trouble. Nobody would go out there acting crazy. She would have her truck [selling food and drink] to make her money back from paying the DJ."[34] Block parties also provided a space for aspiring rappers to polish their material and techniques and build a local reputation. The phenomenon itself has formed the subject of songs such as Partners-N-Crime's "N.O. Block Party" (1998) and Katey Red's "Melpomene Block Party" (1999), among others.

Block parties formed a central axis of many young people's social lives, and they attracted attendees from the general area: "If you stayed in the back, or you stayed up front, or you stayed in Gentilly, you knew that we was having a DJ in the court[yard] on Friday or Saturday night and everybody would come."[35] For many project youths, the block party was not just a way to pass the time, but was "our time to get our shine on," a regular and celebratory high point in the weekly rhythms of life in the city's poor neighborhoods.[36] Gerald Platenburg, a dancer who later performed as part of a group called "The Original Desire," remembered that "our dancing was practice for the DJs in [the housing project] Desire. At least once a week, we would get together to dance."[37]

The frequent use of the term "DJ" to refer metonymically to a block party indicates the centrality of their efforts, but within the vernacular spaces of rap's local evolution the DJs were not the only people actively participating in the creative process. Dancing has always been central to these events and forms a near-universal commonality of experience even as it exists at various levels of athleticism, eroticism, complexity, and organization. Such all-male dance groups as the Parkway Boys, the Nature Boys, and Motown Sound performed tightly choreographed routines that occupied the center of attention at block parties; as Joseph "Joe Black" Baker, cofounder of the Motown Sound group, recalled, "We did a whole lot of different dances as a team. We used to have ladies from all over and people just crowd around us when we started playing and then we used to coordinate stuff together." Individuals who introduced innovative dance steps might have a dance named after them, such as "the Funky Joe Black."[38]

Block parties made substantial positive contributions to the communal experience of black New Orleanians, but these events could not be insulated from the various problems of daily life in the projects or similarly poor neighborhoods. With alcohol, drugs, and gambling sometimes contributing to the mix, block parties were as susceptible as any other gathering of people to the outbreak of interpersonal violence; the chances were increased when they attracted partiers from other parts of town. Their ability to draw neighborhood residents outside made them vulnerable to drive-by vendetta shootings.[39] Uninvolved or otherwise innocent people often become the victims of these actions, as in the case of Raymond Williams, who "got shot out there listening to DJ Carriere" in 1983.[40]

In the block party or nightclub, black youths found community and a release (or at least a distraction) from the challenges of everyday life under material circumstances that ranged from tolerable to bleak. As the comments quoted earlier indicate, block parties and similar grassroots events featuring DJs and dancing provided not only entertainment and opportunities for socializing, but also contributed in important ways to the psychic survival of poor and working-class black youths. Participants in block parties used music and other forms of expressive culture to transform some of the most deprived, stark spaces of the city into festive, multigenerational entertainment venues, as streets and sidewalks became impromptu dancefloors crowded with bodies, contributing to an alternate spatial, social (and, for some, economic) reality created and populated by the city's poor and working-class African Americans.

Nightclubs were essential to the emergence of a local rap scene in New Orleans and played a key role in the careers of DJs in the mid-1980s.[41] In addition to presenting concerts by established regional acts like Miami's 2 Live Crew and Houston's Geto Boys, they more often provided a space for local DJs and rappers to perform. Clubs popular with the rap audience during this period included the Famous Theatre Disco, Club Sinsations, Club Amnesia, Club Adidas, and the sprawling Mirage, at the corner of 17th and Severn streets in the suburb of Metairie. Teen clubs, such as Club Polo on North Claiborne in the Tremé or 18-Below across the river in Gretna, provided space for younger listeners to listen and dance to rap music.

Sal Dimitre's Club Discovery, which opened in the mid-1980s at 2831 St. Claude Avenue, was a hub of the emerging rap music scene in New Orleans. For patrons like Gerald Platenburg, the Ninth Ward club (which also featured a restaurant to provision hungry dancers) served as a weekly place to have fun and socialize. He recalled, "Discovery was known for its dance contests. The [Houston-based rap group The Geto Boys] hosted a contest and the grand prize was five hundred dollars for the winner. I won that one."[42] The size of the purse in this instance is suggestive of the value placed on the embodied contributions of dancers to the nightclub experience, as well as of the scale of the profits that such venues could generate.

Rap music in New Orleans also evolved in the context of talent shows or "gong shows"—open contests featuring stand-up comedians, dancers, singers, rappers (backed by a house band or a recording), and other performers who competed for the audience's response and a modest cash prize. Generally, these consisted of weekly events at bars and clubs, such as the gong shows at Club Discovery hosted by "Brother Randy."[43] Less frequently, higher-stakes contests like the WYLD Talent Show (held annually from 1981 until Katrina) were staged at larger venues. While these events offered opportunities for wider exposure—organizers expected over eight thousand attendees at the 1990 WYLD Talent Show, among them "representatives from most of the major record labels [who] judge the show and scout for acts"—the gong shows at smaller clubs helped build local careers and could also be a source of income.[44] Rapper John "Bust Down" Bickham, who mentioned gong shows at "The Social, The Phoenix, [and] The Other Side" in lyrics on his 1991 album, recalled, "If [the audience] enjoyed your music they would ball up money in small little balls and they would throw the money at you. If you were real good it would be raining money."[45]

Bobby Marchan, a performer and music promoter who "virtually [rode] every trend in black music since the late Forties," was active in organizing weekly gong shows at nightclubs throughout the 1980s and 1990s, and played an important role in the establishment of rap in New Orleans. Born Oscar James Gibson in Youngstown, Ohio, in 1930, he settled in New Orleans after traveling to the city in 1953 with "a troupe of female impersonators called 'The Powder Box Revue' that was booked at [the] Dew Drop Inn for several weeks."[46] As one of the Clowns, he backed pianist Huey Smith in his classic recordings for Ace Records, and developed a solo career around 1960 after his version of Big Jay McNeely's "There Is Something on Your Mind" went to number 1 on the *Billboard* R&B charts.[47]

Marchan's recording career cooled in the 1970s, and he earned a living by touring with a drag act from a base in Pensacola, Florida. He returned to New Orleans in 1977 and found work as the emcee at Prout's Club Alhambra. In the early 1980s he began organizing weekly talent competitions at various clubs around town, including Club 2004 and The VIP New Orleans club.[48] If an artist failed to impress the audience, the acid-tongued Marchan "would come out there and make his little comments, and talk bad about them, and . . . say all kind of bad things to them."[49] Gong shows represented only one of his multi-pronged efforts to make a living in the entertainment business. Under the name Manicure Productions or Manicure Records, Marchan booked and promoted various New Orleans rap artists, including Warren Mayes, Lil' Elt & DJ T, Mystikal, and others, and according to *Times-Picayune* contributor Jeff Hannusch he was centrally involved in the formation of local powerhouse Cash Money Records.[50] If Marchan's laconic assertions are to be believed, his interest in rap music was strictly profit-driven: "I'm not interested in no rap. I'm interested in what they [rappers] do, bring the money in . . . Off the job I stay home and watch TV. There's too much violence in the street for me to be running around out there."[51]

For whatever reason, Marchan stayed active in the local music business until his death in late 1999 at the age of sixty-nine, playing a foundational role in the establishment of many individual artistic careers and by extension the rise of a self-sustaining local rap scene in New Orleans. As rapper DJ Jubilee recalled, "Bobby did a lot for New Orleans. Every bounce artist that went through Bobby made money and became something. Bobby booked shows . . . got you on the radio—Bobby did it all. Bobby was the greatest empowerer of black artists New Orleans ever had. I don't think anyone will ever replace him because he was a hustler and known all over."[52]

Marchan also had a hand in lining up rap acts for the New Orleans Jazz and Heritage Festival (Jazz Fest), which since its inception in 1970 has featured a diverse array of artists based in New Orleans and Louisiana. As one writer observed, the annual event "gained a national reputation during the '80s," a development that "brought the eyes and ears of the music business to our door."[53] But the rewards associated with this heightened interest often favored established genres of "roots" music rather than emergent and explicitly commercial ones like rap. The latter genre has never represented more than a tiny fraction of the vast offerings of Jazz Fest, where locally based artists and cultural groups such as social and pleasure clubs or Mardi Gras Indian gangs share the bill with performers from other parts of the United States and the world.

Nevertheless, Jazz Fest organizers have maintained a "diverse, egalitarian booking policy" that has resulted in a relatively welcoming attitude toward rap in general and local rap in particular.[54] Appearing in 1985, Run-D.M.C. was the first rap group to perform at the festival, but in the years that followed organizers eschewed big-name acts in favor of more obscure local artists.[55] In 1986 Tanya P. appears to have been the first New Orleans–based rapper to perform at the festival; between 1987 and 1991, local rap artists appearing at the Jazz Fest included (in chronological order): Tanya P. & the Mic Conductors; the Rappin Patrol with The Super MC's & The Twins of Spin; MC J' Ro' J & The Gold Rush Crew; Tanya P. & GMS with The Hollygrove Posse; Gregory D & DJ Mannie Fresh; Li'l Mac & Warren Mayes; and E.R.C., Baby T. & Devious D.[56]

As rap gained popularity in the mid-1980s, New Orleans saw a variety of nationally popular acts come through town. The "Jam-A-Tron" concert (featuring UTFO, Kurtis Blow, and Doug E. Fresh, among others) in late August 1985 was held at Municipal Auditorium (located behind the French Quarter near the site of Congo Square); other large venues included Kiefer University of New Orleans Lakefront Arena and the Superdome. Many of these events were promoted by Junius Eli Jr. through his Ghost Productions company, including the "Rap Attack" show in March 1986 and the "Christmas Rap Spectacular" (featuring Public Enemy, EPMD, and others), held in late 1988. While these touring arena shows usually featured well-known national performers, they sometimes provided valuable opportunities to local artists seeking wider exposure. In addition to stars like LL Cool J and Dana Dane, the "Rap Attack" show included two local performers, New York Incorporated and DJ Slick Leo, while a show in December 1990 headlined by gangsta rapper Ice Cube included "New Orleanian Warren Mayes," who was riding the popularity of his single, "Get It Girl," discussed later in this chapter.[57]

In New Orleans, media coverage of rap and its audience in the 1980s revealed the ways in which the genre focused tensions related to race, class, youth, and the use of public space. Teenaged carousing and street crime were reported after several large rap events in the later 1980s; these events and the tone of their coverage in the local press contributed to a growing perception of rap fans and concerts as violent and dangerous and a related reluctance to book rap shows at large, mainstream venues.[58] Another catalyst for tension was the use of portable radios, or "jam boxes," which allowed music to be played on city streets and in other public places, an example of how rap music listeners have used advances in commercially produced audio technology to effect "transformation of the urban sound-scape."[59] In an installment of his weekly "Around Town" local color column from early 1985, *Times-Picayune* writer Bill Grady used a bemused and vaguely sympathetic tone in his description of encounters with young African American men broadcasting rap music in central, public places in New Orleans; the article was the subject of several letters to the editor, in which readers criticized and derided the type of behavior it portrayed.[60]

Whether at block parties, on the street, or in other venues, the rap music played in New Orleans in the early and mid-1980s reflected New York's monopoly on talent and organization. At a Marrero middle school where students were allowed to bring records to play at lunchtime, "DJ Shane Gros, sporting a black felt hat, gold earrings and chains, said he knows what turns the crowd on." Interestingly, Gros identified the crowd's preference as "funk and soul music" but then named "the Fat Boys, Doug E. Fresh and M.C. Ricky D."—all artists clearly within the rap genre—as examples.[61] In this article (as well as Grady's 1985 piece discussed earlier), the words "rap" or "hip-hop" were never used despite the (retrospectively) obvious appropriateness of such labels. Even to aspiring participants in the scene such as Gros, rap music at this time was still in a transitional phase in terms of its status as a recognized genre of music in its own right, forming a conceptual extension of prior genres such as soul and funk.

Participants in the block parties of the mid- to late 1980s recalled the kinds of music played at these events: "all the early hip-hop—Grandmaster Flash, Curtis [Kurtis] Blow, and Run DMC"; "it was the era of tight pants and everybody was into breakdancing, the electric boogie, rap."[62] For many, such as dancer Gerald Platenburg, New York retained an iconic and mythical status as the fount from which rap music culture flowed: "I'd been thinking about New York and breakdancing for years and years." His recollections of music popular in late 1980s New Orleans reflects the growing influence of rap produced in California and, to a lesser extent, Florida: "You had some pretty good rap music back then—L.L. Cool J. [New York], Too Short [Oakland], 2 Live Crew [Miami]. I used to like to dance to N.W.A. [Compton] or Public Enemy [New York]."[63] Artists and groups such as these, from the established centers of rap production, set the standards to which local performers aspired in New Orleans during the 1980s.

Early Rap Recordings and Groups in New Orleans, 1983–1988

Rap was popular with young African American listeners in New Orleans from its inception, but, as in other places, many of the early rap releases in the city were made by artists, producers, or record label owners who already had some experience in the field of popular music. In 1983 the Superdome label (owned by R&B/soul artist and producer Senator Jones) released one of the earliest New Orleans rap records, a twelve-inch single by Parlez, "Make It, Shake It, Do It Good!" The lyrical content of the record (which bears the subtitle "Mardi Gras Man" on its cover) consists of an extended and artful description of New Orleans at carnival time, in which the unidentified rapper refers to white carnival krewes like Rex and Momus as well as black traditions like the Zulus and Mardi Gras Indians.

While the lyrics focus exclusively on New Orleans's distinctiveness and party atmosphere, the stylistic qualities of the vocal performance and the backing music (in which a group of studio musicians performs a funk/disco backing track to support the rapped lyrics) are indistinguishable from their national counterparts. Rather than representing any sort of connections to or inspiration from a local grassroots hip-hop scene, "Make It, Shake It, Do It Good!" instead remains more of a novelty record, written and performed by artists rooted in earlier genres of black popular music. The same can be said for the similarly themed "Mardi Gras Rap," by the Jones & Taylor Experience, which was released on Isaac Bolden's Soulin' Records label in 1985.

These exploratory efforts to exploit rap's novelty and to harness it to a touristic portrayal of the life and culture of New Orleans drew little notice in the early 1980s, and the people that produced "Make It, Shake It, Do It Good!" and "Mardi Gras Rap" remained relatively disconnected from the grassroots hip-hop scene taking shape in the city. In contrast, DJ groups like New York Incorporated, Masters of the Turntables, and the Brown Clowns enjoyed widespread popularity with teenagers and young adults; rapper Bust Down recalled that "hundreds, . . . maybe a thousand people would show up to see them" when they performed at high school dances or other venues.[64] These groups did more than play and mix recordings from rap's centers of production; they also often included "live" elements such as rappers and backup dancers.

Active between 1984 and 1986, New York Incorporated set the standard for DJ groups in 1980s New Orleans. Its organizing force was Denny Dee, a rapper and DJ from Queens, New York, who "transplanted himself" to New Orleans around 1980, bringing with him "all the equipment and skills (such as transforming and battle mixing) that were essential to a budding turntablist."[65] The group also included Denny Dee's cousin, DJ Wop, DJ Mannie Fresh (Byron Thomas), as well as several rappers (including Mia "Mia X" Young, under the stage name Polo B) and male dancers known as "Country" and "Mike."[66] Although they never released any recordings, the group was widely popular on the local scene, frequently opening touring concerts by national rap acts when they came to New Orleans.[67]

New York Incorporated disbanded in 1986, and its members enjoyed varying degrees of success in their endeavors. Denny Dee, the group's founder, descended into obscurity, but other members were able to use their experience in the group as a springboard for successful careers in the local, regional, and (eventually) national/global markets.[68] As Mia X, Mia Young went on to become the most successful female rapper in the history of the Gulf Coast after several nationally distributed albums on Master P's No Limit label in the late 1990s.[69] The group's DJ, Mannie Fresh, became a pivotal figure in the emergence and crystallization of the local style called bounce in the early 1990s, as well as the successful marketing of bounce-inflected rap to national audiences later in the same decade. New York Incorporated deserves mention not only for its pioneering role and the later success of several of its members, but also as an indication of the ways in which New Orleans artists and audiences understood the relationship between place and rap music during this period. Both the name and history of New York Incorporated demonstrate how notions of authenticity were supported by conceptual and biographical connections to New York.

New York Incorporated enjoys the distinction of being the first well-known rap act in New Orleans. Along with other DJ groups, it was part of a transitional phase in local hip-hop, helping to popularize rap and providing opportunities for aspiring rappers, dancers, DJs, and producers to gain exposure and experience. The performances of New York Incorporated were supported by the Rescue Crew, which subsequently led to the formation of another group, Ninja Crew, who became "the first New Orleans rappers to expand beyond the city limits."[70] The trio performed in "ninja" costumes and included rappers Gregory "Gregory D" Duvernay and Terence "Sporty T" Vine, backed by Terrence "DJ Baby T" McKenzie. They caught the attention of the South Florida label 4 Sight Records after an extemporaneous phone audition for label owner Billy Hines, and traveled to Fort Lauderdale to record, releasing a twelve-inch single with "We Destroy" on the A-side.

As Roni Sarig notes, "The record did well among 4 Sight's core audience in Florida and Georgia, and also wound up on AM 940 WYLD in New

Orleans."[71] The style of music on the recording is firmly anchored within the national conventions of the period and shows little to no influence from the New Orleans local vernacular music environment. It consists of beats derived from records manipulated on a turntable by DJ Baby T, who adds "scratching" techniques in the DJ spotlight track on the B-side, "Baby T Rock." The song's lyrics are rendered in impressive back-and-forth patter, a presentation comparable with contemporaneous work by nationally popular groups like Run-D.M.C. or the Beastie Boys. Except for a brief mention of New Orleans by Gregory D in "We Destroy," the lyrics avoid any references to the local context, boasting instead of the performers' superior abilities.

Ninja Crew's recording career began and ended with their 4 Sight single, and, like New York Incorporated, the group (together for less than two years) disbanded without achieving any substantial success except on the local level. Still, the individual members of Ninja Crew—rappers Gregory D and Sporty T, and DJ Baby T (who later changed his stage name to DJ Lil' Daddy)—went on to have prolific careers in rap music at the local and regional levels. After Ninja Crew's demise, Gregory D teamed up with former New York Incorporated DJ Mannie Fresh to form a duo that quickly became the most prolific New Orleans–based rap act of the late 1980s—as Lil Wayne recalled in 2011, "Gregory D was . . . New Orleans's first real big hip-hop artist."[72] While Gregory D and Mannie Fresh generally aspired to make music that was stylistically and thematically similar to that being made in the major centers of production, they were also responsible for several early and influential expressions of locally oriented rap in New Orleans. A brief review of their recorded output during this period is instructive for the insight it provides into the strategic decisions that artists and companies engage in at particular times to privilege or deemphasize local content.

Like Ninja Crew, Gregory D and Mannie Fresh looked outside of New Orleans for support and signed with the Los Angeles–based independent D&D Records. The duo enjoyed moderate success with the 1987 single "Freddie's Back," inspired by the *Nightmare on Elm Street* films.[73] While Mannie Fresh classified "Freddie's Back" as "a southern song" based on its use of the Roland 808 drum machine, its lyrics and music, like those of the full-length album, *Throw Down,* released on D&D the same year, are geared toward the imagined tastes of national audiences.[74] An exception is the song "Never 4-get Were I Come From," a tribute to the support that the rapper (imagined as "world-renowned and [having] millions of fans") received from his hometown crowds. In his narrative, Gregory D's exploitation of the local relies on his own connectedness and loyalty to his hometown and neighborhood, rather than any particularity of the New Orleans rap scene or cultural environment in itself.

Nevertheless, "Never 4-get" contained several musical elements that increased its relevance to local audiences. Near the end of the song, Gregory D leads a male group in a "roll call" of New Orleans's black neighborhoods, with the names of places representing the identities of the people who live there; as he calls out the name of a neighborhood (e.g., "That third ward!"), the chorus responds, "Can't never forget!" Alternating in this fashion, the list covers most of the predominantly black areas of the city (the third, seventh, ninth, twelfth, thirteenth, seventeenth, and fifteenth wards, as well as the middle-class Seabrook subdivision), then moves to higher-level categories such as New Orleans East, Uptown, and Downtown. The rapper breaks off from this list of neighborhoods to include a cluster of references to the early rap groups in New Orleans, or at least those that Gregory D and Mannie Fresh were closely tied to ("That Ninja Crew! . . . New York Incorporated! . . . That Rescue Crew!"), and the list ends with a jubilant shouting out of the name of Gregory D's high school, "Kennedy!"

This is the first known recorded instance of this specific lyrical device— a semi-comprehensive listing of black neighborhoods and communities in New Orleans that alternates between solo performer and audience/group response—which in the years that followed would become a common feature of songs that attempt to exploit the values, preferences, and subjectivities of local audiences. It is a particularly effective device for connecting with local audiences' attachment to the city's various wards, projects, and neighborhoods, but its appeal is equally rooted in its call-and-response-based structure, with chanted and repeated phrases that energize a sense of collective participation.

D&D Records did not release Gregory D and Mannie Fresh's salute to their hometown as a single, and while it does deserve credit as the first song to include a roll call, it could justifiably be viewed as a filler track among the more commercially viable offerings on the *Throw Down* album. But another New Orleans rap song, released in 1988 on the independent Rosemont Records, spoke much more directly and exclusively to local sensibilities. In the seven-inch single "Let's Jump," MC J' Ro' J (Roy P. Joseph Jr., now known as Abdul Malik) represented the city's African American vernacular culture through lyrics, backing music, and the organization of the vocal performance. While the cover image of the rapper wearing a New York Yankees baseball cap and a thick gold chain situates him within rap's

RS 1288

MC
J' RO 'J

"LET'S JUMP"

The cover image of J' Ro' J's 1988 single "Let's Jump" shows the influence of New York–based hip-hop culture, but the song's music and lyrics grounded it firmly in New Orleans and local forms of vernacular expressive culture. Courtesy of Abdul Malik.

stylistic mainstream, the narrator of "Let's Jump" positions himself at the center of the local rap sensibility and scene through the use of musical and lyrical content keyed to the social geography and the vernacular, "street parade" sensibility of working-class black New Orleanians.

While Gregory D's lyrics in "Never 4-get Were I Come From" held few specifics about New Orleans, the lyrics of "Let's Jump" take the city and the particular musical and celebratory traditions of its black neighborhoods as its primary subject, with the narrator's authenticity deriving from his adept participation in these types of events: "This is the truth, it's an actual fact / That we will buck jump to a drop of a hat / As we clap our hands and stomp our feet / I said, this is how we roll to the buck jump beat." Even when they serve the classic rap function of self-aggrandizement, the lyrics of "Let's Jump" maintain a particularity with regard to New Orleans's black culture ("I'm the uptown ruler, I'm cool and I'm hard / I'm well known in every ward"). While many of the song's lyrics speak to the experience and perspective of working-class black New Orleanians, others frame local identity within the dominant images of the expanding tourism industry: "New Orleans is full of happenings / Smiling faces, jamming places, all sorts of things / If you ever decide to come to New Orleans / Sit and try a taste of our native cuisine." These lyrics and others like them mentioning local landmarks are reminiscent of Parlez's 1983 "Make It, Shake It, Do It Good" single and demonstrate the ways in which New Orleans rap music incorporated and strategically deployed more widely held and commercially inflected notions of the city's cultural and historical distinctiveness.

In "Never 4-get Were I Come From" and "Let's Jump," Gregory D and J' Ro' J refer to the practice of "buck jumping," described by Abdul Malik (J' Ro' J) as a solo dance form involving "hops and leaps and . . . a lot of footwork," which was closely connected to New Orleans's "second line" culture.[75] Writing about the rap-influenced Rebirth Brass Band, Ben Sandmel observed that their "young peers [have] developed a unique solo dance called 'buck-jumping.'"[76] It remains unclear how directly this dance draws on earlier, similarly named African American traditions from the area: WPA-era interviews with former slaves from the South Louisiana sugar country include reference to "the buck dance that . . . evolved as a flexible fluid dance in which the slaves, bending low to the ground, pounded the earth with rhythmic intensity."[77] Shane and Graham White, in their study of slavery-era musical practices, describe a "widely popular slave dance-form known as buck dancing," which if nothing else bears an archetypal resemblance to the highly competitive, public dance battles sometimes associated with rap: "Attention was initially fixed on the fast-stepping dancer, a solo performer, who beat out exciting rhythms with his feet. But, typically, buck dancing took place within a communal context . . . As the dance progressed, the spirited participation of onlookers invited others to jump into the central space, challenging the current performer's dancing skills."[78] Possible associations with aesthetic competition are also suggested in the meaning assigned to the verb *to buck* in the jazz era, when competing brass bands would "'buck' (compete against) one another" in public spaces.[79]

"Let's Jump" is also noteworthy because of the ways it represents the idea of local culture and experience through musical (rather than lexical/textual) signifiers. Produced by DJ JMK, the song was the first to use samples of the music of New Orleans brass bands as a way to connote the vernacular traditions of the city's black communities, an idea that was continually employed in recordings by a variety of other artists (39 Posse, Big Heavy, Da' Sha Ra', Ricky B, and 2 Blakk, among others) over the decade that followed. Samples of several songs from the Rebirth Brass Band's 1984 debut *Here to Stay!* surface in different parts of "Let's Jump," including "It Ain't My Fault" and a (tuba) bass line from "Shake Your Booty" that exemplifies the fondness on the part of Crescent City musicians and audiences for "vocally suggestive horns."[80] The chorus of "Shake Your Booty"—which includes collective vocal performance alternating with horn lines—is also appropriated in "Let's Jump," adapted to a new antiphonal structure in which the rapper answers the band's exhortation with one of his own, the title phrase, "Let's jump!" Like "Never 4-get Were I Come From," the tempo of "Let's Jump"—98 beats per minute (b.p.m.)—is also within the range that would become established as a defining local preference in the early 1990s.

Another highly distinctive feature of the song that connects it to earlier forms of local musical identity is its propulsive rhythmic pattern (made with the Roland 808), which resembles the New Orleans "walking rhythm" described by R&B-era drummer Jabo Starks as "a beat that's not on, but it's not off—it's in between.[81] In "Let's Jump," this effect is produced by heavily syncopated, parade-inflected electronic snare and bass drum patterns, which form the foundation for a mixture that includes hi-hat, clave, and electronic handclaps. A connection to New Orleans's nascent rap scene is also established through the use of a small vocal sample from Gregory D and Mannie Fresh's "Never 4-get Were I Come From." Additionally, the song concludes with a "roll call" similar to that featured in Gregory D's song, in which the rapper uses call-and-response structures to encourage audience members to represent their wards.

Because of its unmistakably local orientation (both in terms of content as well as marketing and distribution), it is doubtful that "Let's Jump" received much exposure beyond New Orleans, but it represents an important link in the chain of early expressions that attempted to define and exploit a local musical sensibility. But the song marked the high point of MC J' Ro' J's engagement with the musical, thematic, and social elements of New Orleans vernacular carnival and parade traditions. In the early '90s, he abandoned his career as a solo rapper and founded several record labels, including Emoja and Slaughter House, which released seminal recordings by artists including Mia X, the Bally Boys, Lil' E, and Fila Phil in the early to mid-1990s.

"Buck Jump Time (Project Rapp)" (1989)

About a year after the release of "Let's Jump," a two-song single by Gregory D and Mannie Fresh further elaborated and celebrated a distinct local sensibility through a combination of explicit lyrical references and implicit qualities on the level of style or concept. The duo had departed from Los Angeles–based D&D and signed with the local Uzi Records label, headed by Brian Smith. Their sole release on the label was a twelve-inch single containing the songs "Buck Jump Time (Project Rapp)" and "Where You From? (Party People)," both of which encapsulated the distinctive sensibilities of the emerging New Orleans rap scene.

"Buck Jump Time" and "Where You From?" are similar and easily confused. They share a tempo of around 112 b.p.m., and both rely on refrains chanted in a call-and-response pattern that alternates between an individual and a group. Both songs also include prominent references to various New Orleans wards, neighborhoods, and housing projects. While relatively complex and nonrepetitive lyrical content linked these songs to rap's mainstream, their articulation of a local New Orleans sensibility unfolded forcefully along multiple dimensions: participatory, group-based vocal performance; rhythmic devices such as clapping and propulsive bass and snare drum beats to connote the New Orleans street parade; and lyrics that include references to street life in the city's black neighborhoods and housing projects.

In the lyrics of both songs on the twelve-inch, Gregory D contextualizes his discussion and celebration of New Orleans's "hardness" and neighborhood culture within a national rap industry dominated by the established centers of production—"New York this, California that / Forget that talk, this is where it's at." In "Where You From?," discussion of New Orleans— "the city of doom"—is prefaced by references to several established places on the rap map: "The city that is overlooked / But from this point, the stand has been took / I know you heard of Strong Island [Long Island, home of Public Enemy] and Hollis, Queens [home to Run-D.M.C.] / But let's talk about New Orleans!"

The lyrics of "Where You From?" begin by asserting the uniqueness of New Orleans and the desire on the part of its young people to participate in the "scene," understood here as the national rap music culture and industry. In his verses, Gregory D describes house parties in different parts of town (including the Seventh Ward, Hollygrove, and New Orleans East) where conflicts occur between rival groups representing different housing projects or wards. While the narrator and his group of friends try to leave before violence breaks out, they are obviously fascinated with the charged atmosphere that surrounds these clashes. The exploration and celebration of local neighborhood- or ward-based rivalries contained in the songs serve both to "represent" New Orleans textually as well as to establish the city's position in rap's symbolic economy of outlaw authenticity in which the dangerousness of a place elevates its credibility.

The expression of a particularized local identity in "Where You From?" is also achieved through musical devices. The song's prominent featuring of background chanting by a group of males places the emphasis on call-and-response-based collective participation and dynamic communication between an individual performer and competing groups of audience members. While the lyrics feature complex and nonrepetitive narrative portions, they also include important sections in which phrases (usually names of places) are repeated rhythmically in a chanted fashion. These "war chants"—ward or neighborhood names chanted by a group of male backup singers—are voiced over a stripped-down backing track consisting of syncopated bass drum notes and handclapping in an eighth-note pattern, which, in combination with collectively voiced chants, serves to connote the sense of collective energy and enthusiasm expressed in the city's black parade and carnival culture.

In a similar vein to "Where You From?," the song on the flip side of the record, "Buck Jump Time," was composed "to put the city on the map and represent New Orleans," and uses lyrical and musical devices to establish connections with the traditions and culture of black New Orleans.[82] In addition to the centrality of the "buck jump" concept and the use of synthesizer-generated sounds that suggest a trumpet, the song's connection to second line culture was established though its beat, made with the Roland 808 and featuring a propulsive bass drum layered with snare drum and highly syncopated sixteenth notes played on the ride cymbal. The song has enjoyed enduring popularity in New Orleans for years, and is considered by producer Mannie Fresh to be "one of [his] biggest accomplishments" in a career that encompasses more than twenty years of New Orleans–based rap music.[83]

"Buck Jump Time" begins with an antiphonal roll-call in which Gregory D calls out the names of the city's housing projects ("That Callio!" "That Melpomene!") and is answered by the male chorus chanting the song's title in response. The lyrics consist of listing and (briefly) describing some of

New Orleans's black neighborhoods and housing projects, as well as some of the criminal activities (such as robbery or drug trafficking) of their inhabitants. As the song progresses through several distinct parts, Gregory D portrays himself addressing a crowd and stoking its collective energies to ever-higher levels.

As with "Where You From?," the lyrics of "Buck Jump Time" construct a volatile and paradoxical representation of black life and experience in New Orleans. Both songs ultimately celebrate inner city New Orleans as a cultural whole (albeit a neglected, misunderstood, and somewhat pathological one), but they are animated by creative tension derived from the documentation, celebration, sonic recreation, and (potential) incitement of the potent rivalries between opposing neighborhood groups. According to Gregory D, "When that record came on, motherfuckers went crazy," and veteran DJ Captain Charles lamented that he could not play "Buck Jump Time" without a fight breaking out in the club.[84] In several cases reported in the *Times-Picayune,* this and similar songs that feature the chanted names of wards or projects seem to have been particularly effective at setting off the volatile mixture of neighborhood pride, gun violence, and vendetta killing that plagued the city throughout the early 1990s, spurring participants and journalists alike to frame the relationship between musical representations of ward-based conflict and real-world violence as directly causal.[85] Needless to say, these tensions between neighborhoods or groups of people—and the easy access to powerful firearms that transformed their release from fistfights to much deadlier forms—existed prior to being represented in song. But in consideration of music's transformative potential theorized by Charles Keil, Sara Cohen, and others, it is likely that these songs do more than passively reflect an existing social reality and have a significant potential to catalyze real-world action, including violence.

Gregory D and Mannie Fresh left Uzi Records after the untimely demise of label owner Brian Smith, a suspected drug dealer who fell to his death in June 1989 from a hotel balcony as he tried to escape from U.S. Drug Enforcement Administration agents.[86] Dallas-based entrepreneur Kim Bihari quickly signed the duo to his newly formed independent label, Yo! Records, and they released the full-length *"D" Rules the Nation* later that year. Chicago-based house music producer Steve "Silk" Hurley engineered and mixed the album, which featured few lyrical or musical references to New Orleans.[87] The album's visual presentation also does little to establish a clear relationship between the artists and their hometown, although Mannie Fresh does appear on the cover wearing a cap bearing the name of the New Orleans Saints football team. With several images of the African continental outline, the cover imagery of *"D" Rules the Nation* touches on another, more abstract geographical imaginary, the Afrocentrism of nationally popular late '80s groups like Public Enemy and A Tribe Called Quest, among others. Gregory D's local affiliation was enough to make the record popular in New Orleans, and it received "heavy airplay on WYLD and WQUE," the two stations competing for the city's rap-urban market in the late 1980s.[88]

The duo recorded a new version of "Buck Jump Time" for their album on Yo!, which, when compared with the earlier twelve-inch single on Uzi Records, yields a unique perspective on the ways in which local and mainstream sensibilities were mediated by New Orleans artists during this period. While the lyrics on the twelve-inch began by listing New Orleans's housing projects, the album version starts by naming some of the major cities of the United States, placing emphasis on the potential contributions of the U.S. South in general to the rap music form. Whereas the twelve-inch version represented a charged musical exploration of the creative and destructive energies that animate New Orleans's deeply felt neighborhood-based affiliations, the album version introduces outsider audiences to a more generically southern form of rap expression. The musical content of the song, however—in which Scott Aiges found "clear second-line influences"—remained largely the same in the single and album versions.[89]

"Buck Jump Time" and "Where You From?" hinted strongly at the possible future development of a highly localized interpretation of the rap form in New Orleans, but these songs remained in the background of Gregory D and Mannie Fresh's attempts to forge careers within rap's mainstream, especially after Gregory D signed as a solo artist with the major label RCA. He subsequently toured nationally with West Coast rappers Too Short and Spice-1, and filmed a music video for his single "Crack Slangas" in the gangsta rap capital of South Central Los Angeles. The release in 1992 of his full-length album *The Real Deal* was celebrated in New Orleans with "an autograph signing party at Odyssey Records [and] a party at the downtown Sheraton" arranged by RCA, but the album's sales fell far short of expectations.[90] Producer Mannie Fresh attributed the disappointing result to a dilution of the duo's original sound and artistic vision at the insistence of RCA, who "started telling us what we should be doing . . . [That] we need to change our sound."[91] For whatever reason, a national following failed to materialize for Gregory D, and by 1994 he was back with Kim Bihari's label (now renamed Midwest), struggling to carve out a slice of the New Orleans market that he had largely been able to take for granted in the 1980s. His Midwest album *Niggaz in da Boot* was marked by explicitly local expressions, in its title (which includes a popular slang term for the boot-shaped state of Louisiana) and in its inclusion of the 1989 twelve-inch (local) version of "Buck Jump Time."

"It Was a West Bank Thing" (1989–1991)

As the 1980s came to a close, more and more skilled rappers and producers emerged from the New Orleans area. Groups like Full Pack, ERC, and 39 Posse built local reputations, while other rappers, including MC Thick, Bust Down, and Warren Mayes, made records subsequently picked up by major labels or large independents from outside New Orleans in the years 1989–1991. Like "Let's Jump" or "Buck Jump Time," the work of these pre-bounce rap artists and groups contained musical and lyrical elements that foreshadowed the emergence of a more particularized local music sensibility.

The most prominent members of the next generation of rap performers in the city came from one part of town, the West Bank. Despite its name, most of the area is located to the east and south of central New Orleans, from which it is separated by the meandering Mississippi River. The West Bank includes a small part of Orleans Parish, where Algiers and the site of the now-demolished Fischer Projects are located. To the west, in neighboring Jefferson Parish, lie the suburbs of Gretna, Harvey, Marrero, and Westwego. A cohort of rappers from this part of New Orleans, including MC Thick, Bust Down, Ice Mike, and Tim Smooth, built on local fame to attract the attention of major labels or large, out-of-town independents in 1990 and 1991.[92] Their success inspired others' efforts, and their geographic concentration on the West Bank made easy fodder for rivalries between them and rappers across the river, as documented in the song "It Was a West Bank Thing," by the Ninth Ward–based group Most Wanted Posse.

MC Thick (Stewart Glynn Harris) grew up in Marrero, an unincorporated part of Jefferson Parish with around 45,000 residents. The portly Harris "began his career in the ninth grade by forming the rap group Thick and Thin," but he soon developed a career as a solo artist, honing his skills at talent shows and nightclubs.[93] MC Thick's career took off in early 1991, when the nineteen-year-old released his debut single, "Marrero (What the F— They Be Yellin)." Produced by J. "Diamond" Washington for his Alliv Records label, the song features a loping beat with a relatively slow tempo (88 b.p.m.). Its chorus consists of a complex montage of samples, which ultimately concludes with a group chanting, "Marrero!" in response to the leader's question, "What the fuck they be yellin'?" References to specific places within Marrero and individual law enforcement officers contributed a sense of documentary realism to the lyrics of the gangsta (or "reality") rap song, which revolved around the local drug trade and its byproducts of crime, violence, and aggressive police tactics. They express an ambiguous social commentary that simultaneously criticizes and glorifies the excesses of the crack-fueled drug trade in Marrero.

By August 1989, the *Times-Picayune* reported, MC Thick's single on Al-liv had sold three thousand copies, and the song was "among the top five most-requested songs on radio station WQUE," leading to "heightened interest in his nightclub performances." Several months later, the newspaper reported that the rapper had signed a deal with "giant record company" Atlantic, which released "Marrero" nationally in late November 1991.[94] Another single, "From the Brick Jungle" (a "Marrero" knock-off) soon followed. MC Thick's debut album, *The Show Ain't Over till the Fat Man Swings,* came out on Atlantic's Big Beat subsidiary in 1993.

MC Thick's ascent boded well for the New Orleans rap scene, but his depiction of Marrero as a war zone where cops and drug dealers vied for dominance was greeted unenthusiastically by local civic leaders. "Marrero" drew the ire of Jefferson Parish councilman James Lawson Jr., a white Democrat who asserted that "Marrero is a good place to live[,] with numerous beautiful subdivisions," and vowed to "ask WQUE to stop playing" the song.[95] But these sentiments had little effect on MC Thick's popularity; he placed first in the "best rap" category in the Big Easy Entertainment Awards in 1992, and performed at the New Orleans Jazz and Heritage Festival soon afterward.[96] "Marrero" represented the peak of his popularity, however, and despite the release of full-length albums in 1993 and 1996, he remained a marginal figure until his death in 2001 at the age of twenty-nine. To an important extent, "Marrero," with its lyrical focus on the local environment and a chorus organized around chanted, call-and-response vocal performance, expressed some of the values that would come to define the intensely local bounce subgenre in the early 1990s.

John "Bust Down" Bickham Jr. was another West Bank–based rapper who rose to local popularity in the years preceding the emergence of bounce. He debuted on the local Disotell label around 1990, and in 1991 he signed with Effect, a subsidiary of Miami-based independent Luke Skywalker Records (home to the raunchy 2 Live Crew). Working with producer Herbert Michael "Ice Mike" Scott, Bust Down's best-known effort is the grotesquely humorous and misogynistic "Nasty Bitch." In addition to its over-the-top lyrics, the song's appeal was augmented by the huge booming bass tones punctuating its slow (around 80 b.p.m.), ponderous beat. In a move that again points to the underdevelopment of New Orleans's rap music infrastructure, producer Ice Mike flew to Dallas to use a mastering studio where he could ensure that the bass would be as powerful as technology allowed.[97] The combination proved successful: "Nasty Bitch" became a regional club hit, popular enough in the U.S. South to inspire a female "answer song" eight years later in the form of Memphis-based rapper Gangsta Boo's 1999 single "Nasty Trick."

Explicitly local references, while absent from "Nasty Bitch," were most prominently featured in Bust Down's song "Putcha Ballys On." Dedicated to "the whole New Orleans," it contains "shout outs" to locations on the West Bank ("Marrero, Harvey, the Heights [Kennedy Heights], Algiers") and "'cross that water" ("Ninth Ward, Hollygrove, Uptown"). The rapper voices these place names in call-and-response phrases in which a male chorus responds with the song's title. The inclusion at the beginning of the song of a trumpet sample from the 1970s Mardi Gras song "Second Line" by Senator Jones's group Stop, Inc. connoted the city's carnival culture for local listeners.

Warren Mayes became locally famous in 1990 with a song, "Get It Girl," that, while lacking explicit references to New Orleans, formed an important and influential expression of a local rap music sensibility.[98] Mayes relied heavily on simple, repeated refrains intended to inspire dancers; these "chanted" vocals form a defining element in the song that connects it to the city's vernacular music traditions such as brass bands (who often rely on chanted, repeated refrains for lyrics) or Mardi Gras Indians. For this reason, "many consider ["Get It Girl"] to be the forerunner of bounce."[99] The song was originally released on Bobby Marchan's Manicure Records label, before being licensed to Atlantic Records for national distribution.

Largely adapted from the 1988 Too Short song "I Ain't Trippin'," the song's bass-heavy, swing-shuffle beat creates a relaxed mood conducive to dancing. At around 96 b.p.m, the tempo of "Get It Girl" is in sync with the distinct preferences of New Orleans audiences that would crystallize in the early 1990s. Mayes's exhortative narrative voice, his dance-oriented lyrics, and his fondness for various musical devices that encourage collective participation, made him a local favorite. When compared to the other New Orleans–based rappers who achieved prominence during this period, Mayes deemphasized lyrical complexity, instead foregrounding chants, grooves, and a participatory attitude toward music, aspects that support his classification as an influential forerunner to the bounce style.

While "Get It Girl" made little impact outside of New Orleans, "the record burned up local charts and airwaves" in 1991. Male and female backing dancers supported his live performances, which drew on Mayes's ability to "get the crowd hype . . . [and] the whole club rowdy," and helped fuel his celebrity status.[100] Mayes performed at the New Orleans Jazz and Heritage Festival in 1991, headlined a talent revue at the State Palace Theater, and produced an "answer record" to "Get It Girl"—"Get It Boy" by The Get It Girls & M.C. Donna.

The success of "Get It Girl" in the local market suggests that Mayes's approach to making rap resonated with local audiences, and along with "Marrero," "Get It Girl" was one of the two records produced in New Orleans between 1989 and 1991 that caught the ear of national music companies. While MC Thick's appeal rested on a thinly politicized interpretation of the standard gangsta rap concept, however, Mayes's music featured neither angry rhetoric nor sensationalized imagery of crime and violence. For this reason, "Get It Girl" was out of sync with the rap music conventions of the New York/Los Angeles axis, while displaying much more of an affinity with Miami bass. Mayes could not match the dazzling verbal dexterity of other New Orleans rappers like Gregory D or MC Thick, a fact that led some to view the song as an anomaly in its catchiness and its apparent simplicity.

Mayes came of age in the Tremé (one of the city's most intensive areas of distinctive cultural and musical practices and a stronghold of the city's Creole community) in the late 1970s, when the vernacular culture of black New Orleans was experiencing an exciting revival, transformed by the efforts of funky brass bands like the Dirty Dozen and "second line" groups like the Tambourine and Fan club. Mayes enjoyed strong ties to these neighborhood institutions and traditions—he collaborated with the Rebirth Brass Band, and in the early 1990s he often organized concerts with both brass bands and rappers on the bill. In addition to his extensive connections to the city's vernacular, parade-based expressive cultural traditions, Mayes's ability to please local crowds drew on his long involvement with the city's rap music and club scene. He promoted concerts, founded several small record labels, and worked in nightclubs, eventually opening his own Club 88, among other ventures. A mover and shaker in the New Orleans club scene, the tall and handsome Mayes (a former football player) was also a ladies' man; according to his 1999 obituary, he was survived by thirteen children when he died at the age of thirty-three, shot to death in his car while stopped at a red light at two in the morning.[101]

The releases discussed in this chapter do not cover the entirety of rap music production in 1980s and early 1990s New Orleans. In addition to countless amateurs who aspired to careers in rap during this period, other artists were able to obtain record deals with out-of-town companies, such as Tim "Tim Smooth" Smoot and producer/rapper Ice Mike, both of whom released material on Kim Bihari's Yo! Records. Other local groups, such as 39 Posse and Full Pack, capitalized independent record labels (Parkway Pumpin Records and Pack Records, respectively). These labels initially allowed them to release their own records, but the involvement of talented producers like Craig "KLC" Lawson and "Don Juan" Henry soon led them to record and market music by other artists as well. All of these efforts contributed to the vibrant local scene that existed in the several years prior to the birth of bounce.

3

"Where They At"

In the years between 1992 and 1995, New Orleans's rap scene was transformed by the sudden emergence and rise to widespread local popularity of a distinctive style of rap music, eventually labeled "bounce." Driven by the collective efforts of "independent production networks and links between artists, studio producers, nightclubs, radio programmers, and an eager audience constituency," bounce emerged and "took over" within a relatively short period of time.[1] The new style was oriented toward the musical preferences and narrative perspectives of residents of New Orleans's housing projects and other poor neighborhoods, and it proved to be an enduring and profitable feature of the local music landscape. Its popularity soon spread through concerts and airplay on local radio and helped build a local music infrastructure in the form of clubs, record labels, and retail outlets. Like jazz, R&B, and funk from New Orleans, the distinctive features of bounce stem from its connection to the city's vernacular forms of expressive culture and music.

Rapper MC T. Tucker, backed by DJ Irv, catalyzed the emergence of bounce as a distinctive local subgenre in late 1991 with a song called "Where Dey At." While it built on earlier expressions of a local rap sensibility in songs like "Let's Jump," "Buck Jump Time," and "Get It Girl," "Where Dey At"—which featured chanted lyrics and relied heavily on a 1986 recording called "Drag Rap" for its backing music—crystallized a new set of priorities that would shape rap music in the city for several years to come. In this period, the preferences of New Orleans audiences—which included polyrhythmic layering of musical elements, tempi between 95 and 105 b.p.m., vocal performances in cellular structures, an emphasis on collective experience based in call-and-response rather than individual narrative—were, to an important extent, distinct from those associated with national, mainstream audiences. Artists or companies in New Orleans who ignored these preferences did so at their peril; engagement with audiences at the grassroots level of nightclubs and block parties was a crucial first step for aspiring artists, producers, and label owners, regardless of their personal artistic aspirations, and bounce was quickly becoming central to the expectations of local audiences.

Tucker's "Where Dey At" was quickly followed by a number of similar recordings (by DJ Jimi, Silky Slim, Juvenile, and others) that indulged the increasingly well-defined appetites of New Orleans rap audiences. The "explosion" of the rap scene and local industry in the city that began in 1992 was matched by a corresponding surge in press coverage. Writing in the daily *Times-Picayune* and the free monthly magazine *OffBeat: New Orleans and Louisiana Music, Food, and Art News,* local music critics documented the extent of the genre's popularity and the contested politics of style that it entailed.

During this period, the distinct values and preferences of New Orleans audiences coalesced into an identifiably local interpretation of the rap genre. This development was not universally celebrated; criticisms of bounce abounded, rooted in a hierarchical understanding of musical complexity. That the period in question saw the national exposure of New Orleans–based artists drop from its late-1980s levels, rather than increase, fueled dissatisfaction with the possibility of bounce "representing" the city. Rappers, producers, and record label owners whose aspirations went beyond local or regional markets were especially sensitive to these concerns. Their views were sympathetically received by music critics who disliked bounce and were eager to see New Orleans established as a home of more "serious" rap in an era when African American popular music and vernacular traditions were becoming increasingly central to the city's self-image and marketing as a tourist destination. Of several local critics whose views are examined in this chapter, only one—*Offbeat* columnist and one-time WQUE music director Karen Cortello—approached bounce with anything resembling an open mind. For *Times-Picayune* music critics Scott Aiges and Keith Spera, the local genre was an atavistic embarrassment, "cookie-cutter" "rap lite" with a dance orientation and meaningless lyrics.[2]

Bounce entailed continuities as well as disjunctures in musical style and lyrical content, but it ultimately produced a radical shift in the career trajectories of both established and emergent rap artists and labels in New Orleans. In late 1989 Aiges lamented, "New Orleans isn't known as a center of rap music, by far the most important musical genre to emerge from the decade," but by 1994 he looked back nostalgically on the period "before

Backed by Irvin "DJ Irv" Phillips, bounce pioneer Kevin "MC T. Tucker" Ventry originated the bounce style in New Orleans in the early 1990s. Catch the Wall Productions.

bounce hit, [when] New Orleans rap artists Gregory D, Bust Down, MC Thick and Tim Smooth were signing deals with major record labels such as Atlantic and RCA."[3] The emergence of bounce interrupted the process of connecting these and similar artists to national audiences, as new generations of performers trading in more explicitly local priorities and values rose to unexpected prominence within the New Orleans rap scene.

New Orleans–based artists and owners of independent record labels were often dissatisfied with their continued inability to move beyond the regional level in the early 1990s, but the prevailing circumstances also offered certain advantages. Cultural and geographic distance made it more difficult for national companies to extract talent or ideas from New Orleans's rap scene, allowing local independents to rise to the top of the food chain. They enjoyed a near-monopoly in their access to New Orleans's market and talent pool and had the opportunity to establish creative and commercial networks that could contribute to long-term viability and profit. On the other hand, these companies and entrepreneurs dealt with uniquely negative aspects of the local environment, including poverty, violence, and economic underdevelopment.

In the three or four years after bounce had energized the New Orleans rap music scene and industry in late 1991, a number of labels, including Cash Money and Big Boy, expanded rapidly, building their rosters of artists and producing a steady supply of popular releases. While some companies active in the late 1980s and early '90s (including Pack, Parkway Pumpin, and Soulin') dropped out of the scene, many new record labels—Take Fo', Mobo, Slaughter House, and others—were formed during this period in order to capitalize on the thriving demand for locally oriented rap and to exploit the seemingly endless supply of talent held by New Orleans's projects and black neighborhoods.

Bounce Beginnings

Though bounce did not "explode" until 1992, it built on many years of collective efforts to explore and refine local preferences. To a large extent, these were expressed and reinscribed through recordings like "Buck Jump Time" or "Get It Girl" in which performers used particular themes or stylistic approaches that local audiences found compelling. The New Orleans rap sensibility was also expressed more subtly, through the differential ways in which audiences responded to the work of artists from other cities.[4] Songs that resonated strongly might inspire similar compositions and performances on the part of local producers and artists, or they might be more directly appropriated through electronic sampling. In the case of the song "Drag Rap" by the Showboys, New Orleans more or less adopted a song from New York and made it an anthem of local identity that persists to this day.[5]

"Drag Rap" was part of a small body of work produced in the mid- to late 1980s by the Showboys, a duo from Queens, New York, consisting of Orville "Buggs Can Can" Hall and Phillip "Triggerman" Price. The song made little impact on the national scene when it was released by Profile Records in 1986, selling fewer than five thousand copies, and the group became inactive not long afterward.[6] But unbeknownst to the song's creators, its popularity continued to grow during the late 1980s in the South, especially in Memphis and New Orleans. As John "J-Dogg" Shaw observed in late 1997, "Drag Rap" "became a smash club hit, influencing the local rap scenes [in Memphis and New Orleans] which were to follow."[7] Among rap listeners in these cities, the song was often referred to as "Triggerman." As DJ Jimi remembered, in nightclubs during the late 1980s, "you had to play

'Triggaman,' you had to do that shit for 'bout four hours straight, nonstop, nothin' else, *all* night!"[8]

In terms of its lyrical themes and imagery, the Atlanta-based journalist Roni Sarig writes, "'Drag Rap' was perhaps the first gangsta rap song," although it lacks the genre's defining characteristic of implicit or explicit linkage between the performer's real-life biography and the narrative characterization.[9] Loosely set in the Prohibition era, the song consists of an elaborate exchange of threats between two "gangstas fightin over territory," which are made ironic through levels of rhetorical violence that border on the absurd.[10] A "commercial break" that makes reference to television commercials for deodorant soap and a hamburger chain humorously calls attention to the most basic function of the sensationalized portrayals of crime on shows like *Dragnet:* to promote and sell products that are often quite mundane.

According to producer Mannie Fresh, "What made ['Drag Rap'] so hot around New Orleans was just the [Roland] 808" drum machine.[11] As the Showboys' Orville Hall explained, "At the time there was a new drum [machine], the 808 with that boom sound. We was the first ones to use it where it didn't just come in and go out, it was constant."[12] The tonal qualities of the bass drum and its swinging cadence were central features of the song that drove its popularity in New Orleans, along with its mid-tempo (around 96 b.p.m.) orientation. The "Drag Rap" bass drum pattern was made even more propulsive when combined with a drum break known colloquially in New Orleans as "Brown's Beat," taken from Derrick B's single "Rock the Beat."[13]

Another influential element of "Drag Rap" was a running, ascending and descending ostinato pattern of high notes, "a line that went 'digidigidigidigi,' . . . a constant [that the Showboys called] the bones on the keyboard."[14] This feature would become better known in and around New Orleans as the "bells," and was described by Scott Aiges as a "xylophone arpeggio."[15] The "bones" motif is one of the most persistent and frequently quoted elements of "Drag Rap," contributing a continuous, melodically inflected strain within the polyrhythmic layering that is a central and long-standing feature of the New Orleans sensibility generally. Through repetition, the sample has become an icon of the bounce style, to the extent that even in isolation it connotes New Orleans for rap aficionados.

In addition to the bass drum, the "bones," and "an electro-cowbell on the first and (swung) fourth 16ths of the '4,'" "Drag Rap" contains a large number of distinct musical elements and breakdowns, almost all of which have been subsequently stripped out, sampled, and recombined for use in bounce songs by New Orleans DJs and producers. Other frequently sampled elements include vocal snippets, a powerful break that is played simultaneously on the snare and bass drums, and a version of the thematic motif from the television show *Dragnet* (*dum, dah dum dum*), which, as Ned Sublette indicates, invokes both "a lexical meaning: crime" and the "*habanera* or *tango* [rhythm that] has been part of New Orleans music probably since the late eighteenth century."[16]

The influence of "Drag Rap" on the lyrics and vocal performance style of New Orleans–based rappers remains debatable; nevertheless, the song had a profound effect on the instrumental content of rap music from the city in the early 1990s, and is widely recognized as "the foundation of New Orleans bounce music."[17] Veteran club and party DJ Charles "Captain Charles" Leach recalled in 2005, " 'Triggerman' was such a huge, huge, *huge* song . . . If you was a young kid who came up and wanted to be a rapper or a beatmaker . . . that would be one of the songs you would want to use . . . That was the song everybody related to."[18] Writing about the bounce scene at its creative peak in 1994, Scott Aiges claimed that "Drag Rap" samples were no longer fashionable in music produced for local audiences, but this turned out to be a premature conclusion.[19] While the use of the song may have waned in the mid-'90s, it continued to resurface regularly, especially in the work of artists and record labels oriented toward local audiences. In 2007 Mannie Fresh insisted, "That shit is still a big impact right now," and "It's been heard so much now, it's just programmed into you. A party ain't a party without Triggerman."[20] "Drag Rap" retained its mythical status several years later; as Lil Wayne observed, "You play this song right now, 2011, people will go bananas . . . We took that song and we fell in love with it, man."[21]

Given the evident popularity of "Drag Rap" in New Orleans, it is not surprising that local rappers supported their own performances with the instrumental version of the Showboys' song. Used in this manner, the record was central to a key transition in New Orleans rap that began in December 1991 with the release "Where Dey At" by Kevin "MC T. Tucker" Ventry (sometimes called "T.T. Tucker" or, as in the following pages, simply "Tucker") and Irvin "DJ Irv" Phillips, which catalyzed dramatic stylistic and organizational changes in New Orleans rap. The song, "recorded . . . within 15 minutes," re-created their club performance and relied exclusively on portions of "Drag Rap" for its musical backing, as Phillips kept the groove going continuously for long periods of time using the technique known as "backspinning."[22] The combination of the Showboys' song with Tucker's exhortative, chanted raps made "Where Dey At" a local favorite that, like "Drag Rap," continues to be popular.[23]

Tucker traced his career back to 1989, when he began performing at block parties in the St. Thomas housing project where he lived, and he further honed his skills and developed his repertoire in local bars.[24] It was in one of these, Junius Eli Jr.'s Ghost Town Lounge (located at the intersection of Edinburgh and Eagle Streets in the Carrollton neighborhood in Uptown) that he and DJ Irv became known for performing "Where Dey At." Initially released as "a cheap demo tape" and then as "a hastily recorded single on local label Charlot Records," the song quickly became a local sensation.[25] Despite the technical limitations of the recording, it was put into heavy rotation at the two stations in New Orleans programming rap music in the early 1990s, WQUE and WYLD. On the latter station, "Where Dey At" was "the most requested song"; on WQUE, host Wayne "Wild Wayne" Benjamin and DJ Davey Dee generated a similar level of popular response when they played the record on-air "against the judgment of [their] management team."[26] The radio airplay was matched by brisk sales of the cassette: the owner of Odyssey Records estimated, "Just out of my stores, I would say it sold 500 copies a week . . . This was something that sounded like nothing else, and they had to have it." The song remained a top seller for about three months, and over that time Tucker became a local rap celebrity.[27]

In contrast with earlier New Orleans rappers like Gregory D, Tim Smooth, or Bust Down, whose appeal rested on the complexity or richness of their narrative constructions, T. Tucker asserted in 1994 that his famous performance "wasn't no rap at all," but instead "just talking a gang of bull stuff."[28] With regard to lyrics, his approach consisted of "chanting common phrases heard on the street rather than written raps."[29] The most prominent of these was the title, "Where they at." To describe Tucker's performance as "chanting," however, glosses over the fact that he was using simple, repeated phrases as the basis for extended percussive improvisation within the vocal performance, intercutting them in ways that simulate the manipulation of a recording on a turntable.

Tucker's lyrics in "Where Dey At" consist of an open-ended string of seemingly unconnected phrases (some of them explicitly borrowed from other texts), repeated rhythmically within an open-ended structure based on crowd response and the backing music provided by the DJ. Within the context of an evolving New Orleans rap sensibility, "Where Dey At" shares some of the central elements of such precursors as "Get It Girl" or "Buck Jump Time" (e.g., chanted phrases designed for call-and-response participation alongside local themes and references). Still, "Where Dey At" stood out for its unmitigated indulgence of local musical and lyrical preferences and its raw simplicity, in terms of the conception of the musical and textual dimensions of the song as well as in regard to the production and reproduction of the recording.

The lyrics in "Where Dey At" lack explicit narrative cohesion, but they take on a more unified quality when viewed as music rather than as text. Tucker's lyrics are constructed with an expectation of audience participation within a call-and-response structure. While not immediately discernable in the four-minute version of "Where Dey At" released as a single, this feature is clearly evident in an undated, twenty-six-minute long live recording of Tucker and Irv performing at a club—the crowd can be heard chanting back to the rapper in response to key phrases. It is also likely that, as in Afro-Caribbean forms like dancehall reggae, "vocal and musical quality [were] as important to listeners as [was] the strictly lexical register" in Tucker's performance, and textual meaning was often secondary to the sonic value of a lyric or phrase.[30] The success of Warren Mayes's "Get It Girl"—which mixed more conventional rapped narratives with chanted, repeated phrases—hinted at the readiness of New Orleans audiences to deemphasize explicit lyrical meaning and prioritize "vocal and musical" qualities like rhythmic inflection, timbre, and repetition.

Tucker's vocal performance can also be connected to Afro-Caribbean musical values based on its cellular, rather than linear, structure, "meaning that pieces tend to be constructed by repetition and variation of a short musical cell or ostinato. Variety is provided by altering the pattern or by combining it with another feature." Rather than contributing to tedium, repetition enhances the enjoyment of these short musical elements; as Peter Manuel observes with regard to Caribbean music, "From the aesthetic point of view, the individual polyrhythmic cell is interesting enough that one does not mind hearing it repeated again and again."[31] In one of many instances of this concept in "Where Dey At," Tucker riffs off of the phrase "I'm the nigga you love to hate" in various rhythmic permutations for twelve measures. His extemporaneous performance shows the influence of a groove-centered New Orleans musical sensibility, a collective fascination with the "endless repetition of short motifs" that can be traced back through the twentieth century and beyond.[32] Similarly, the use of repetition in his performance speaks to a deeper, Afro-diasporic cultural context; as Hansen writes, "reduplication in Louisiana Afro-French, as in the Gullah dialect of Georgia and South Carolina and in the West African languages, most often intensifies the meanings of words."[33]

Tucker's voice was as much a percussion instrument as it was a source of textual meaning, and by improvising rhythmic patterns consisting of repeated phrases, he put his vocal performance into dynamic interaction with the backing track and with the audience's verbal and embodied responses. Not only did Tucker include lyrical content that provided a degree of local representation unavailable elsewhere, he also performed in a manner that resonated with the tastes of black New Orleans audiences for participatory, group-based musical expression. The connections between Tucker's style and the vernacular musical traditions of New Orleans were not lost on Scott Aiges, who observed that Tucker's "sing-song chant . . . wasn't too distant from the repetitive call-and-response songs of the Mardi Gras Indians he grew up watching."[34]

The lyrics of "Where Dey At" existed at a level of casual abstraction that accommodated a wide range of literal meanings as well as connoted moods or feelings, including electoral politics, social control, male sexual desire, the hustling lifestyle, the worthiness of the performer, and the city's neighborhood culture. Aiges speculated that the question " 'Where they at?' . . . might refer to 'fly' (pretty) girls, homeboys or the police," an explanation that downplays one of the central meanings of the phrase (especially in light of the longer live recording of the song) as referring to "posses" or groups of audience members who "represent" different wards, neighborhoods, or housing projects.[35] Other lyrics alternately serve the ends of self-aggrandizement and fantasy, the encouragement of the audience to dance, and sexualized commands to an imagined female addressee.

Early in the song, Tucker moves to another lyrical riff—"Fuck David Duke"—that takes the embryonic bounce genre in an explicitly political direction. Duke's status as the only individual named in "Where Dey At" speaks to the depth of feeling generated by the unrepentant former Klansman's campaigns for governor and president in the early 1990s. The infusion of this crude politicized rhetoric into a song dominated by boasting and sexual themes helped make the lyrics a collection of "non sequiturs" for Roni Sarig.[36] But the pairing of the phrases "Fuck David Duke" and "Fuck 5-0" [i.e., the police] later in the song posits a connection between overt anti-black racism represented by Duke and the everyday interactions of police and citizens in New Orleans's poor and working-class black communities, which were marked by long-standing distrust, corruption, and violence. As with New Orleans jazz and R&B, however, the political significance of bounce is not defined by lyrics about David Duke or the police, but rather by the autonomy with which African American youth created participatory adaptations of rap music that spoke to their own particular experience and cultural frame of reference.

Despite their meteoric rise in the local market, Tucker and Irv were unable to capitalize on their newfound fame. An offer by Miami-based Luke (formerly Luke Skyywalker) Records held out the possibility of further regional exposure, but their manager, Louis Phillips III (Irv's brother), rejected the terms of the agreement.[37] At the peak of his fame, Tucker violated his parole and was jailed for a year and a half, spending his time "working in the kitchen of the state penitentiary" in Winfield, Louisiana.[38] He was released around late 1993 or early 1994; in a March 1994 article Aiges notes, "Tucker returned from prison calling himself 'the father of bounce,' and began work on his first full-length album, which was expected to be released in late March [1994]."[39] A single featuring "Let the Booty Shake" and "Where Dey At? Part 2" was all that materialized, however, and his career stalled. The rapidly changing local rap market, combined with Tucker's repeated episodes of incarceration, contributed to the rapper's inability to regain the prominence that he had attained in late 1991 and early 1992. For his part, Phillips was convicted of sexually assaulting a fan in Texas during the summer of 1992 and served eight years in prison. He was shot to death in 2001, less than a year after his release.

The raw qualities of the performance and recording, the adherence to local stylistic and thematic priorities, and a heavy reliance on "Drag Rap" have all hindered the widespread exposure or reproduction of "Where Dey At" outside of New Orleans. As of 2010, nearly two decades after the song's initial release, it had only been released sporadically, in limited quantities, as the product of fly-by-night companies or as a bootleg. Despite its apparent lyrical, technical, and conceptual simplicity, however, Tucker and Irv's song introduced radical changes in the city's rap scene, and put emerging local preferences into sharp relief. For these reasons, "Where Dey At" stands as the single most influential rap song to come out of the New Orleans market.[40]

The Scene Expands

The subsequent production of a number of songs in 1992 and 1993 that responded or referred to Tucker and Irv's song was a telling indicator of the extent of its influence on the local scene in the early 1990s—as rapper Floyd "Everlasting Hitman" Blount put it, "Everybody runnin' 'round town bitin' [i.e., appropriating] Tucker rap." Ramona "Silky Slim" Mark's song "Sister Sister," released in February 1992 on Mugz Records, was probably the first knock-off, coming out just months after Tucker and Irv's "Where Dey At." The song's title and chorus adapted the concept and borrowed the rhythmic cadence from Tucker's lyric, "I'm the nigga / The nigga nigga," a connection that was strengthened by the inclusion of a cameo appearance by Tucker himself on the recording. "Sister Sister" did not use any samples from "Drag Rap," but a short ostinato motif repeated throughout the song achieved a similar effect to the Showboys' "bones" and further linked Silky Slim's song to the emerging conventions of bounce.

"Sister Sister" presented some of the core ideas and themes of "Where Dey At" in a less concentrated and more professionally produced form. Sonic variety and extended narrative verses increased its potential for wider appeal and marketability. While not the first female rapper on the scene in New Orleans, Silky Slim was the first to record in the bounce genre, which benefited from the contributions of many women performers during the first half of the 1990s. Tucker and Irv's "Where Dey At" had resisted facile commercial exploitation, but "Sister Sister" demonstrated the possibility for wider success held by recordings that presented the distinctive New Orleans approach to rap within more polished arrangements. Silky Slim signed a deal with New York–based independent Profile Records, which released "Sister Sister" as a single, "with an LP option" based on sales of the twelve-inch, making her one of the few performers in this period to attract attention outside of New Orleans with locally oriented style or content.[41] The song garnered a positive (if brief) review in *Billboard* and received radio airplay in Louisiana and neighboring states, but its sales fell short of expectations, and Profile released Silky Slim from her contract.[42] Mark resurfaced in 1994, when she released an album (*Bouncin' in a Six Tray*) on Big Boy Records under the name "Silky."

Building on these efforts, the next important step in the establishment of bounce began with a local music entrepreneur, Isaac Bolden, who, sensing the commercial possibility in Tucker's song, released a similar recording by an artist named Jimi "DJ Jimi" Payton. Bolden was an experienced song-writer and arranger who since the 1960s had produced R&B, soul, funk, and disco records on his Soulin' label by artists including Tony Owens and Jean Knight. Ever attuned to the shifting terrain of the music business, he had ventured into rap in 1989, releasing a single and album by the duo Devious D & Baby T (Dion Norman and former Ninja Crew DJ Terrence McKenzie). Despite their impressive skills at rendering complex, extended raps and smoothly blended sample collages and beats, they achieved only a moderate level of success at the local level. Undaunted, Bolden continued to keep his ear to the ground for an artist or song that would produce a hit for him in this era when "the industry was changing" as a result of shifting music styles and generational taste patterns.[43]

Bolden became aware of the potential marketability of Tucker's song in the summer of 1992 while eating at a local seafood restaurant. When

"Where Dey At" was played on the radio, he noticed that "all the customers—you had a lot of young people in there, customers—would be dancing." He inquired about the song at Peaches Records, a hub of the local rap music scene, and was told that the artist was in jail. "Rather than have that record die," he instructed Dion Norman to "cover it," with the caveat, "Don't do the same thing because then it's their song." Citing his distaste for the song, Norman balked at rapping on the record, so Bolden instructed him to "get somebody else." Norman recommended DJ Jimi, "a guy who works at a place called Big Man's . . . a place where a lot of teenagers would go," and who had also worked with DJ Irv. Bolden booked studio time and Norman (with the help of Derrick "Mellow Fellow" Ordogne) produced Jimi's "(The Original) Where They At."[44]

Tucker's and Jimi's songs shared important thematic and stylistic similarities, including the prominent use of samples from "Drag Rap" and the "Where they at?" chorus or hook. Their lyrics consisted largely of phrases intended to encourage dancing and evoke participation on the part of audience members, as well as examples of the "ribald sexual scenarios [and] crude humor . . . in the dirty blues tradition" that would become stock elements of the bounce genre.[45] Still, substantial differences in style and content marked the two versions of "Where They At." Recorded and mixed by an experienced production team, DJ Jimi's song was more polished, with less rhythmic improvisation a more relaxed vocal style than Tucker's raspy monotone. Musically, DJ Jimi's song was slightly slower in tempo and had a more complex backing track, with the "Drag Rap" bass drum, "bones," and cowbells augmented by many other samples, including the theme from the horror movie *Halloween*. An introductory section, as well as the use of effects and the interjection of a variety of sampled sounds (including snippets from Bronx-based B.D.P. as well as local New Orleans rapper Bust Down) helped to further build richness and variety in the song and differentiate it from the earlier single by Tucker & Irv.

With local radio exposure, the recording quickly became an overnight sensation. According to Bolden, "That's all you would hear . . . They played the clean version on the radio . . . [and] the next morning they had orders at the distributor for the record. It was . . . like magic."[46] The fact that DJ Jimi's recording took off in New Orleans even after the apparent saturation of Tucker's song further demonstrates the extent of the local market for this type of material. Jimi's career was transformed from that of a struggling nightclub DJ to a regional celebrity, a status that was enhanced by his raunchy live shows, in which his mother and grandmother often performed as his back-up dancers.

Despite Jimi's growing popularity, Bolden's attempts to license the single to a major label for distribution—something he had achieved with Jean Knight's "My Toot Toot" in 1985 (like Jimi's, a slicker cover version of a song already popular locally) and that he had facilitated with Warren Mayes's "Get It Girl" in 1991—met with resistance: "I talked with the people with Universal, because I did business with them before, Atlantic, and all—'No, too vulgar.' " Even with the inclusion of a clean version suitable for radio play, the majors' response was, "Too vulgar!" Eventually Bolden struck a deal for national distribution with the Memphis-based independent Avenue Records, which helped the record reach the middle regions of *Billboard*'s "Hot R&B singles" chart, where it hovered for around six months.[47] In places that were within New Orleans's regional sphere of influence, such as Houston, the single did significantly better.[48] While it did not garner the major label interest that Bolden hoped for, DJ Jimi's "(The Original) Where They At" helped to further establish the conventions of the emerging bounce style that Tucker's song had initiated. The success of the single led Bolden to release an album of material by Jimi and others, which became another important vehicle for the development of bounce as a distinct and lasting local subgenre.

Owing in part to DJ Jimi's limited experience as a songwriter—he described his own efforts as "acting a fool"—and also to the prevailing ethos of experimentation, the 1992 album *It's Jimi* included several guest appearances by other artists who had never recorded previously.[49] On the single release of "(The Original) Where They At" and on the *It's Jimi* album, an uncredited female rapper performs a song called "Bitch's Reply," a parodic female response to T. Tucker's "Where Dey At." Like Silky Slim's "Sister Sister," "Bitch's Reply" interpolates Tucker's "nigga nigga" motif (a feature that did not appear in DJ Jimi's version). A more serious attempt at a female retort to "Where They At" was included on the *It's Jimi* album, in the form of "Lick the Cat," a song by a performer named MC E. Released as a single in early 1993, the song's lyrics include a chorus that rhymes with and uses the same rhythmic phrasing as Jimi's and Tucker's. In a description that fits much early bounce material, a *Billboard* reviewer wrote that "Lick the Cat" "derives catchiness from repetition with a nursery-rhyme quality to it."[50]

In common with "Sister Sister" and other, later songs by New Orleans–based women rappers, the lyrics of "Lick the Cat" feature a reversal of the themes of male gratification and exploitation of women that mark early bounce recordings by male artists, with a chorus that demands cunnilingus (often figured as the ultimate in sexual submission) from the imagined male listener. The proliferation of female "answer songs" and the aggressive sexuality that they expressed speak both to the popularity of the "Where They At" concept as well as the degree to which women performers promptly and effectively countered the misogynistic aspects of Tucker's and Jimi's songs. "Lick the Cat" quickly faded into obscurity, however, and of the two songs by women on *It's Jimi*, it is the novelty "Bitch's Reply" that has been remembered (faintly, at least) in rap circles. Regardless, both songs demonstrate the potential of bounce and local rap to provide a forum for negotiating and contesting gender roles and sexuality.

Another guest appearance on Jimi's 1992 album, by Terius "Juvenile" Gray, had far-reaching effects on the stylistic and commercial development of bounce. The rapper, who was seventeen at the time, "was approached by D.J. Jimi to record the song [he] had been performing at clubs." The result, "Bounce (for the Juvenille)," became "one of the most requested local songs at radio, record stores, and clubs."[51] Like Tucker's and Jimi's songs, the lyrics of "Bounce" feature no perceptible narrative arc and show an eclectic range of influences, including several lines from a nursery rhyme as well as a quoted riff from the chorus of Shabba Ranks's song "Housecall" (1991). The teenaged rapper told a journalist that "he gets most of his musical ideas from the projects, and that he tries to keep an original New Orleans sound," and in both content and conception his performance was keyed to local tastes and preferences.[52]

"Bounce (for the Juvenille)" became a local sensation in its own right when, according to Karen Cortello, "radio stations and clubs started playing the LP cut, and it caught on."[53] Scott Aiges confirms this account: "Commercial radio has been wearing out the wax on 'Bounce,' but it hasn't been released yet as a single. So all those Juvenile fans have had to buy Jimi's album to hear their song, and Jimi is laughing all the way to the bank"—and indeed, the older rapper was reported to have earned over $200,000 in 1993, when his career was at its height (although much of this income likely derived from live performances).[54] Interviewed in 2000, Juvenile complained, "The song that I put on [DJ Jimi's] album made him a star . . . [but] I didn't make any money back then." Still, he was happy to take credit for originating the local style: "I started chanting, and after a while, everybody started doing it. And it feels good to know that I was doing something right."[55] While his statements amount to a gross oversimplification of the collective and incremental efforts through which a local rap sensibility emerged, Juvenile nevertheless played an influential role in this process. DJ Jimi's career peaked around 1992 or 1993, but his young protégé went on to become one of the most successful rappers in the history of New Orleans and "helped bounce blow up around the country" in the process.[56]

Beginning in late 1991, then, a series of recordings jump-started the bounce genre in New Orleans. Tucker and Irv's local hit "Where Dey At" combined the music of "Drag Rap" with chanted lyrics in call-and-response structures that were familiar to local audiences. In 1992 the "Where Dey At"–inspired "Sister Sister" was one of several early bounce records that garnered attention outside of the city in the form of distribution deals or chart position and coverage in *Billboard*, a fact that would seem to bode well for the future prospects of artists emerging from the local scene. DJ Jimi's subsequent song "(The Original) Where They At," though similar in many ways, attempted to overcome the limitations of Tucker's efforts. With Bolden's substantial experience in the music business, DJ Jimi's release was recorded professionally according to prevailing technical standards and was promoted on local radio. Further, because Bolden had paid for clearance of the samples used in the song's composition, its exposure was unimpeded by legal stumbling blocks.

The early bounce recordings by Tucker & Irv, DJ Jimi, Silky Slim, and Juvenile enjoyed immense local popularity, and in several cases drew notice and sales outside of the regional hinterland—in the distant locale of Cincinnati, *It's Jimi* was for a time the top-selling album by a new artist, although it reached only number 39 in the national charts.[57] Other aspiring rappers were quick to follow on the heels of this foundational group with similar releases, backed by record label owners eager to cash in on the bounce craze. In August 1992 Scott Aiges reported, "New Orleans rap is booming. The number of local artists increases daily. Records are being released on homespun labels almost as fast as stores can stock them, and fans are snapping them up."[58]

Some of these records, like Everlasting Hitman's "Bounce! Baby, Bounce!" (1992) and Lil' Slim's "Bounce, Slide, Ride" (1993), helped to further establish the genre's name and central concepts. In the early years of bounce, the style was defined and elaborated by rappers including Edgar "Pimp Daddy" Givens, Joseph "Daddy Yo" Howard, Papadoc, Terence "Sporty T." Vine, Philip "Fila Phil" Anthony, James "Magnolia Slim" Tapp, and others. Female rappers proliferated in 1993 and 1994, including Mia "Mia X" Young (whose song "Da Payback" was "the No. 1 selling local record of 1993 at Odyssey Records"), Trishell "Ms. Tee" Williams, Angela "Cheeky Blakk" Woods, Cicely "Ju'C" Crawford, and the duo Da' Sha Ra' (Danielle Eugene and Rene Porche).[59]

Opinions varied on the artistic worth of bounce, but one metric of the genre's success in New Orleans—sales—was beyond dispute. Local audiences greeted the efforts of the early bounce artists with enthusiasm, and encouraged the emergence of artists peddling similar material. Owners of local record stores like Odyssey, Peaches, Groove City, and Brown Sugar were understandably pleased. Odyssey's Gary Holzenthal reported in 1992 that "of his 12 top-selling cassettes . . . , nearly all are rap and eight of those are by local artists." An incredulous tone pervades the animated descriptions of "local rap releases [that] fly off the shelves" in unanticipated numbers, "kicking [every major record label] in the butt," especially given the sparse efforts at marketing and low production values that characterized these recordings in comparison with their national competitors.[60] Bounce built up considerable momentum with surprisingly little promotion in the traditional sense. Holzenthal marveled, "The word-of-mouth is so phenomenal, I've never seen anything like it."[61] Despite this remarkable success in the local market, however, reaching national audiences seemed close to impossible. Until Juvenile broke through with "Ha" in 1998, no rapper trafficking in a locally oriented style was able to match the relatively modest achievements of Silky Slim, DJ Jimi, and Juvenile in the early 1990s.

Defining Bounce: Musical Style and Lyrical Themes

By the summer of 1992 collective and dialogic effort between and among audiences, performers, and entrepreneurs had established the basic contours of the new local style of rap, in a process heavily marked by imitation and artistic borrowing; as Scott Aiges lamented, New Orleans had become "a city where rappers by the dozen get by with insipid, simple rhythm tracks" and derivative, uninspired lyrics.[62] Musically, bounce relied on tempi between 95 and 105 b.p.m. and multiple simple percussive patterns (often using handclaps and elements from "Drag Rap," including the "bones" and bass drum) repeated within a cellular structure and combined in a layered, polyrhythmic fashion. The bass drum patterns inflected to accent the end of the measure (similar to "the second line beat—the accent on the two and the four instead of the one and three") creating a propulsive and swinging beat with ties to the city's parade culture.[63] While bounce producers often used samples of other recordings, they also relied heavily on sounds generated by sequencers and drum machines.

The stylistic conventions that generally applied to vocal performance in bounce were also distinctive. Extended narratives were often replaced by a string of shorter, chant-friendly phrases, hooks, or choruses that lend themselves to call-and-response participation. These are rendered in a manner that is more heavily melodic (resulting in frequent use of the adjective "singsong" in describing bounce vocals) and in the early years lyrics were often rendered within specific sixteen-bar rhythmic and melodic patterns that ultimately form another self-reinforcing element of bounce's particularity.[64]

While there was considerable variety in New Orleans rap during the early 1990s, the lyrics of bounce songs have several core themes, with dance being one of the most prominent (DJ Jubilee's 1993 "Stop, Pause [Do the Jubilee All]" was described as "a typical bounce track that simply chants the names of dance styles").[65] Rappers often exhorted listeners at the collective or individual levels to dance, encouragement that was sometimes localized to particular parts of the body ("Shake that ass like a saltshaker"). The representation of various places within the city's African American social geography, which includes housing projects ("Melpomene," "Calliope"), neighborhoods and parts of town ("Uptown," "West Bank"), and even particular intersections ("Sixth and Baronne"), was another defining feature of the bounce style, one that could be employed in multiple ways. The names of these places often form the text of basic call-and-response structures designed to encourage collective participation; at other times, the city's map of wards and projects serves as the contextual setting for linear, "gangsta" narratives.

The lyrics of many of the early bounce recordings revolved around a particular representation of male-female relationships, which resembles the "culture of sexual exchange" described by Rose.[66] Men voiced their sexual and material demands in songs including "Where Dey At," "(The Original) Where They At," "Bounce (for the Juvenille)," "Bounce, Slide, Ride," and even "Stop, Pause (Do the Jubilee All)" by the famously clean-cut DJ Jubilee. These existed in conversation with similar expressions by women rappers, including Silky Slim, MC E, Mia X ("Da Payback"), and Females in Charge ("Where's My Bitch?").

These songs portray a ruthless and mercenary battle between the sexes in which men and women attempt to exploit one another for the commodities they offer. Men who dole out money or other gifts in return for sex ("tricks") and women who engage in sex and demand nothing in return—or, even worse, who reverse the dominant scenario by providing cash or material possessions to their male partners—are all figured as foolish within a logic of exploitation that, like the jargon of "tricking" and "treating," can be understood within New Orleans's history as a center of prostitution, a reputation established during the era of slavery.[67] These statements are almost always intended to be humorous as well as demeaning, however, and they exist in continuity with various African American oral traditions (such as "the dozens") involving hyperbolic, combative verbal exchange. The theme also resonates with the historically rooted understanding of the pimp as a "culture hero" within urban African American culture, whose motto is, according to Roger Abrahams, "The one who does best is the one who manipulates most and is manipulated least."[68]

The career aspirations of Tucker, Irv, and Jimi were vaguely defined and evolved over the course of the 1990s. Scott Aiges emphasized the unexpected nature of their initial success, which he described as "a surprise" or "a fluke" rather than the product of strategy, calculation, or ambition.[69] To the extent that we can accept this explanation, it suggests that specific local audience preferences exercised a pronounced influence on the direction of the local music scene, much more than that wielded by music critics, promoters, or record label owners. While many of the latter were unable to resist expressing their contempt for bounce (and by extension its audience), the genre's resonance with the values and preferences of inner-city youth was strong enough to propel it and the artists associated with it forward on a local and regional level. By attending concerts, purchasing records, and requesting songs on the radio, New Orleans audiences drove the emergence of bounce as the dominant force in the local rap music market.

The press coverage of bounce touched on some of the central dimensions of the music's appeal for local audiences. The most obvious and taken-for-granted of these was the fact that the music was "easy to dance to"; asked to explain "why they listen to bounce music," two eighteen-year-old girls responded, "Because you can bounce to it!"[70] The music's dance orientation is evident in its emphasis on continuous grooves within a particular range of tempi, which facilitate transitions between stylistically similar recordings in a club, party, or radio broadcast setting. The use of highly inflected bass drum patterns and the layered combination of these with other rhythmic and melodic elements all helped to cement the appeal of the music, which combined ideas and preferences drawn from the national/global rap music context with those tied to the historically rooted vernacular music traditions of New Orleans. As Scott Aiges wrote, "Bounce . . . is dance music in a dance city. The shuffle of a second-line beat will turn a New Orleans street into a block party in minutes."[71]

Observers and participants made frequent reference to another aspect of bounce that was thought to explain its appeal among the city's young rap audiences: its reliance on lyrics referring to various housing projects, neighborhoods, and wards within New Orleans. As one local producer explained, "People just chant what we like to hear down here—the wards

and the neighborhoods and all that."[72] Though Aiges clearly did not identify with the "emphasis on local references" that marked bounce, he per-
ceptively identified "inclusiveness" as key to the music's appeal, a value that
structured lyrical as well as musical composition and performance. For
Aiges, however, these participatory elements produced a democratizing or
leveling effect that, by implication, drained rap of its artistry and complexity, reducing it to an "anyone can do it" art form.[73] Aiges also ignored the
ways in which the "inclusiveness" engendered by neighborhood shout-outs
both depended on and contributed to a sense of divisiveness and rivalry
between groups of audience members associated with different neighborhoods or parts of town. This pathological side of neighborhood culture
was the subject of Joe Blakk's 1993 song, "It Ain't Where Ya From," which
sharply criticized black-on-black violence.

Articles on local rap in written by New Orleans–based journalists in the
early 1990s were generally marked by a focus on the issue of bounce and
its distinctiveness, artistic worth, and potential effect on markets and careers. The emergent local style was a phenomenon too imposing to ignore,
simultaneously enabling and constraining the efforts of local artists and
companies. Commenting on his 1993 Big Boy Records release, Sporty T
explained, "I had to give them (the audience) what they wanted . . . They
want bounce, nothin' but bounce."[74] Similarly, a description of a performance by rapper Dion "Devious" Norman asserted that he "left the stage
unfulfilled" despite having driven "thousands of bounce fans . . . into a
frenzy," emphasizing the concessions that bounce demanded from artists
and the resulting diminution of creativity. The rapper complained, "It's
easier for me to bounce and make the crowd get hyped and talk about their
territories than it is for me to get on the mike and talk about something
knowledgeable."[75]

Critics assumed that rappers shared their view of bounce as an unfor-
tunate but unavoidable career necessity imposed by local audiences. As
one journalist noted, "Bounce has become so dominant that local rappers
hoping to establish themselves have adopted it, chanting simple lines over
the 'Drag Rap' beat or something similar with the hope of crossing over to
more conventional rap later."[76] In the same vein, Karen Cortello observed,
"For some reason, many New Orleans rap fans have adopted the 'Drag
Rap' beat as a local theme song. So rappers like [Joe] Blakk use the beat
to get strong local support, which translates into radio airplay and record
sales. It also sets the stage for original, more creative releases later on."[77]

While these descriptions laid the blame for bounce's supposed shortcomings—repetitiveness, musical and lyrical simplicity, lack of creativity—

at the feet of immature and unenlightened audiences, others focused on unscrupulous agents of corporate mediocrity: paraphrasing the opinions of unspecified "underground rappers," Aiges wrote, "Listeners' tastes are shaped by what they hear on the radio, and . . . if radio stations play only pabulum, then that's what listeners get used to and request. If exposed to more adventurous rap, these artists argue, the audience would embrace it," instead of the "simpler stuff" they seemed to prefer. But Cortello made it clear that agency lay in the hands of local listeners: "We [at WQUE] have to play the hits and the records the audience wants to hear . . . The 39 Posse [a local group whose biggest hit was 'Ask Them Hoes'] may not be considered progressive or whatever, but if that's what the audience wants to hear, that's what we play."[78]

These comments and others indicate that the emergence and rise of bounce caused a significant amount of upheaval and conflict within the New Orleans rap scene even as it fueled expansion and growth in the local music industry. To some extent, participants' opinions of the genre were shaped by whether they personally stood to gain or lose ground in the new, bounce-centered environment. Rappers who had cultivated the ability to write and perform extended, nonrepetitive narrative material often derided the new local style as not "real rap"; Timothy "Tim Smooth" Smoot remarked, "[Bounce] should be labeled dance music," as if this alone were enough to disqualify it from serious consideration as rap. He further complained that the new crop of bounce artists "really [doesn't] rap—it's more like cheerleading, like chants."[79] Given the feminized association of "cheerleading," such comments (and similar ones by music journalists) illuminate the gendered dimensions of sense-making and evaluative processes as they relate to the music scene.[80] The conclusions of Peter Stallybrass and Allon White regarding the importance of "interrelating and dependent hierarchies of high and low" in the symbolic representation of culture and society apply to the discourse around bounce, which was often represented in an inferior position within a series of pairings (including but not limited to male/female, mind/body, listen/dance, rap/chant, national/local, creative/derivative, authentic/commercial, serious/silly, heavy/light) that expressed and structured understandings of musical value.[81]

Rappers also complained about the effects of bounce on New Orleans's reputation and identity within the wider rap geography and industry. The popularity of bounce, it was feared, "[diluted] the definition of the local rap sound" and may have "sullied the New Orleans scene in the eyes of some national labels" and other outsiders. As Tim Smooth complained, "The people from other states [who] come here to check our scene out . . .

don't think nothin' comes out of here." Gregory D also had a negative perspective on the emerging local style, insisting that New Orleans–based artists must be able to "create national material that's gonna sell national" to achieve true success. But he also acknowledged the determinative role that music corporations play in terms of their willingness to invest in artists emerging from marginal local scenes: "They don't give a fuck about New Orleans, that's the bottom line."[82]

At times, artists who stood to lose the most from the ascendance of bounce nevertheless tempered their criticism of it with grudging acceptance or even admiration, based on their own sense of hometown pride and an understanding of the music's widespread grassroots appeal. Regarding the use of "Drag Rap" in local rap, Tim Smooth described the "Triggerman" beat as "the cornerstone of the local sound": "Once they put that in, that's New Orleans music—it's like Mardi Gras music. Anybody who uses it will sell." While predicting that the "chant artists, the 'Where They At' people . . . ain't gonna get far from here," producer and rapper Ice Mike conceded, "At the same time, for New Orleans, that's working." For some, like rapper Larry Birden, the fact that they were "not really into" the local style of music did not stop them from seeing it as contributing positively to stylistic diversity and local cultural expression, with potentially marketable results: "There is a totally different sound coming out of New Orleans compared to the industry . . . People looking into New Orleans are like, 'What are they doing down there? That's live, I like that.' That's what's going to be what draws a lot of attention to New Orleans. It's a totally different flavor, a totally different concept."[83]

The response of producers and label owners to the rise of bounce was also multidimensional, often combining a desire to profit from the expanding local scene with attempts to distance themselves or their companies from the music's negative connotations. Ronald "Slim" Williams, president of Cash Money Records, chose to hedge his bets with regard to the possible connections between bounce and the music on his label (some of the most popular in the local market in the early 1990s): "We took it from chanting—what they call 'Where They At'-style—and added lyrics . . . But by us swinging our lyrics, they call it bounce. Other than that, it ain't no different from rap."[84] This description might apply to some songs released under the Cash Money imprint, but others (including those by Pimp Daddy, Ms. Tee, U.N.L.V., Lil' Slim, and even Williams himself, under the stage name B-32) are, in retrospect, not only solidly within the bounce genre but were also instrumental in defining the local style during the years 1992–1994.

James Joseph, a self-described gangsta rapper and president of Pack Records (a company that released several influential bounce recordings in 1992 and 1993), declared that "bounce music . . . is just stupid," made by artists who are "not showing any real talent."[85] The hyperbolic label owner assured a journalist that his group Full Pack would "never stoop to doing a bounce song," although they included one ("Slide, Giddy Up") on a 1993 single. Setting aside his personal feelings, Joseph conceded that "bounce is what's making money now," because "the people who buy rap music down here, they prefer to buy bounce music." Rather than stand on principle, Joseph acceded to the clear preferences of local audiences and advised other interested parties to do the same: "The hip-hoppers, the gangsta rappers—whatever type of music you doing, if it ain't bounce, you going to have a problem. It took over."[86] After selling thirty thousand copies of DJ Jubilee's debut single, Take Fo' Records president Earl Mackie expressed a similar sense of resignation and bafflement toward the popularity of bounce: "The people just like it."[87]

Both Mannie Fresh and Leroy "DJ Precise" Edwards—the "busiest bounce producers" in early 1990s New Orleans—attempted to distance themselves from some of the production values of the local style, particularly the use of the "Drag Rap" record and other sampled sources. Both asserted that they "use only live instruments on their tracks, no samples from other records" (a claim that is contradicted by several subsequent recordings).[88] While DJ Precise observed that "if you do a bounce song locally, independent, you'll make more money than if you do a rap song on a national record label," he also made clear his preference for producing "national sounding" material: "Every time you put out a project, you're really educating the consumer and gettin' them prepared for upper level stuff."[89] Nevertheless, Edwards remained optimistic about the possibility for bounce to catch on in other places, even if the style had peaked in New Orleans: "If you take it into Buffalo, it's something new."[90] For his part, Mannie Fresh, who characterized bounce as "the silliest thing in the world," acknowledged the dynamic nature of the evolving local rap scene, and the push-and-pull between imitation and innovation involved in its development: "Bounce has "got to change, or the public is not going to go for it . . . If you do something simple, they'll say, 'That was two years ago' or 'He ain't saying nothing.' It used to be that you could say the same lyrics that somebody else did and get over, the same little chants. Now you can't say the same old things."[91]

P-Popping and Bounce Dancing

The ways young New Orleanians have danced to local rap and bounce have changed over time, often in response to ideas drawn from the wider national media sphere. Still, they also express significant continuities with earlier genres of popular music in the city and ultimately with their Afro-Caribbean and West African roots. Particular dances of local or extralocal origin have waxed and waned in popularity over time; in the early 1990s these included the Eddie Bauer, the Cabbage Patch, the Beenie Weenie, Bootin Up, the Shackle, the Neck, the Whop, and countless others. Dances might be named after the person who introduced or inspired them, such as the Josephine Johnny, or, as in the case of the Discovery Shuffle, the club in which they emerged. The prolific invention and popularization of new dances continued apace in new generations of bounce dancers: in a 2009 interview Javae Turner mentioned the "Swiggle" and "Iggy Pop" as two of his favorites.[92]

While African Americans in New Orleans have been adept at minting and mastering new dance steps and forms, they have also engaged in more general types of embodied response to local rap—to use the words of Dawan "DJ D-Boi" Gibson Jordan, "bending over, shaking and clapping"—which have been continuously present since at least the early 1990s.[93] In New Orleans, a variety of words suggestive of shaking or similar motion have been used with reference to dance, including "twerk," "work," "wobble," and of course, "bounce." With the emergence of bounce in the early 1990s, a highly suggestive female shaking dance called the "Pussy Pop" or "P-Pop" became an enduring aspect of the audience response to bounce.

P-Popping is performed by women who use their hands to anchor themselves on a wall or floor while isolating and shaking their buttocks. Evidence suggests that the P-Popping dance was present in New Orleans at the time that bounce emerged; in late July 1991 Miami-based journalist Greg Baker noted that the new 2 Live Crew single "Pop That Pussy" was (like the group's earlier hit "Throw the D") "another groin-oriented dance song, inspired during a trip to New Orleans, where a dance by that name is already making the club rounds."[94] While "Pop That Pussy" is musically distinctive from the contemporaneous and similarly themed song "Pop That Thang" by New Orleans–based rapper Bust Down (signed at the time to Luke Records), both songs were inspired by the erotic dances performed by women in New Orleans clubs. "Hey P-Poppers" (1993) by Devious, one of several rap songs by New Orleans–based artists that make reference to the dance, testified to both its widespread local popularity and the

Residents of the Melpomene (later C. J. Peete) housing project dance to music played by Jerome "DJ Jubilee" Temple at a 2002 block party. Catch the Wall Productions.

rivalry between Miami and New Orleans based on their claim to primacy in emerging forms of African American popular culture.

P-Popping existed at a grassroots level in New Orleans before it was appropriated into a wider arena of southern rap music and strip club culture, and (like many aspects of the city's contemporary African American musical culture) it draws on traditions, practices, and embodied cultural memories that connect modern residents to their West African and Afro-Caribbean heritage. The anthropologist and African studies pioneer Melville J. Herskovits, in *The Myth of the Negro Past* (1941), maintained that "recognizable African dances in their full context are probably entirely lacking in the United States, except perhaps for the special area constituted by Louisiana," and it is likely that P-Popping constitutes an expression of what Chadwick Hansen identified in the late 1960s as "a long tradition of erotic shaking dances in America," which "have clearly been continuous within the Negro community."[95] The connection between P-Popping and a West African cultural heritage was not lost on contemporary observers within the New Orleans club and party scene: as Lorén K. Phillips

Fouroux recalled, in the early 1990s "everybody just started dancing. It became more erotic and you really got to see more of New Orleans['s] island heritage—it was more Caribbean, the way people would dance. But no one looked at it like, 'What are you doing?' "[96]

Like other habitués of New Orleans nightclubs, Philips understood and accepted P-Popping, but the frank eroticism of this and similar dances performed by "utterly liberated young women" became more problematic as it moved to more widely accessible venues. Interviewed in a 1998 article on block parties, Barbara Jackson, president of the resident council at the St. Thomas public housing complex, insisted, "I don't have anything to do with them, but a lot of people say they're too vulgar." Rapper Mia "Mia X" Young countered, "It's not sexual; dancing to bounce is about freedom." For some, the public context was more problematic than the dancing itself—as one local mother noted, "I don't let my kids do that dance outside . . . Only inside."[97] The divergent views on dancing, eroticism, and appropriate public behavior often broke down along generational lines, but social class, education, and religious orientation also exercised significant influence. As in the jazz era, local popular music in late twentieth-century New Orleans served to focus deeper and long-standing tensions between divergent attitudes and perspectives. These conflicts sometimes erupted across a black/white divide; at other times, they occurred between different factions within the African American population.

Through public dancing at block parties or in clubs, young African Americans in New Orleans maintain or challenge boundaries of gender and sexual identity. The explicitly submissive and presentational nature of P-Popping makes it the exclusive province of women or gay men. Bounce rapper Josephine Johnny observed, "No real brother is going to do that pop or shake their butt," and for this reason the dance that he introduced was "cool" and "laid-back," allowing men to respond to the music without endangering their sense of authentic, heteronormative identity.[98] While young men who showed an interest in or talent for dancing sometimes had to fend off attacks on their masculinity, they found increased acceptance when they joined a dance crew or group, which allowed them to engage in the art form within a structure built around performance and team-based or individual competition in the form of "battles" showcasing their "shoulder work and shaking."[99] Highly sexualized dancing by women was prevalent on the dancefloor and at block parties, but performances by rappers like Warren Mayes, DJ Jubilee, or Choppa were often supported by all-male dance crews whose moves titillated the female members of the audience.

The Business of Bounce: Record Labels, Radio, Concerts

As with prior genres of black popular music, small, locally owned independent record labels formed a crucial link in the productive nexus between artists, radio programmers, music retailers, and local audiences in New Orleans's rap scene. Some of the earliest rap record labels in the city were owned by individuals who had a toehold in the music business in the 1960s and '70s. Isaac Bolden's Soulin' Records is one case that has already been discussed. J. "Diamond" Washington, owner of the Alliv, Lamina, and Rap Dis! labels, was an accomplished producer by the early 1990s, contributing to the creation of such popular records as MC Thick's "Marrero," Everlasting Hitman's "Bounce! Baby, Bounce!," and Mia X's "Da Payback," among others.

In the early 1990s a number of other labels were capitalized by members of a younger generation of aspiring entrepreneurs. Many of these, including Pack, ERC, and Parkway Pumpin, were owned by artists who used them to release their own work as well as, in some cases, that of other artists. But the stakes were raised considerably over the course of 1992 and 1993, when the local market for rap recordings demonstrated new levels of profitability, and several labels were formed as more serious business ventures. Cash Money, Big Boy, and Take Fo' were some of the most prominent local labels during the period from 1993 to 1995, but they were far from monopolizing the New Orleans scene. A long list of smaller labels came and went, including Mobo, Slaughterhouse, Hit 'Em Up, Mugz, Tombstone, Ready-Or-Not, Disotell, Terrible T, and Mr. Tee Records. Some of these labels predated the emergence of bounce, but made important contributions to the new style nonetheless.

Cash Money Records, started in 1992 by brothers Ronald ("Slim") and Bryan ("Baby") Williams, became the most successful label to emerge in the early 1990s, producing a variety of bounce, gangsta rap, and every imaginable fusion of the two by artists including Kilo G, Lil' Slim, Ms. Tee, U.N.L.V., and others. Veteran DJ Mannie Fresh became Cash Money's in-house producer soon after the company's founding, a position he would hold for over a decade and one that would allow him to exercise an influential role in the evolution of a local rap sound. While many of the other record labels serving the local market in the early years of bounce released music on generic-looking cassettes, Cash Money invested in artwork and packaging; record store owner Gary Holzenthal recalled, "It was the Cash Money guys who started to really make some nice-looking product."[100] These investments gave Cash Money a competitive advantage in the local market, where the company "dominated the local charts by consistently claiming four of the top five spots" in 1994.[101]

Big Boy Records, which would grow to become Cash Money's closest competitor, was capitalized by California native Charles Temple and his partner Robert Shaw, reportedly after Temple won $20,000 at a casino.[102] The label's debut release, Sporty T's "Sporty Talkin' Sporty '93," hewed closely to the conventions established by earlier bounce artists, while subsequent releases on the label by artists including Silky and Partners-N-Crime mixed bounce-inspired hooks and concepts with extended narrative raps and diverse thematic orientation. The style and content of other Big Boy releases, such as those by G-Slimm and Black Menace, were much closer to West Coast–based gangsta rap but were nevertheless locally popular. Like Cash Money, Big Boy benefited from the efforts of an experienced in-house producer, Leroy "Precise" Edwards, who grew up in the Hollygrove area and who had deep roots in the local rap scene. As Karen Cortello observed, "By the late '80's, Precise was producing the majority of local rap acts—everybody from DJ Jimi to Fullpack."[103]

Bounce flourished on the margins of established networks of production and marketing, but the emerging genre benefited from widespread exposure on local radio in the early 1990s. In 1993 Scott Aiges reported, "Radio has played a key role in solidifying bounce's hold on New Orleans."[104] The desire on the part of inner-city New Orleanians to hear their local sound and place names on the radio helped further diffuse bounce within the New Orleans area and helped to solidify its status as a representative local subgenre. Radio's role was more significant in New Orleans than in other places: a 2001 *Mediaweek* profile noted that "the region's scorching heat and humidity in the summer" produced levels of television viewing that were "much lower . . . than in other markets. As a result, New Orleans media is largely dominated by radio during the summer months."[105] Competition in the urban radio market helped fuel the "explosion" of local rap that bounce entailed. The exposure of New Orleans–based artists on commercial radio reached a high point in 1991 and 1992, years when WYLD and WQUE vied for the city's rap audience. In 1993, however, WYLD underwent a change of ownership and eliminated rap from its format. With the consolidation of WQUE's hold on the rap radio market, the amount of local music being played on commercial radio decreased.[106]

Critics writing about the local rap scene in the early 1990s often framed bounce as competing for audience and airtime with "local hip-hop," material with extended narrative raps and an emphasis on textual meaning.[107] Commercial stations like WYLD or WQUE played bounce because of its overwhelming local popularity, and did not play the "underground" rap championed by local music journalists such as Aiges and Spera for the simple reason that it did not make good business sense to do so. In the nonprofit sector, however, bounce was kept at arm's length; Jeff Bromberger, host of a rap show on the Tulane University station WTUL, gave airtime to "local hip-hop but [banned] bounce because he thinks it's 'stupid.'"[108] For such hip-hop purists, bounce was suspect for reasons including its relationship to dancing, its deviation from a preferred set of conventions with regard to musical structure and lyrical themes, and even the extent of its grassroots popularity. The latter threatened the relevance of would-be gatekeepers like Aiges, Spera, and Bromberger, who were largely ineffective in their efforts to promote what they saw as more authentic rap music. Local rap audiences had a clear idea of what they wanted to hear and dance to, and local artists, producers, and record labels often chose to cater to these preferences.

Just as in the early years of rap, live appearances at house or block parties, clubs, talent shows, and other local spaces played a central role in artists' efforts to establish careers. Within New Orleans, the nightclub and talent show circuit provided a basic and constant forum for aspiring rappers seeking places to perform, while more established artists performed at "1,000-person-capacity dance clubs."[109] Descriptions of early bounce performances indicate the dynamic nature of the performer-audience relationship and the crowd's ability to influence the evolution of the local rap scene rather than merely passively observing change. In the narrative of Tucker's ascendancy, crucial turning points are marked by audience response: he persevered as a rapper because "the crowd reaction was enthusiastic" at his early block party performances; he and DJ Irv decided to record "Where Dey At" after "the audience went crazy" when they performed the song at the Ghost Town Lounge.[110]

Despite the importance of these live encounters between performers and audiences, Aiges reported, "scheduled concerts are rare."[111] Occasionally, larger events were staged at venues including the Municipal Auditorium or the Pontchartrain Center and featured multiple artists. Warren Mayes, who had prior experience in promotion and the operation of nightclubs, organized some of these shows, such as the "Summer Jam '92" in mid-August. The ticket price was only five dollars, and the bill touted performances by ten rap acts, including Mayes, as well as the Rebirth Brass Band, which enjoyed close ties to the New Orleans rap scene.[112] Similarly, in late 1993 Mayes put together a "special Christmas concert" at the Tremé Community Center, featuring "eight of the hottest-selling local bounce rappers" in addition to "a couple of local non-bounce rappers as well as live funk from three brass bands."[113]

The days of these extravaganzas were numbered, however, as the local scene matured and began to fuel wider commercial aspirations. In 1992 a writer for the *Times-Picayune* cited several local rappers in an article that claimed that the fabled "house party" that "once served as a proving ground for local rappers" had declined, as "the lure of bigger dollars elsewhere and increasing violence have sent many rappers looking for new ways to promote themselves."[114] But enough bars and nightclubs (including Club Discovery, Club Sinsations, Newton's, Flirts, Club Rumors, and countless other short-lived endeavors) existed in the city that such decisions did little to slow the expansion of the local scene. The city's Jazz and Heritage Festival continued to provide an important platform for local rappers, especially those promoted by the well-connected Bobby Marchan. Artists associated with the bounce scene dominated the festival's rap offerings after 1992, which included Silky Slim, Lil' Elt, DJ Jimi, DJ Jubilee, and Ricky B.[115]

The hinterlands connected to the emerging New Orleans scene were determined by geographical proximity, cultural affinity, and specific connections at the level of commercial networks. As early as 1992 a local commentator observed, "Bounce artists regularly travel throughout Louisiana and neighboring states drawing thousands of fans," and New Orleans–based artists reached audiences in "Louisiana and parts of Texas, Mississippi, Alabama, Florida, Georgia, and Tennessee."[116] While bounce concerts in New Orleans were relatively infrequent, "out-of-town concerts throughout Louisiana and neighboring states [were] nearly weekly affairs."[117] New Orleans–based artists performed together in "little country towns in St Charles Parish, St. James Parish," and other nearby locations, with some shows featuring "an entire roster of artists" from a given record label, events that "often [earned] $15,000 to $20,000 per show."[118]

The appeal of bounce was highly constrained within the Gulf Coast region. As the local scene matured in the early 1990s, its already tenuous contact with the wider national music industry and audiences dwindled; as Ice Mike recalled, "We couldn't understand why they couldn't understand us."[119] The New Orleans music scene remained largely isolated from mainstream exposure in the early and mid-1990s, sustained by strong local sales based on word-of-mouth and radio promotion. The isolation was compounded by the limitations of local and regional music industry networks: "New Orleans's labels' dependence on Gonzales Wholesale, whose distribution area was primarily limited to Louisiana and southern Mississippi," was one of the factors that "widened the gulf" between the city and nearby potential markets like Memphis.[120]

Bounce: Evaluation and Criticism

Since the 1970s, New Orleans's rich traditions of vernacular music culture, in combination with a growing understanding on the part of civic leaders of the central role of music and cultural tourism in the city's economic future, have fueled increasingly thorough (and mostly positive) coverage of local performers and musical events in a variety of print media. This category includes the daily *Times-Picayune,* the "alternative" *Gambit Weekly,* the free monthly music magazine *OffBeat,* and the African-American-owned *Louisiana Weekly,* as well as other, shorter-lived publications devoted specifically to the city's rap scene, like *Da R.U.D.E. Magazine.*

An examination of the critical writings of three prominent New Orleans music journalists—Scott Aiges, Karen Cortello, and Keith Spera—reveals the ways in which they understood and evaluated the emerging local scene and style and contributed to the discourse around it. The relationship of bounce to the New Orleans music journalism establishment in the early and mid-1990s was not a smooth one. Artists, producers, and audience members working in the local scene relied more on word-of-mouth and radio play than on print media for publicity. On the other side of the equation, journalists like Aiges, Cortello, and Spera were separated from bounce's core audience along multiple dimensions—most centrally race, class, and age—in ways that ultimately influenced their evaluation of the music, although important differences obtained between their views.

As the main music critic for the *Times-Picayune,* Scott Aiges was "the gatekeeper to the most visible print media outlet in the area" in the early 1990s. In the hundreds of articles on local and national music he wrote before leaving the paper in late 1995, he displayed a keen grasp of musical style and history in general and New Orleans's traditions in particular. In addition, Aiges, who grew up in New Jersey, was "a dyed-in-the-wool, Adidas-wearing rap fan" with a keen appreciation of the genre.[121] But while Aiges understood the connections between bounce and the historical-cultural context of New Orleans's black communities, he never seemed to warm up to actually liking the music, which he dismissed as "inane," "insipid," and formulaic "cookie-cutter" music "with seemingly interchangeable music and words."[122] In his conviction that "the so-called 'bounce' style of local rap—the sing-song chanting that is popular on the radio . . . is uncharacteristic of true hip-hop, which emphasizes wit, creativity and social consciousness," he promoted an essentialist understanding of the rap form informed by geographical and cultural biases and a particular interpretation of "musical sophistication."[123] These views colored his coverage of bounce, in which he often stressed the music's idiosyncrasies and surprisingly strong local sales rather than any musically innovative or interesting qualities it might embody.

Aiges had several related complaints about bounce. First, that it was simple and simple-minded. He criticized practitioners of the "spare and dirty" local style for "[ignoring] the sonic complexity of the national scene," and eschewing the "funky grooves with brave musical choices" and "increasingly diverse selection of musical backdrops" found in "state-of-the-art rap."[124] He dismissed bounce rappers' lyrical content along similar lines: in contrast with "the best rap artists [who] show off their poetic skills with intricate, witty word play" and use rap to issue "calls for justice, equality and peace," local rappers craft "lyrics that are no more complex than a few phrases repeated as refrains. The local rap hits that have actual story lines rarely go deeper than the usual complaints about gold-digging women, challenges to other rappers or neighborhood cheerleading."[125] A review of material produced between 1992 and 1994 in New Orleans, however, demonstrates that Aiges vastly overstated both the musical and thematic simplicity of the local style.

Aiges reacted negatively to the frequent use of the "grating" "bones" sample from "Drag Rap," which was "trotted out again and again by local rappers." In early 1994 he wrote, "For the first 18 months or so of [the genre's] existence . . . all bounce records relied on two elements: a snippet of a xylophone arpeggio electronically 'sampled' from . . . 'Drag Rap,' and one- or two-line chants that were sung rather than spoken."[126] In another article on the rise of bounce, he lists seven songs that "use the same electronic drum beat and synthesized xylophone sound" taken from "Drag Rap."[127] Close listening to the recordings in question, however, reveals that only four of them sample the Showboys' recording, with only one of these (T. Tucker's "Where Dey At") depending entirely on "Drag Rap" for its musical content. The remaining three combine the "bones" and other samples from "Drag Rap" with a variety of other musical elements.

Three of the songs cited by Aiges as relying on "Drag Rap" samples ("Sister Sister," "It Was a West Bank Thing," and "Get the Gat") do not actually contain any samples from the song at all. Aiges's oversight can be partially attributed to the fact that all of the songs listed share a similar tempo and swinging bass drum beat. Further, some of those that do not employ "Drag Rap" samples contain short motifs repeated within a cellular structure similar to the iconic "bones." Still, in his confident assertions about the ubiquity of "Drag Rap" samples, Aiges minimized or ignored the complexity, variety, and sophistication (both technical and conceptual) represented by the recordings in question. His conviction that all of the early bounce material sounded the same, said the same thing, and drew from the same sources clouded his ability to hear evidence to the contrary, making his pre-formed conclusions effectively self-fulfilling. Through his position, these opinions and mischaracterizations were widely disseminated.

Aiges's lack of attention to nuance and subtlety within the style led him to compare it unfavorably to national or mainstream recordings and artists. On the other hand, he did provide basic coverage of the bounce scene and in that way helped to further establish the genre in New Orleans. For Aiges, the most appealing aspect of bounce was its compatibility with a historically rooted narrative of New Orleans as a site of distinctive expressive cultural forms and musical innovation based on cross-cultural contact: "Rap in New Orleans is different from rap just about anywhere else. Here, the preferred style has a jaunty, rolling beat with musical influences from the blues, Jamaican dance-hall reggae and Mardi Gras Indian chants as well as gangsta rap."[128]

Interviewed by his colleague Keith Spera, Aiges commented on what the appropriate "hybrid" coming out of New Orleans should sound like: "The city would seem to be fertile ground for the further development of the rap/jazz merger propagated by national acts like Digable Planets." Referring to a local group that mixed hip-hop vocal performances with "live" instrument playing (a concept popularized by the Philadelphia-based group The Roots), he conceded that Kipori Funk "may not be a great band, but at least they are . . . delving into that scene, and that is brilliant news to me. I would love to see 10 bands like that playing around town." For Aiges, Kipori Funk represented a more authentic and progressive alternative to bounce, which he generally dismissed as mediocre, derivative, "cookie-cutter" music that all sounded the same.[129]

Aiges left the *Times-Picayune* in late 1995, but he remained a fixture of the local music landscape in a variety of positions with city government and other music-related nonprofits. He was succeeded at the paper by Keith Spera, a New Orleans native who had previously written for *Off-Beat*. Spera's views on local rap were similar to Aiges's and informed in important ways by the perspective of his predecessor. The overlap is evident in Spera's 1993 *OffBeat* cover story, an interview-based article on "New Orleans hip-hop," which begins with Aiges before moving on to other participants in the scene, including rappers, producers, and engineers. In the article, Spera described a New Orleans "rap and hip-hop community . . . roughly divided between the lightweight 'bounce' artists whose repetitive, crowd-pleasing cheers are the most successful at winning local airplay and generating local sales . . . and the more serious, harder-edged rappers."[130]

The equation of narrative complexity in the lyrical dimension with artistic worth and seriousness continued to pervade Spera's treatment of bounce in the years that followed as he became one of the city's most prominent music critics. Based on bounce's "repetitive, sing-along choruses," and "relatively simple musical arrangements," he consistently labeled the music "rap-lite" and "hybrid."[131] Like Aiges, Spera gave positive coverage to acts that most closely resembled (in musical style and lyrical content) their national counterparts. Both critics shared the opinion that bounce artists were not noteworthy for their creative contributions, which were largely minimized or ignored, but instead for their inexplicable local popularity and concomitant sales.

While the passing of the torch to Spera did not signal any major change in the critical perspective on bounce in the pages of the city's daily paper, some local journalists were less pessimistic about bounce. When she began writing her "Street" column in *OffBeat* in late 1992, Karen Cortello was the "music director/assistant program director" at WQUE, and had been instrumental in getting local bounce artists on the air.[132] Her columns were characterized by informational rather than evaluative content, and while she actively promoted the work of women artists in the local rap scene, she hesitated to scrutinize or condemn other rappers for misogynistic or violent lyrics. Cortello's general willingness to take bounce at face value and to accept (for the most part) the local style without forcing comparisons with the dominant style of rap music helped her achieve a relatively unbiased perspective on the bounce scene as it emerged in the early 1990s. Until her departure in 1998, her "Street" column retained its status as a relatively comprehensive chronicle of the local New Orleans rap scene.

By 1994 bounce had become the dominant force in the New Orleans rap marketplace, although no artist had managed to break through to national audiences to any significant degree. But the production of music in other cities that was clearly influenced by the New Orleans sound bore witness to its spread through informal and "underground" networks. In 1992 Memphis-based rapper FM released the single "Gimme What You Got! (For a Pork Chop)," billed as "the answer to 'Where They At'" but almost entirely derivative of DJ Jimi's song. A more original attempt to adapt the bounce concept to a different location came in the 1994 single "Georgia Bounce" by the group N.P.C. A 1999 song by Miami-based rappers the 69 Boyz (featuring Luke), "Don't Start No Shh," was based on a common brass band or second line chant, and began with a rendition of Tucker's "alright, alright" introductory riff.

Once dismissed as a passing fad, by 1994 bounce had become an entrenched local subgenre in New Orleans, and a contested process of historicization began. Originary narratives focused on the efforts of an individual or a small handful of people. Interviewed after his release from jail in 1994, T. Tucker expressed satisfaction that "everybody knows who started it." His claim was quickly contested by DJ Jimi's aunt and manager, Gayl Payton, who contacted the newspaper to insist that "Jimi influenced Tucker before either ["Where They At"] single was released."[133] Juvenile, whose influential song "Bounce (for the Juvenille)" gave the genre its name, insisted, "I started it . . . I am bounce."[134] Soulja Slim made similar claims in the lyrics of his song "Make It Bounce," included on his 2001 release *The Streets Made Me.*

Rappers were not the only participants to stake discursive claims to the origins and history of bounce. Local record labels were essential to the diffusion of these songs, and credit is justifiably claimed by label owners like Isaac Bolden, who remarked about Jimi's song, "That's the first rap record to come out of New Orleans to make the national trades. And Master P [the New Orleans rap mogul who rose to prominence in the mid- to late 1990s] and all them other people now, [have] followed that."[135] With the use of "Drag Rap" samples established as one of bounce's central features, members of the group 39 Posse asserted their status as the first to appropriate the "bones" on record (in their 1991 song "Ask Them Hoes"). For those involved in the production side of the rap scene, the credits are given to seminal DJs. Ice Mike asserted, "A guy named DJ Lowdown [Dwayne Jackson, of the late-1980s group The Famous Low Down Boys] . . . was actually the originator of bounce. He used to backspin 'Triggerman' and other guys, DJ Irv, would do the same thing out on the other side of town at Ghost Town. And T. Tucker started rapping over it. So, that's the three people who you could actually say are the originators of bounce."[136] When all of these claims are assembled and compared, however, the incremental, collective, and collaborative nature of New Orleans's rap music scene in the early 1990s seems beyond dispute.

4

"Bout It"

New Orleans Breaking Through, 1995–2000

Between 1992 and 1994 the rise of bounce transformed rap as both an art form and a business in New Orleans. The increasingly well-defined preferences of local audiences encouraged particular kinds of musical and lyrical content. While constrained in their ability to move beyond New Orleans and its hinterlands, the artists and companies that flourished during the early 1990s were able to exploit these idiosyncratic local tastes and, to an important extent, dominate the local market. This period of incubation and intense activity around locally oriented rap music set the stage for a transformation of a different kind that would take place beginning in 1995. The long isolation of New Orleans artists and independent labels from national markets and audiences was broken, and within a few years the city was home to two of the most successful independent record labels in the business, No Limit Records and Cash Money Records, which had each succeeded in launching New Orleans–based artists into the national mainstream. In 2000, journalist Neil Strauss told readers of the *New York Times* that "Louisiana is fast becoming the nation's capital of filthy-rich rappers."[1]

In this chapter I examine three central contributions to the process that changed New Orleans from a rap backwater to a celebrated center of the "Dirty South" in the second half of the 1990s: Michael "Mystikal" Tyler, No Limit Records, and Cash Money Records. Differences in timing, background and experience, business models, and access to capital and commercial networks meant that in each of these cases, the intersection of the local with the national/global nexus through which the New Orleans rap scene connects with national companies and audiences would unfold according to its own particular logic. Although their collective efforts boosted the exposure of New Orleans rap in the national arena, the artists and record label owners associated with these cases drew on the local rap scene and sensibility in different ways.

In the years 1991–1994 national companies had shown little to no interest in the New Orleans rap scene, which remained largely a world unto itself, with the ambitions of record companies and their artists constrained to a local or, at best, regional level. The conservatism of the major labels—based in "anxiety, lack of expertise and incomprehension"—allowed or even encouraged a scene to develop in which locally based record companies could dominate the market by catering to local preferences, often racking up higher sales numbers than their national competitors.[2] Had they been located closer to New York or Los Angeles, Cash Money, Big Boy, and No Limit Records would likely have been approached by larger companies much earlier in their history; as it was, these companies were able to grow and prosper by exploiting a remote and idiosyncratic market, and they enjoyed exclusive access to the city's rap and production talent. The rise of No Limit and Cash Money also influenced the ways in which the New Orleans scene was organized, resulting in significant concentration of production and rapping talent on the two labels, to the detriment of second-tier independent labels.

The ways in which the New Orleans rap scene intersected with national companies and audiences over the course of the 1990s can be understood in the dual contexts of the business practices and culture of the rap industry and the historical circumstances of cultural production in New Orleans. As Keith Negus has observed, major music companies "tend to allow rap to be produced at independent companies and production units, using these producers as an often optional and usually elastic repertoire source."[3] In New Orleans, however, this kind of relationship between the local music scene and the wider music business was in keeping with historical trends that stretched back at least to the rhythm and blues era, if not further. Geographical and cultural distance kept the majors at bay during the early 1990s, and when they belatedly caught on to the potential for profit that the city's rap represented, they preferred to deal with well-connected intermediaries rather than try to navigate the murky waters of New Orleans's local scene on their own. For their part, independents like No Limit and Cash Money had years of experience and a store of available capital; for these reasons, they wielded a substantial amount of leverage in the bargaining process.

Mystikal: "The next big thing in New Orleans rap isn't bounce."

By 1994 bounce had proved to be more than just a passing fad, and it continued to dominate the local New Orleans rap market.[4] The idiosyncratic
local genre had displayed a surprising amount of longevity and stylistic diversification, enabling the establishment of several profitable independent
record companies in the city and driving an expansion of the production
base generally.[5] In terms of their connections with national companies and
audiences, however, bounce artists seemed unable to recapture even the
relatively meager possibilities that existed for performers like MC Thick,
DJ Jimi, and Silky Slim in the early 1990s. No New Orleans–based artist
gained national exposure in the years 1992–1998 with anything resembling a locally oriented, bounce-flavored style. The artists who did break
through to national audiences during this period seemed to confirm the
growing understanding of bounce and marketability on the wider level
as mutually exclusive. "In 1995," wrote Karen Cortello, "New Orleans's
local rap scene finally got some of the national attention it deserves," but
for an artist—Michael "Mystikal" Tyler—who explicitly framed himself
outside of the bounce subgenre and who shunned its signature formal and
thematic elements.[6]

Mystikal first entered the local rap scene as a breakdancer and later
moved on to try his hand at rapping under the name "Mystical Mike"
as a member of the group 39 Posse, with whom he recorded "Ask Them
Hoes." Having previously left New Orleans only once in his life (for a trip
to Disneyland), Tyler's perspective was broadened by a four-year stint in
the army that took him to Iraq as part of Operation Desert Storm in 1991.
His time in the army also provided opportunities to build his repertoire
and hone his performance skills during open-mic contests while stationed
in Georgia.[7] By 1993 he was finished with his army commitment and had
returned to New Orleans, where he found work as a security guard. His
rap career took off in early 1994 after he was invited to open a concert by
the legendary '80s group Run-D.M.C. at the Tremé Community Center,
where his performance caught the ear of Leroy "Precise" Edwards, the in-
house producer for Big Boy Records.

Within several weeks, Edwards had signed Mystikal to a contract, and
soon afterward released the rapper's debut single, "Not That Nigga." Mystikal was "an immediate sensation in the New Orleans rap community,"
and Big Boy released an eponymous full-length album in late 1994, which
by the early part of the next year had risen to number 56 on the *Billboard*
"Top R&B Albums" chart without national distribution.[8] Amid these suc-

cesses, he experienced personal tragedy when his sister Michelle Tyler was stabbed to death at the age of twenty-nine in September 1994, an event the rapper ascribed to the pathological social conditions in his hometown: "That's the story of everybody in New Orleans: If it ain't your immediate family, it's your cousin or your buddy—if it's not you. That's something we all understand down here, so we bond and make something positive from it."[9]

During the late spring and summer of 1995, after the release of his full-length debut, Mystikal was "one of the top-selling artists in New Orleans, of any genre."[10] Big Boy had sold over 300,000 copies of the record by the time the local company sealed a distribution deal with Jive Records, an independent distributed by RCA (itself a property of the German-owned BMG).[11] The signing of Mystikal conformed to Jive's "A&R philosophy of spotting developing regional performers, signing them, then building onto their respective bases," which had helped the company build a reputation for "high-caliber rap acts."[12] With the addition of several new tracks, Jive re-released Mystikal's debut with the title *Mind of Mystikal* and a cover image that (unlike the Big Boy release) included several signifiers of New Orleans and (black) Louisiana identity in the form of a Grambling University jersey and the backdrop of the Greater New Orleans Bridge. The album was distributed nationally in September 1995 and sold over 500,000 copies, enough to qualify for gold-record status. The rapper filmed a video for the song "Here I Go" in late 1996 in which he and the director "chose to highlight the city's landmarks—Bourbon Street, the Lakefront, the Piazza D'Italia, and others," presenting a generic, timeless, and picturesque New Orleans rather than any specific references to the city's distinctive rap scene or the black neighborhoods where it flourished.[13]

Tyler drew early stylistic inspiration from New Yorkers Das EFX and LL Cool J, and he developed a style marked by unpredictability that at times resembled aural pastiche. In comparison to the sing-along chants of bounce, which often unfolded according to thematic, rhythmic, and melodic patterns already familiar to New Orleans audiences, Mystikal crafted complex, largely nonrepetitive lyrics that drew on eclectic and diverse sources for inspiration. The result included dramatic shifts in register, timbre, pacing, and volume, and an agile movement between different subjects and narrative voices. Robert Shaw, a partner in the Big Boy Records label, commented on Mystikal's "voice control, what he can do with his mouth—you might listen to his CD and think you're hearing sound effects, but it's his voice."[14] In the content and delivery of his lyrics, Tyler mixed popular culture references (e.g., the sitcom nerd Urkel) with an array of ideas and stylistic approaches drawn from the local world of African American vernacular expressive traditions, including the Baptist preaching and singing that he was exposed to as a child.

Mystikal's composition and performance style challenged the values and conventions that had become established in local rap. According to producer Precise, because the rapper's "wording, . . . style and . . . lyrics" were "so different" from what he was accustomed to working with, they required a different approach to composition and the creation of custom-made backing tracks.[15] Fellow Big Boy Records artist Michael "Misdemeanor" Patterson (of the group Partners-N-Crime) marveled, "It's just the emphasis that he puts on so many words that makes the music so different. Mystikal can do tongue-twisters, break it down, slow it down, speed it up . . . he's got his own style." For some, the fact that Mystikal's style was "unusual for New Orleans" was tied to geographically inflected hierarchies of style and artistic merit. Patterson's description of Mystikal's relationship to the conventions of the local rap scene illustrates the intertwined and mutually dependent nature of ideas of place, identity, and musical style: "I heard him rap, and I was like, 'Man, where did *this* dude come from?' . . . It was a certain type of sound that I had never heard from New Orleans . . . New Orleans had its own flavor—bounce. Or people try to rap hardcore, but it all sounds the same. When he came along, it was a hardcore style that was different. I thought he was from New York or somewhere like that."[16]

Mystikal also distanced himself from the local rap scene in more explicit ways. In mid-1994, when Karen Cortello first reported on his career in her "Street" column, the rapper emphatically described his music as "original hardcore hip-hop . . . NOT bounce."[17] Mystikal eschewed bounce's characteristic chants and local perspective, and the production behind his rapping contained few if any of the signature elements of the genre. His ambivalent relationship to bounce is put into relief in the song "Never Gonna Bounce (The Dream)," one of several added to the original Big Boy release to fill out Jive's *Mind of Mystikal.* The song's title makes obvious reference to New Orleans's native rap style, insinuating a rejection or disconnection from it. But it also signifies on another meaning of the verb *to bounce* in the wider rap subculture, which is *to depart.* The song's lyrics revolve around the rise of bounce icon T. Tucker and his subsequent incarceration and commercial marginalization, with the majority narrated from Tucker's first-person perspective. At the end of the song, however, it becomes clear that he is telling his story over the telephone from jail. These lyrics portray Tucker's perseverance and eventual triumph; however, through its delivery, composition, and musical backing, "Never Gonna Bounce" also expresses Mystikal's distance from the style Tucker started.

Mystikal's breakthrough to national audiences built on the local and regional success of his record label, Big Boy Records. Established in 1993 and based in the New Orleans suburb of Kenner, it was one of several local independents—including Cash Money, Take Fo', Mobo, and Mugz—that had blossomed during the formative years of the bounce genre. The label's owner, Charles Temple, had roots in the local music scene that extended back to 1990, when he partnered with rapper and producer Ice Mike in the C&M label. Prior to the release of Ice Mike's single "I Got Game," the entrepreneurial Temple "wasn't really interested in [the] music business at all. He was into tow trucks . . . that was his thing."[18] In the early to mid-1990s Big Boy and Cash Money vied for dominance in the local scene. Songs dedicated to the rivalry between the two labels and their respective artists included "Pussy N a Can (Fuck U & LV)" (1993) and "Talk That Shit Now (Fuck U & LV)" (1995) by Partners-N-Crime; "Come Like Me" by female rapper Silky (1994); "F**k Big Boy" by B.G. (1995); and "Nigga I'm Bout It" (1995) and "Drag 'Em 'N' tha River" (1996) by U.N.L.V.

Big Boy looked like the wave of the future for New Orleans's rap in-dustry, as Mystikal's rise to national prominence seemed to confirm the wisdom in the label's strategy of moving away from the values of bounce. With the exception of the duo Partners-N-Crime, whose music retained a substantial amount of bounce influence, the label generally moved away from the local flavor that characterized many of its earlier releases (such as those by Sporty T or Silky from 1993 and 1994, respectively) with West Coast–flavored gangsta rap from the likes of Black Menace, G-Slimm, and the female duo Ghetto Twiinz, a trend that was greeted with thinly veiled jubilation on the part of Scott Aiges. "Rap newcomer G-Slimm's debut," the *Times-Picayune* critic wrote in late 1994, "isn't just a great New Or-leans rap record—a contradiction in terms to those who hate this city's homegrown 'bounce' sound," but instead "can stand proudly with records on the national charts and has not a trace of bounce."[19]

By 1996, according to label owner Charles Temple, Big Boy was poised for "a total takeover" of the New Orleans rap scene.[20] In addition to having brought Mystikal to national audiences, the label's roster featured several other promising artists, such as the duo Black Menace, who charted in *Billboard* in early 1995. The label's in-house producer, Leroy "Precise" Ed-wards, had developed his local career as part of the group ERC ("Everyone Receives Cash"), and had produced most of DJ Jimi's debut album, *It's Jimi* (1992). In terms of technical skill and creativity, the quality of his production work, while not completely devoid of locally oriented content, was often equivalent to or better than much of that in the national market.

Despite the promise of its beginnings, however, Big Boy never achieved the anticipated "takeover" of the local rap scene. The company's roster took a hit when up-and-coming gangsta rapper Kenneth "G-Slimm" Jackson Jr. was murdered in late 1996 at the age of twenty-two. At the same time, its profile was rapidly being eclipsed by the rising stars of Cash Money and No Limit. The highly capitalized Master P lured several of Big Boy's most promising rappers to his label. Not long afterward, Big Boy foundered in the wake of conflicts between Temple, his label partners Precise and Robert Shaw, and some of the label's top-drawer artists.[21] By 1997 Precise and Shaw had left to form Upper Level Recordings, bringing with them former Big Boy artists the Ghetto Twiinz (Tonya and Tremethia Jupiter) and building on a relationship with Houston-based Rap-A-Lot Records. Around 2002 Big Boy reappeared on the New Orleans scene but remained far less influential than in its mid-1990s heyday.

No Limit Records: "It ain't about where you're from"

In 1995 and 1996, while Big Boy and Cash Money were locked in a battle for dominance of the local market, another independent rap label seemed to come out of nowhere, rapidly becoming a dominant presence in the world of New Orleans rap and the main conduit connecting the local scene to mainstream, national audiences. No Limit Records enjoyed spectacular growth between 1996 and 1998, making founder and sole owner Percy "Master P" Miller a multimillionaire and elevating the profile of New Orleans rap in general. But the label's relationship to New Orleans's rap scene and vernacular culture was always tentative, qualified, and carefully managed for maximum strategic effect.

Born in 1969, Miller was "about 5 years old" and had three younger brothers when his parents divorced. He and his brother Kevin moved into his paternal grandmother's apartment, where Maxine "Big Mama" Miller and her husband, Claude, raised him along with several other children. "This meant that young P often slept in the hallway of the three-bedroom home" in the Calliope Projects.[22] His grandmother worked multiple jobs in order to send Miller to a nearby private Catholic school.[23] Under the iron discipline of his grandparents, who "wanted us to get out of the project," he finished high school and went to the University of Houston on a basketball scholarship, but a knee injury forced him to abandon the sport temporarily. Returning to New Orleans, he studied business at the

Southern University of New Orleans and, with his younger brother Kevin, dabbled in the street life and drug dealing that were nearly ubiquitous in the city's poor neighborhoods. Sometime around 1988, however, Miller concluded that New Orleans was "too hot . . . Everybody was dying there." He moved to Richmond, California (north of Oakland in the San Francisco Bay Area), to be near his mother. His brother Kevin joined him, but after a week decided "it was too slow for him And when he went back home, he got killed the next day."[24]

In Richmond, Miller and his wife, Sonya, opened a record store, and they soon found that they were selling large quantities of "underground" gangsta rap tapes, the production and distribution of which were, for the most part, disconnected from major companies and their commercial networks. To tap this market, Miller founded the No Limit Records label. His first full-length release, *Get Away Clean* (1991) featured his brothers Corey ("C-Murder") and Vyshonn ("Silkk the Shocker"), who along with Master P made up a trio called TRU ("The Real Untouchables"). Another album, *Mama's Bad Boy,* followed in 1992; like its predecessor, it was released in conjunction with In A Minute Records. Thematically and musically, these recordings (as well as another in 1993 by Sonya Miller under the name "Sonya C") were heavily influenced by the gangsta rap of West Coast artists like N.W.A. and, later, Tupac Shakur, although on a technical and a creative level they lagged behind the industry's standard bearers. As Miller's experience grew, No Limit's recordings became more technically sophisticated, and he began to develop his own career as a solo artist. He sold over 100,000 copies of his third album, *The Ghetto's Tryin to Kill Me!* (1994), which cost a mere one thousand dollars to produce. Sales doubled with his next effort, *99 Ways to Die* (1995), the first No Limit title to penetrate the *Billboard* charts; combined, the two releases had achieved total sales of 350,000 copies.[25]

Increasing sales fed into an expanding business plan; in addition to developing himself and various members of his family as rap artists, Miller also tapped into the Bay Area's vital underground rap scene. In 1994 No Limit released a compilation, *West Coast Bad Boyz: Anotha Level of the Game,* featuring prominent Bay Area rappers such as Rappin' 4-Tay, JT the Bigga Figga, C-Bo, and E-40. As his business grew, Master P began to establish connections with artists and producers back in his hometown of New Orleans. These included Mia "Mia X" Young, one of the city's most popular female rappers, as well as Craig "KLC" Lawson, an accomplished DJ active in New Orleans since the late 1980s who had honed his abilities as part of the group 39 Posse (named for the 3900 block of Washington

Avenue, where the group members grew up) and as a producer for the Parkway Pumpin Records label.

In 1995, Master P organized a compilation of up-and-coming southern artists in the mold of *West Coast Bad Boyz. Down South Hustlers: Bouncin' and Swingin'* featured an impressive selection of New Orleans talent, including KLC, Mia X, Magnolia Slim, Joe Blakk, and Skull Dugrey, as well as rappers from Baton Rouge, Texas, and (in a departure from the ostensible geographic theme of the release) even the Bay Area. While much of the material for *Down South Hustlers* was recorded on the West Coast, Master P was strengthening his ties with New Orleans during this period, most significantly through his increasingly close relationship with KLC. The decision to move strongly into southern regional rap at this time was prescient, as the tastes of national audiences were in the process of shifting in this direction. According to Roni Sarig, "The success of Third Coast gangstas like the Geto Boys and Eightball & MJG convinced [Master P] there might be some opportunity in the South where he'd seen none back in 1989."[26] *Down South Hustlers* was forward-looking in terms of both its regional orientation and—as one of rap's earliest double CD releases—its ambitious scale.

The song "Bout It, Bout It," produced by KLC and included on TRU's 1995 album *True,* marked an important moment in Master P's ascent as well as in his shifting relationship to New Orleans, one in which he found his niche between "Louisiana bounce," on the one hand, and California G-funk (slow gangsta rap music characterized by "a heavy bass sound . . . and laid-back tempo") on the other.[27] Several dimensions of his vocal performance in the song—including reliance on a simple, repeated motif and the inclusion of a prominent and extensive roll-call of the city's wards in a participatory, antiphonal structure—suggest connections to the grassroots New Orleans rap subculture. Within the backing music, stylistic elements tied to the local New Orleans environment are combined with ideas drawn from rap's stylistic mainstream. A tempo of 76 b.p.m. and the use of soaring, portamento-inflected single-note synthesizer lines situate the song within the West Coast gangsta rap aesthetic. In contrast, the propulsive bass drum pattern and the rhythmic, simple organ chords suggest connections to New Orleans's "parade beat" and the syncopated funk of groups like the Meters. The song, one writer claimed, "synthesized three styles of hip-hop production: New Orleans 'bounce,' Oakland 'dopefiend beat,' and L.A. 'G-funk.'"[28]

In its lyrics and concept, "Bout It, Bout It" represents Master P's most explicit and direct attempt to situate himself within the local rap milieu and served to announce his return (physically and stylistically) to his hometown. He introduces himself as a "native of New Orleans," and vows, in an echo of Gregory D's 1987 tribute, "I could never forget where I came from." In "Bout It, Bout It," Master P portrays New Orleans as the "murder capital of the world," emphasizing the toughness and ruthless opportunism of the gangsters and hustlers in the city's housing projects and poor black neighborhoods, places where there "ain't no love." A mention of Mardi Gras only serves to make the point that "some tourists don't make it back."

In her lyrics on "Bout It, Bout It," Mia X departs from Master P's gritty realism, and peppers her rap with references to iconic touchstones of New Orleans's cultural particularity (such as "gumbo, gris gris, [and crawfish] etoufee") that resonate with a touristic portrayal of New Orleans in the wider cultural imagination. Nevertheless, "Bout It Bout It" presents a darker and more narrowly focused portrait of local criminality than earlier efforts like Gregory D and Mannie Fresh's "Where You From (Party People)" and more closely resembles the Atlanta-based Goodie Mob's contemporaneous song "Dirty South," in which the criminal subculture of southern, urban blacks (as well as the South's history of racism) is used as a starting point for discussing the invisibility of southerners within the wider rap music geography and imaginary.[29]

No Limit's growth did not escape the notice of California-based Priority Records. Owned by former employees of the budget label K-Tel, the company had its first taste of success in 1987, when it released the first of several compilations by The California Raisins. The animated classic soul "group" (which used the vocal talents of Buddy Miles, among others) produced a hit single in the form of a cover of Marvin Gaye's "I Heard It through the Grapevine" and eventually sold over a million copies of their debut *The California Raisins Sing the Hit Songs*. Priority then forged a deal with Eric "Eazy E" Wright of N.W.A., the seminal "West Coast" gangsta rap group. Their 1988 release *Straight Outta Compton* was the first of several multi-platinum releases by the group, generating profits that financed Priority's further pursuit of partnership and distribution deals with smaller companies and of contracts with individual artists.[30]

Like other major labels, Priority used "street teams . . . for information gathering and feeding that data back to headquarters" as a way to spot emerging market trends.[31] According to label executive Bryan Turner, "We have . . . promotion guys out in the field, and one of our employees saw P's records in stores and inquired, 'Who is this guy?'"[32] Shortly afterward, Turner offered Miller "a typical boutique-label deal that heavily favored Priority," which was "promptly declined." Building on his impressive history of underground success with minimal marketing and radio support, Master P leveraged a deal with Priority in 1996 in which he retained "100% ownership of the master recordings, which allows [No Limit] to profit from future sales such as catalogs and reissues"[33] Priority pressed and distributed his releases, but Miller earned eighty-five cents on the dollar for the sales of No Limit products. The first album to be released under the new arrangement, *Ice Cream Man* (1996), "sold 32,000 in the first week [and by late 1999 had] sold nearly one million units."[34]

With Priority's backing, No Limit cranked out a string of million-selling albums. In its first week on the market, Master P's 1997 album *Ghetto D* "sold a staggering 256,000 copies, surprising many music industry observers by vaulting to No. 1 in *Billboard* magazine," becoming "the first release by a Louisiana artist to do so in more than 30 years."[35] In addition to topping the R&B charts, "where rap artists generally appear," the album also penetrated "the *Billboard* 200, [and] the mainstream pop and rock charts."[36] To some extent, this success was understood as carrying the New Orleans rap scene along with it; in 1997 the *Times-Picayune*'s Keith Spera reported that "business is booming for local rap in general," and claimed that "P and his organization are riding atop this bull market—and are largely responsible for calling national attention to New Orleans rap."[37]

Throughout the late 1990s Master P pursued a strategy of branding and diversification into products beyond music. One of his earliest efforts in this regard was the 1997 straight-to-video project *I'm Bout It*. The promise of street-level authenticity and the power of underground promotional networks helped push the sales of the low-budget feature into the multimillions. The success of *I'm Bout It* was due not only to Master P's seemingly unstoppable marketing genius, but also to the power of its subject matter, which was the crack-dealing criminal subculture of the New Orleans projects. In the film, Master P used his own family history and experiences to craft a bleak tale based on the murder of his brother Kevin Miller. The film trades on another form of New Orleans imagery as Kevin's funeral ends with a second line parade with a brass band. The success of *I'm Bout It* helped drive the sales of other No Limit products, and Master P secured a distribution deal with Miramax for his next film, *I Got the Hook-Up* (1998), a comedy about hustlers selling black-market cell phones.

As members of the group TRU and as solo artists, Master P and his brothers C-Murder and Silkk the Shocker retained important positions in the label's roster. This emphasis on providing careers for his brothers and other members of his immediate family is reminiscent of the musical families (such as the Nevilles) that contributed to earlier genres of popular music in New Orleans. 1998 was a banner year for Master P and

No Limit, which "sold 26 million records . . . , more than any other rap label."[38] In that year, C-Murder and Silkk both reached the top spot on *Billboard*'s R&B album chart and "landed in the Top 10 of the pop chart," and Master P sold four million copies of his solo album, the double CD *MP tha Last Don,* which, he claimed, marked his retirement as a rapper.[39] *Forbes* magazine estimated Miller's income at $56.5 million, with the company itself valued at $230 million. In the summer of that year, the label secured a deal for international distribution with Virgin Records.[40] In the three years following its deal with Priority, No Limit generated twenty platinum or multi-platinum albums. Not since the era of Fats Domino and the "golden age of New Orleans R&B" had artists from the Crescent City achieved this level of sales and exposure.

No Limit's growth after 1996 also involved an aggressive strategy of identification and acquisition of the most talented artists operating in the local New Orleans scene. The label negotiated a joint venture with Jive in order to bring Mystikal onto its roster, a deal that resulted in two platinum-selling albums—*Unpredictable* and *Ghetto Fabulous*—released in 1997 and 1998 respectively. No Limit signed several promising rappers away from Big Boy Records, including Awood "Magic" Johnson, Ricky "Fiend" Jones, and the identical twin rappers Kane & Abel (David and Daniel Garcia). Former New York Incorporated member Mia "Mia X" Young had enjoyed a local hit with the 1993 single "Da Payback" and had signed with Slaughter House Records, owned by Roy P. Joseph Jr. (MC J' Ro J'), before moving to No Limit in 1995. That year, she traveled to California to record an EP for the label titled *Good Girl Gone Bad,* which sold 200,000 copies. In 1997 she released her first full-length recording, *Unlady Like,* which eventually hit gold record status, with over 500,000 copies sold, and peaked at number 2 on the *Billboard* "Top R&B Albums" chart. A second album, *Mama Drama* (1998), would be her last No Limit release.

James "Soulja Slim" Tapp, who made his recorded debut under the name Magnolia Slim in 1994 on the Parkway Pumpin Records label, was another established New Orleans artist who joined the No Limit operation in the mid-1990s. Thanks in part to his connection to producer KLC, Tapp was one of several up-and-coming New Orleans rappers featured on *Down South Hustlers: Bouncin' and Swingin',* which included the song "You Got It" (originally released on Tapp's *Dark Side* EP). His career was interrupted in 1995 when he was sentenced to a three-year prison term for armed robbery. In the title track of his 1994 full-length cassette, *Soulja Fa Lyfe,* as well as in the song "Soulja Made for Walkin'," Tapp was one of the earliest New Orleans–based artists to introduce the "soldier" trope into his lyrics and self-presentation. This metaphor of fatalistic militarism would be further elaborated by several prominent artists and record labels in the later 1990s, most notably Master P, who used a diamond-encrusted tank for his company's logo and called his clique the No Limit Soldiers. In 1998 No Limit released Soulja Slim's album *Give It 2 Em Raw,* although the hard-living rapper was back in jail for violating parole before he had time to promote the recording.

In addition to signing these promising artists from the New Orleans scene, Master P also added the iconic "West Coast" gangsta rapper Calvin "Snoop Dogg" Broadus to No Limit's roster in 1998. Not content with these remarkable achievements, and vowing not to "get caught up in the music," Master P used No Limit's reputation for gangsta rap as a starting point for a variety of side ventures and spin-offs, branching out into "phones, . . . beepers, . . . clothes, . . . movies, . . . real estate. Ain't no rappers at No Limit. We're entrepreneurs."[41] His direct-to-video projects earned millions for the label, and his empire grew to include several Foot Locker retail stores, a clothing line, and a sports management company, No Limit Sports, which was (briefly) able to attract the business of several prominent professional athletes. He was possessed of seemingly boundless energy, and his ambitions also included a revival of his own basketball career: he made a respectable showing in the tryouts for the Charlotte Hornets in the summer of 1998, although the team ultimately decided not to sign him.

No Limit and the Local/Global Nexus

For Master P, the flavor and perspective of the New Orleans scene constituted one of several possible marketing hooks. As Roni Sarig observes, "Early No Limit was definitely a West Coast label," with a roster made up of rappers from the local Richmond area. This "West Coast" orientation related to both musical style and the content of lyrics or imagery; "even the Millers [Master P and his brothers] represented for Cali [California] at least as much as they did the [New Orleans housing project] Calliope."[42] But Master P's closer engagement with the New Orleans scene beginning in 1994 and 1995 set the stage for key transitions in the stylistic and geographic associations of his music and provided a profitable new avenue for the development of his company.

As Master P and No Limit's national fame grew, their relationship to New Orleans was represented in contradictory ways. To an important extent, Master P himself contributed to the confusion through his highly selective and opportunistic engagement with the New Orleans scene. The subtitle of the 1995 compilation *Down South Hustlers: Bouncin' and Swingin'* suggests an embrace of the local New Orleans sound, as does Master P's recollection of his awareness in the early 1990s that "we had a big bounce style down there [in New Orleans] that they didn't have nowhere else."[43] The label's wider appeal depended to an important degree on its biographical and stylistic connections to New Orleans and by extension the city's status as representative of a southern gangsta subculture.

But even while *Down South Hustlers* relied heavily on the talents of artists and producers with roots in the local scene, in its content the compilation contained only muted references to the bounce style. No Limit's relationship to the New Orleans rap scene was strategically mediated in ways that attempted to capitalize on the growing appeal of southern rap in the late 1990s, while maintaining distance from the limitations associated with local style and content. The production of music with explicit connections to New Orleans was merely a step toward a global vision that would transcend place: Master P "was determined to surpass the limitations of 'bounce,' the local rap-lite hybrid with sing-song choruses that has not broken beyond its regional base." "New Orleans is my heritage," he remarked, "but you've still got to think bigger . . . You couldn't do the stuff we do if you have your mind focused on New Orleans."[44]

The label's attempts to tap the New Orleans scene for talent became more selective as the decade progressed. While many critics focused on the place-based authenticity and stylistic peculiarities of No Limit's music, Master P understood his and his label's appeal as dependent on the *absence* of a strong regional affiliation: "After a while, with the different tragedies and the battles between the East and West Coasts, I just think I was right in line to say it ain't about where you're from. It's about making good music and representing that."[45] It was only between 1999 and 2000—after Cash Money had won over national audiences with more explicitly bounce-influenced material—that No Limit began to reengage with local New Orleans style.

Critics often failed to appreciate the considerable distance that existed between the music released on No Limit and the grassroots rap of New Orleans. That the label's roster was largely made up of artists and producers with substantial experience in the local scene also served to encourage an understanding of its output as stylistically representative of the wider New Orleans scene, when in fact it was not. In a 1998 *Village Voice* article, Barry Michael Cooper offers a series of interrelated generalizations and distortions related to the stylistic particularities of New Orleans rap in general and No Limit's relationship to them. Cooper describes "the unique

N.O. Bounce" style as "funerary" and "slowed down to a heroin nod," descriptions that match No Limit's music (heavily influenced by West Coast gangsta rap) much more closely than they do bounce in general, with its defining mid-tempo orientation.[46]

As an example of the connections between Master P's work and "New Orleans funk history," Cooper cites the portamento-inflected, minor-key synthesizer lines of "Bout It, Bout It": "If you're familiar with the New Orleans tradition of the mournful, plaintive wail of a jazz band trailing a funeral procession, then you can also hear the synths replacing the brass section." Ironically, the critic's focus here is on a musical element that is clearly within the parameters of West Coast G-funk or gangsta rap. Historically rooted stereotypes inform Cooper's representation of the relationship of place and music in New Orleans rap, as evidenced by his description of rappers "enslaved to the drum" who include "apparent references to voodoo" in their lyrics.[47] These comments gloss over the complexity and contradiction that marked Master P's relationship to the local musical and cultural context, accepting at face value the generally contrived and touristic portrayal of New Orleans that characterized much of No Limit's engagement with the subject.

Many rappers and producers from New Orleans's rap scene benefited from their association with Master P's label, but some were annoyed by the portrayal of No Limit's music as representative of the grassroots culture and music of New Orleans. Joseph "Joe Blakk" Francois, one of several local rappers featured on No Limit's *Down South Hustlers* compilation, insisted, "People in New Orleans didn't know who Master P was until he hit BET [cable network Black Entertainment Television]" with the music video for "Bout It, Bout It." That Master P and No Limit were not mentioned in Karen Cortello's "Street" column in the local monthly *Offbeat* until mid-1995 lends credence to these assertions. Joe Blakk suggests that it was not Master P who brought fame to New Orleans, but the reverse: paraphrasing him, a journalist writes, "[Master] P had that West Coast sound and he had not become nationally recognized until the first dirty South hit 'Bout it, Bout it' was released." Rankled by Master P's willingness to strategically emphasize or deemphasize ties to New Orleans and the distortion of wider popular understandings of music history that resulted from the mogul's high profile across a variety of media, Joe Blakk complained, "He made the world [believe] he was the creator of all this and he wasn't."[48]

The qualified and strategic nature of Master P's relationship to New Orleans and its music scene after 1995 is also evident from changes in the location of the No Limit Records headquarters. In 1998 he moved the label's center of operations from New Orleans to the state capitol, Baton

Rouge, where construction began on a sprawling studio and office complex.[49] Eighty miles to the northwest, Baton Rouge had a cultural history and vernacular music traditions that differed substantially from those of New Orleans. No Limit's executives and top-selling artists moved into mansions in the exclusive Country Club development in Baton Rouge, although Master P's application to join the golf club (all-white until 1993) was denied.[50] At the same time, the number of rappers on Miller's label with local roots declined sharply, as he focused on artists with minimal connections to the New Orleans scene, including his preteen son "Lil' Romeo" and Snoop Dogg. Still, Master P and his company retained their symbolic association with his hometown, and he remains one of the most widely known figures in the history of rap music from New Orleans.

The establishment and expansion of No Limit was due, in large part, to Master P's understanding of the "powers of street-level marketing, cross-promotion and branding." His mastery of these principles allowed him to transcend racialized market divisions: "That was my main concern—creating a brand. I wanted to hit every marketplace, every community that accepted rap music. I didn't care whether it was white, black, Asian or Latino."[51] While his record label cranked out a steady supply of bleak and violent gangsta rap, Miller saw himself in the tradition of American icons of aggressive corporate expansion: "I built my record company like McDonald's and Wendy's: The customer is always right."[52] He frequently analogized the music business to the street-level drug trade (as in the cover image for *Ghetto D,* which shows a crack smoker blissfully enveloped in a digitally generated cloud of No Limit tape covers), but he also called himself "the Ghetto Bill Gates," appropriating one of the blandest public personalities of information-age capitalism.[53]

Miller was attuned to the importance of lifestyle marketing, the idea that "you're unique and you stand behind something." "It's your identity," he told an interviewer, "and I think people were just looking for a different identity."[54] Master P also relied on sheer volume to establish his dominance; he pioneered the double-CD trend in rap, and he packed his releases with as many songs as possible.[55] CD and tape inserts were crowded with advertisements for other No Limit releases in various stages of production, some of which were ultimately never released.

Uncommitted to any particular musical vision, Master P kept rappers and producers around only as long as they furthered his business interests. In a stark contrast to Cash Money's nearly exclusive reliance on Mannie Fresh, No Limit employed a roomful of producers, including a collective known as Beats by the Pound, made up of KLC, Master P's cousin Mo B.

Dick (born Raymond E. Poole; he later changed his name to Ruhi Anubis Yazid), Craig B. (Craig Damian Bazile), and O'Dell (Odell Vickers Jr.). Like the rappers on his label (at least those not in his immediate family), these producers were ultimately expendable; after most of them had left the label around 1999 (when the group changed its name to The Medicine Men), Miller rationalized their departure as "business": "I had producers that couldn't keep up, I got rid of 'em. I had artists that couldn't keep up, I got rid of 'em."[56]

The reasons for No Limit's stagnation and decline (further detailed in the following chapter) were multiple. They related to Master P's tendency toward micromanagement of projects and his failure to establish budgets and to keep track of finances through centralized accounting practices.[57] His pursuit of a strategy of diversification, in which music played an increasingly marginal role, not only failed to slow the label's spiraling decline, but further contributed to crippling confusion and overextension beginning in 1999. A proliferation of ventures could not exist without the core of authenticity that No Limit's music had provided between 1996 and 1998. As the company's fortunes waned, many of the side ventures were abandoned.

The vast differences between Master P and the New Orleans grassroots rap scene with regard to capitalization and music industry connections created a situation ripe for resentment. Many former No Limit artists and producers complained of Master P's exploitative business practices and his lack of commitment to his artists or to making good music generally. James "Soulja Slim" Tapp claimed that No Limit had cheated him on royalties from his two albums with the label (for which he had signed no contracts) and had failed to promote him correctly: "Nigga stuck me out there like a sore thumb." Rather than pursue his royalties in court, Tapp asserted his preference to "get it in blood," although his own murder in 2003 prevented him from acting on this threat.[58]

Among other advantages provided by Master P's access to mainstream channels of distribution and marketing, he was able to turn a catchy song into a mass media phenomenon in ways that ensured that he and his company would reap the biggest benefit. The case of the rapper Awood "Magic" Johnson, the son of a respected local trombonist and one of many New Orleans–based rappers to part ways with No Limit amid allegations of unfair treatment, provides another example of Master P's business practices. Initially signed to Tru Records, a side project managed by Master P's brother Corey "C-Murder" Miller, Magic was pulled onto the No Limit roster as soon as he started to show some promise.

According to Magic, this business decision entailed significant negative consequences on the level of creativity and friendship: "In the process . . . a lotta relationships got destroyed, a lotta bad things happened." One of the "bad things" was the fate of the bounce-flavored song "Wobble Wobble," which Magic had hoped to release as a single. Sensing its potential, Master P instead insisted that his group 504 Boyz (with Silkk the Shocker and Mystikal) record "Wobble Wobble," with Magic appearing as a guest rapper along with Mac and Krazy. Not only was Magic robbed of the song's career-building potential—it reached the number 17 spot in *Billboard*'s "Hot 100" singles chart and helped the 504 Boyz' 2000 album *Goodfellas* reach the number 1 slot on the "Top R&B/Hip-Hop Albums" chart—but Master P compounded the insult by arrogating the publishing credits. As Magic bitterly recalled, "When I say he took it I mean he took it . . . He abused the situation."[59]

It should be noted, of course, that No Limit is not the first or the last rap record label to suffer criticism from former artists alleging exploitative practices, mismanagement, or dishonesty. Still, taken together these experiences express the tension created by massive differences in access to capital and in connections with outside companies and channels of distribution. No Limit sought exclusive access to any individuals or ideas from the local rap scene that might produce a profit, but remained highly tentative in terms of its long-term connections with the city.

No Limit had a profound effect on both the local scene and the perception of New Orleans rap within the wider, national-level rap imaginary. Master P's selective use of local talent, content, and style produced impressive results in 1997 and 1998, but his inability to respond to changes in the tastes of wider rap audiences—changes that he himself had helped catalyze—contributed to a rapid loss of market share after 2000. In that year, facing declining sales of No Limit product, a lack of artistic continuity in the areas of rapping and production, and the rise to prominence of Cash Money, Master P framed the difference between the two companies: "If it's just about rap music, then you need to talk to Cash Money. I wish those guys the best of luck, and I think they're doing a great job. But I'm not in it for rap music. I'm in it to be the best business that I can have. That's what No Limit is about."[60] But his ability to maintain the No Limit brand ultimately rested on the label's reputation for "making good music," which quickly evaporated as the new millennium dawned.[61]

Fortunately, No Limit's decline did not mean that New Orleans would lose its position of prominence in the national rap industry; in the shadow of Master P, another company had been consolidating its hold on the local scene and by 1998 it was ready to pursue wider audiences. Cash Money Records was uniquely positioned to bring the next crop of New Orleans rappers to the national market, for reasons related to its long and successful local track record, the sensibilities of its in-house producer Mannie Fresh and core artists like B.G., Juvenile, and Lil Wayne, and its particular approach to musical style and content. The company's rise also depended on an increasing openness on the part of rap listeners at the national level to music explicitly tied (through lyrics, music, discourse, and imagery) to southern urban scenes such as the one that became established in New Orleans in the early 1990s.

Cash Money: "We wanted to create neighborhood superstars"

As a writer for *Billboard* observed, within the national rap music industry of the late 1990s, "Cash Money/Universal and No Limit/Priority represent the main success stories of independents joining forces with majors and their efforts skyrocketing."[62] But while both labels share a trajectory from humble beginnings in housing projects and poor neighborhoods to groundbreaking deals with national companies, important differences existed between them, especially with regard to their relationship to the local rap scene and style.

Like No Limit, Cash Money was a family business, founded in 1992 by brothers Ronald ("Slim") and Bryan ("Baby") Williams, born in 1967 and 1969 respectively. The two had grown up in the Magnolia (renamed C. J. Peete in 1981) Projects in an Uptown neighborhood called Central City, in the Third Ward. Their mother had died of kidney failure before either boy reached the age of ten, and "their father, Johnny . . . raised them alone while running a neighborhood grocery store and lounge, the Gladys Bar, named after their mother." According to Slim, the single father "was working so much to make sure we had everything that he never really had the time to spend with us"; that the brothers were just two of a dozen or more children that he fathered surely did not help matters.[63]

Still, Johnny Williams (who died in 1995) passed his entrepreneurial spirit on to his sons ("He told us you should have a business of your own"), as well as some of his practical knowledge, such as how "to handle the money, the books."[64] He also imparted lessons about the interpersonal aspects of running a small business in the highly competitive local environment: "He let us know . . . that to deal with people, you never let anybody know your right hand or your left hand. That you had to watch people."[65] Johnny Williams died in 1995, but ideas of father-son relationships remained central to the ways in which Baby and Slim ran their business and dealt with the artists on their label. Like No Limit, Cash Money represented a version of the New Orleans "musical family" updated for the rap era, in which musical practice and cultural production were rooted in tight familial or neighborhood-based networks. As the brothers told an interviewer in 2000, "We wanted to create neighborhood superstars."[66]

The Williams brothers were not able to resist the promise of easy money held out by the illegal drug trade, and Baby spent several years in jail in the late 1980s. By the early 1990s they were looking for a legitimate business opportunity.[67] Inspired by a 1991 concert by local rap veteran Tim Smooth in nearby Opelousas, the brothers founded Cash Money with funds borrowed from their father.[68] They also benefited from the wisdom and experience of promoter Bobby Marchan, whom Hannusch described as "a key figure in the formation and success" of the company.[69] The fledgling label's first release was the maxi-single *The Sleepwalker* by Rob "Kilo G" Johnson Jr., which briefly surfaced on *Billboard*'s "Hot Dance Breakouts" chart in September 1992. Like Houston's Scarface, Kilo G's lyrics combined a celebration of crime and lawlessness with motifs of interior psychological disturbance.

Kilo G's debut was followed in 1993 by an album by Baby (rapping under the name B-32, a reference to the number of gold teeth he claimed to have in his mouth), backed by DJ Byron "Mannie Fresh" Thomas and a mysterious (and possibly nonexistent) producer named "DJ Crack Out." The cassette-only album also featured contributions from a variety of artists who released music for Cash Money in the early to mid-1990s, including Lil' Slim, the singer/rapper Trishell "Ms. Tee" Williams, the group P.M.W. ("Project's Most Wanted," or "Pussy, Money and Weed"), and the trio U.N.L.V. ("Uptown Niggas Living Violent"). The distinct roles of the two Williams brothers in the company's operations and public image began to emerge in these years; the taller, older Slim was known as the "business mastermind" of the company, a reputation enhanced by a taciturn personality and abstemious lifestyle.[70] His stocky, gregarious younger brother Baby served as the public face of Cash Money, flaunting a high-rolling lifestyle and releasing several albums as a soloist or group member despite his limited abilities as a lyricist and performer.

Around 1993 Cash Money's owners made a valuable long-term investment by formalizing their relationship with Mannie Fresh, making him the label's sole producer. His contributions in this role were not only essential to the establishment of a local rap scene and style in New Orleans; they also helped drive the subsequent mediation of New Orleans–based rap for wider consumption over the course of the next decade. Inspired by his father (who had supported his family as a "street DJ" under the name Sabu), Mannie Fresh had built up nearly a decade of experience in the local scene and beyond by the time he signed on at Cash Money, first performing as a member of New York Incorporated and, later, as MC Gregory D's DJ and producer. Subsequently, he spent time in Los Angeles as an understudy to legendary Chicago house DJ and producer Steve "Silk" Hurley and toured as a DJ backing West Coast rappers Spice 1 and Too Short.[71] Through these experiences, he gained technical expertise and creative networking opportunities that further enabled the expression of his keen and lively musical sensibility. Mannie Fresh single-handedly produced almost all of the music released on Cash Money between 1992 and 2005, and in this way he exercised considerable stylistic influence over rap music produced in New Orleans and elsewhere.

The music released by Cash Money in 1993 and 1994 was strongly tied to the established conventions of bounce. As rapper Sporty T recalled, "They were . . . a straight bounce label at that time, except for Kilo G. He was on some gangsta stuff."[72] In these years, the label strengthened its grip on the local scene and released several artists whose work was foundational to the bounce genre, including Lil' Slim, P.M.W., Ms. Tee, and U.N.L.V. The Williams brothers lured Edgar "Pimp Daddy" Givens ("the music's star who most credit for the sing-songy delivery used by many modern bounce artists") away from rival Pack Records, releasing recordings both before and after the eighteen-year-old rapper was murdered by another teenager in April 1994.[73] Within less than two years, Cash Money became the top label in the New Orleans rap scene; as Scott Aiges reported, it "dominated the local charts by consistently claiming four of the top five spots" between 1992 and 1994.[74] While remaining largely a regional force with minimal promotion or media coverage, the company "moved nearly 100,000 units each year between 1991 and '95."[75]

As Mystikal's mid-decade success boosted the profile of competitor Big Boy Records, Cash Money rallied: "We're upgrading our music and our lyrics," vowed Slim Williams in 1996; "We've got some bombs comin'."[76] The period around 1995 and 1996 was a transitional one for the label, during which the Williams brothers made important changes in their roster and the style of music on their recordings. Like Master P, Cash Money's owners tried to find new formulas for a product that could transcend regional markets without losing its grounding in the danger and authenticity associated with New Orleans's neighborhood culture. Part of the process of "upgrading" involved a dramatic reduction in the number of rappers recording for the label, a move that allowed the Williams brothers to devote more resources to promoting each artist. They dropped many of their established local acts and began the process of developing younger artists who could work in a solo or group context and who would, presumably, be less "hard to control."[77] The new direction was indicated in the 1995 album *True Story* by a duo called The B.G.'z (or "Baby Gangstaz"), led by fourteen-year-old Christopher "Lil' Doogie" (later "B.G.") Dorsey.[78]

Dorsey had grown up around the Magnolia Projects, although he and his family later moved to eastern New Orleans. After his father was shot to death in a robbery, his mother enlisted the Williams brothers to help raise the troubled teenager, who was gravitating to the street life of drugs and crime. He was essentially adopted by the aspiring moguls, who "helped raise [Dorsey] like a son, housing him, schooling him and teaching him about hip-hop."[79] Dwayne "Lil Wayne" Carter Jr., a preteen rapper who had come to the label after an impromptu audition for Baby at a record store, made his recorded debut on the *True Story* album as a member of the duo The B.G.'z. An only child, he grew up in the Carrolton neighborhood before moving with his family to eastern New Orleans. While Carter stayed in the background for most of the late 1990s, he later rose to become Cash Money's biggest star ever.

Under the Williamses' tutelage and guidance, Dorsey and Carter honed their rap skills and focused their lyrical efforts on tales of pimps, dealers, and thugs in a ghetto war zone. Like No Limit, the Williams brothers and their artists emphasized the "family" metaphor as their business model, although both labels operated as almost exclusively male enterprises, structured by patriarchal relationships between controlling "fathers" and loyal "sons."[80] Shortly before he left the label, B.G. commented, "I'm Cash Money for life. Baby and Slim is fathers to me."[81] Lil Wayne, who has remained with Cash Money and has adopted "Weezy F. Baby" as one of his aliases, expressed similar sentiments: "I'm always more than just a rapper to Cash Money . . . I'm Baby's son."[82] To an important extent, these expressions are tied to the absence of effective and successful male role models (including fathers), a common experience of many African American youth in New Orleans. As Baby Williams put it, "We act as father figures . . . They didn't really have fathers. So we bring them up."[83]

Building on the local success of *True Story,* Cash Money released *Chopper City,* the solo debut by Dorsey (now operating under the name "B.G.") in 1996 and quickly followed with two additional B.G. solo albums (*It's All On U,* volumes I and II) in 1996 and 1997. The label gained significant momentum with the signing of Terius "Juvenile" Gray in 1996. Both Juvenile and in-house producer Mannie Fresh were keenly attuned to local cultural and musical sensibilities, and collaboratively they created a body of work that would transform the image of New Orleans within the wider national rap market, where mainstream audiences were warming to previously obscure southern interpretations of the genre.[84]

Gray came to Cash Money with substantial experience in the New Orleans rap scene. His local hit "Bounce (for the Juvenille)" was included on DJ Jimi's 1992 album *It's Jimi,* released on Isaac Bolden's Soulin' Records. Bolden licensed other Juvenile material from these sessions to the New York–based independent Warlock Records, which released an album, *Being Myself,* in 1995, which suffered from disappointing sales and a lack of critical interest. After graduating from high school, Gray worked in the oil and gas industry to make ends meet before finding a home at Cash Money.[85] Local and regional sales of Juvenile's debut album for Cash Money, *Solja Rags* (1997), were driven by the success of a single, "Solja Rag," which took as its theme the street-hustling "solja" and his iconic accoutrement of a bandanna. In its delivery and concept, the song bears many similarities to Juvenile's 1998 hit single "Ha" (a key turning point in the rapper's career), and its lyrics contain several phrases that would later be adapted for use in "Ha." In both songs, the lyrics took the form of an imagined conversation between male participants in the New Orleans street life.

In *Solja Rags,* and in subsequent releases for the label, Juvenile helped Cash Money develop a new approach to the marketing of local culture to wider audiences. In contrast to the relatively thin veneer of touristic views of local culture and pathological ghetto authenticity put forth by Master P, Cash Money's artists engaged more substantially with the expressive culture of the local environment as a central subject in itself. Imagery and concepts typical of gangsta rap maintained a presence in Juvenile's lyrics, but his overall presentation was oriented less toward first-person narratives of violence and criminal activity and more toward description of and commentary on the everyday life of people in the communities he grew up in. In interviews, the rapper frequently identified his "people" in and around the Magnolia/C. J. Peete housing project where he spent much of his childhood as his main source of lyrical and conceptual inspiration: "Growing up back there, I had a chance to see how the people are. My people played a big part in my career"; "I like to talk about my people, how we doing, how we enjoying ourselves."[86]

Juvenile's description of his style as "off-the-porch flowing" further establishes his grounding in the spontaneity of public, communally oriented oral culture as it exists in the grassroots milieu of New Orleans's projects and poor neighborhoods. His allegiance to this vernacular is a proudly held part of his self-presentation: "I basically use broken English in all of

With roots in the early 1990s bounce scene, Cash Money Records won over
national audiences with music, lyrics, and imagery infused with New Orleans's
musical sensibility and neighborhood culture. Standing behind producer
Mannie Fresh, from left to right: B.G., Juvenile, Lil Wayne, Turk, Bryan "Baby"
Williams. Copyright 1995, *The Times-Picayune*. All rights reserved.
Reprinted with permission.

my songs. I try to get you my way rather than trying to talk proper."[87] This
connection to the expressive sensibility of the black poor and working
class informed the title of his 2001 album for Cash Money, *Project English*.
The rapper's heartfelt appreciation of (and related talent for exploiting) the
everyday culture of one of New Orleans's poorest and most violent areas
may relate to the fact that his childhood experience was not narrowly constrained to this context. His family sent him to a private Catholic school
in nearby LaPlace for his elementary school years, after which he attended
Fortier High and graduated from Booker T. Washington High. Not only
did these experiences (and the family support that they suggest) provide
Gray with a broader perspective on the social environment in and around
the Magnolia Projects, they also helped him cultivate an awareness of the

socioeconomic condition of its residents. "New Orleans has extreme poverty," he stated flatly; "all my people are struggling."[88] These comments give voice to a sociopolitical consciousness that underlies many of his party-oriented songs.

A lyrical emphasis on the everyday activities, attitudes, and expressions of project dwellers was one of the ways in which a sense of place was communicated in Juvenile's work, but this was not the only way he and critics understood his creative relationship to his hometown. His performance style (or delivery) and approach to composition incorporated catchy riffs, hooks, and chants that lent themselves to call-and-response. Like Mystikal, Juvenile's performance on *Solja Rags* and subsequent releases featured complex narrative constructions. Unlike Mystikal, however, Juvenile relied heavily on melodically inflected, repetitive rhythmic cadences in his lyrics. His sense of rhythm (in hip-hop terms, his "flow") and his nuanced use of accents and offbeats to create a "swinging" effect cemented the connections between Juvenile's music, the New Orleans sensibility that informed it, and a wider, Afro-Caribbean cultural context. As one critic observed, Juvenile's style was shaped by his "husky voice and . . . offhanded delivery that switches between chanting and singing like a Jamaican dancehall rapper."[89]

Juvenile's ability to build on the success of *Solja Rags* was greatly enhanced by a deal between Cash Money and the global entertainment company Universal (itself a part of the Seagrams empire) in early 1998, "a three-year, $30 million pressing and distribution contract . . . which provided upfront financing" for the New Orleans label.[90] Universal took over the manufacturing, distribution, and promotion of Cash Money's product, but (as in Master P's deal with Priority) the Williams brothers retained ownership of their master recordings, which allowed them to collect healthy percentages of the income from royalties and publishing.

Dino Delvaille, Universal's senior director of A&R (Artists and Repertoire), reportedly "'discovered' Cash Money while on vacation in New Orleans" in 1998.[91] Given the New Orleans company's prolonged dominance of the local rap scene at this time—"the label was six years old and moving between 50,000 and 150,000 albums per release," figures that would be available through SoundScan—as well as the fact that Priority's deal with No Limit was at the peak of its profitability, it strains credulity that Universal was not more deliberate in seeking out a New Orleans–based business partner, especially considering Delvaille's stated strategy: "research, research, research."[92] Regardless, the deal between Universal and Cash Money was another coup for a New Orleans–based independent record company. Like No Limit's deal, and (to a lesser extent) Mystikal's signing to Jive, the agreement bridged the geographic, cultural, and economic divides that separated the New Orleans rap scene from the established mainstream music industry.

The Cash Money–Universal partnership resulted in a string of highly successful releases in 1998 and 1999, beginning with Juvenile's breakthrough album *400 Degreez*. The local flavor in the hit songs "Ha," "Back That Azz Up" and "Follow Me Now" drove sales of the record as it rose to the top of both the rap and pop charts. It was covered by critics from a diverse range of publications, including rock magazines such as *Rolling Stone* and *Spin*. *400 Degreez*, which by 2004 had sold over 4.7 million copies, marked the moment when "Cash Money surpassed No Limit Records as the dominant force in New Orleans rap." Based on the popularity of Juvenile and, to a lesser extent, B.G., "Cash Money's variation on the city's homegrown bounce style came to define Big Easy rap for the nation."[93]

The following year, the Williams brothers released B.G.'s fourth solo effort, *Chopper City in the Ghetto*, which sold over a million copies. The lyrics of the first single from the album, "Cash Money Is an Army," used a military metaphor for discipline and competitiveness, a common trope within the New Orleans rap scene of this period. But the album's biggest hit was "Bling Bling," with a concept based in "onomatopoeia, mimicking the imaginary sound of light hitting diamonds."[94] "Bling Bling" featured guest appearances by the Big Tymers and Hot Boys, and relied on a hook sung by Lil Wayne to set off B.G.'s rapped verses. Over the course of a few years, "bling bling" as a term for flashy or expensive jewelry crossed over into general usage in the wider media and popular culture environment, and it was added to the *Oxford English Dictionary* in 2003.

Part of Cash Money's strategy in the late 1990s involved maximizing the potential of their relatively lean roster by uniting their solo artists in a label "supergroup" called Hot Boys. Led by marquee artists Juvenile and B.G., the quartet also included Lil Wayne and Tab "Turk" Virgil Jr. Hot Boys released their debut album, *Get It How U Live!!*, in 1997; it sold around 200,000 copies. Not content to remain on the sidelines, label co-CEO Baby Williams formed a duo, Big Tymers, which featured himself and Mannie Fresh. They debuted in 1998 with the album *How You Luv That* (subsequently rereleased with added tracks as *How You Luv That v. 2*), and in 2000 released *I Got That Work*.

Energized by the new arrangement with Universal, Cash Money's ascent continued in 1999. That summer, the second album by the Hot Boys, *Guerilla Warfare*, reached the number 5 position on the pop albums chart and the top of the rap/R&B albums chart. Propelled by singles "I Need a Hot

Girl" and "We on Fire," the album sold 2.4 million copies and reached the number 5 spot on the *Billboard* 200 pop albums chart. Lil Wayne's debut as a soloist, *Tha Block is Hot,* rocketed toward platinum sales, and, just in time for Christmas, a third Juvenile album, *Tha G-Code,* hit record store shelves. The combined sales totals for the year topped 9 million.

Cash Money and the Local/Global Nexus

The imagination and representation of Cash Money's relationship to the local music scene and style by critics (as well as the company's owners and artists) have been marked by baffling contradiction. By many accounts, the label sought to avoid being pigeonholed as "regional" or "local," despite its key role in the rise of bounce. On the other hand, the label and its artists are often credited with bringing the distinctive local values of bounce to a wider, national audience. In reality, while Cash Money stayed much more closely grounded in the local scene and its stylistic particularities than No Limit, the ways that the label's connections to New Orleans and bounce were negotiated depended changed over time depending on prevailing attitudes in the wider sphere of the rap industry.

According to some critics, B.G.'s 1996 album *Chopper City* signaled a transition in Cash Money's relationship to the particular stylistic and thematic dimensions of bounce. In 2000 *Rolling Stone*'s Jason Fine wrote that the record "marked a major change in direction for the label, mixing New Orleans bounce with hardcore, gangsta-style rhymes, and introduced the melodic synth-and-guitar party sound that has become Fresh's trademark." This assertion of a stylistic shift is confirmed by Mannie Fresh, who asserted that he and his Cash Money bosses were "kind of scared" by the departure from their previous orientation: "We were always known as a bounce label. But when it hit the street, it was like the new craze. It left all the other cats that was doing bounce, like, five years behind."[95] When examined in the context of other Cash Money releases that preceded and followed it, however, *Chopper City* sounds less like a radical departure from previous stylistic and thematic preferences and more like one step within a general progression toward a more subtle use of local signifiers and preferences in lyrics, musical style, imagery, and artistic personae. The backing music remained highly danceable, with tempi that often conformed to the general orientation of bounce.

In B.G.'s album and other mid-1990s releases, Cash Money's artists moved away from bounce's collective, dance- and party-oriented chants and cultivated a narrative voice and thematic orientation that was keyed to the isolated perspectives of street-corner hustlers and aspiring dope kingpins. This shift encompassed important gendered dimensions; the innuendo and insult that focused earlier efforts on issues of sexuality and male-female relationships was phased out in favor of narratives animated by tension related to the individual struggles of male subjects who vied for dominance in an environment shaped by treachery, ruthlessness, and violence. The change in lyrical focus further constrained the already narrow set of possibilities enjoyed by female artists, who experienced increased marginalization as New Orleans rap moved closer to the thematic conventions of the commercial mainstream.

Much of Cash Money's success can be attributed to the musical sensibility of Mannie Fresh, who engineered and produced dozens of albums for the label between 1992 and 2005. His approach to production was heavily dependent on "instruments" (a category that includes programmable drum machines, synthesizers, samplers, and sequencers as well as guitars, bass, and keyboards) that he used to compose original backing music, sometimes using studio musicians.[96] While he did occasionally sample sounds from other recordings, he more often used his skill at playing, composing, and arranging his own original music to borrow ideas and "feel." His ability to capture the dynamic polyrhythm of bounce without using any of its key samples contributed to Cash Money's reputation as a source of exciting and original rap music.

For Mannie Fresh, musical style, place, and identification on an individual level were inextricably intertwined and interdependent. Interviewed in 2003, he rejected ideas of musical diversification or change in favor of consistency and reflective musical expression of his own identity. When asked to quantify the stylistic differences between two of the label's releases, the prolific producer replied that they amounted to "almost nothing. Because that's the way we do it, we aren't going to go forward with it [,] you know? It's just me and my life, that's the way it is. If the other one was Tuesday, this one is Wednesday."[97]

As Cash Money's artists became more familiar to national audiences, critics' attention sometimes focused on the label's stylistic relationship to New Orleans's vernacular music traditions. Ironically, while some earlier successes had been attributed by critics and label affiliates to a brave move away from bounce and local content, Juvenile's national breakthrough pushed the discourse in the opposite direction, making Cash Money "the label that brought bounce music to the nation."[98] Journalists at the national level understood the company and its artists as representing authentic, unmediated ties to New Orleans and its expressive cultural forms, an assertion that those associated with the company were careful not to contradict.

Having risen to national prominence, Cash Money's owners and artists helped to perpetuate the idea of their label's music as an unchanging and organic representation of their own place-bound identities. As Juvenile explained, "Down here we always stuck to our own thing, and it finally broke for us."[99]

Critics and audiences responded to the distinctive qualities of "Ha," which were tied to both Juvenile's vocal performance and composition (the lyrics consisted of a string of phrases or questions ending in the affirmative interrogative, "ha?") and Mannie Fresh's production work, which featured a propulsive beat driven by handclaps and (at 94 b.p.m.) within the range historically defining bounce. Slim Williams recalled, "When we were in New York, watching people react when they first heard 'Ha.' They couldn't understand it, because they hadn't heard anything like it before."[100] *Times-Picayune* critic Keith Spera recognized Juvenile's 1998 album *400 Degreez,* with its singles "Ha" and "Follow Me Now," as "an undeniable *refinement* of bounce's call-and-response," but other commentators often understood it as a representative example of the local genre.[101]

In the wider context of the national rap marketplace in the late 1990s, the expression of ties to a local rap sensibility and the portrayal of Cash Money's artists and producer as representative of a local, organic music scene—as "remaining true to their New Orleans sound and style"—underwrote the authenticity and distinctiveness of the company's music, during a period in which certain key cities in the southeast were rising to become the new capitals of rap production.[102] After Juvenile's breakthrough in 1998, critics in mainstream, nationally circulating publications often blurred the lines between Cash Money's music, the grassroots New Orleans bounce scene, and the rap music of the wider U.S. South. One alluded to the influence of distinctive climatic and social dimensions on the label's music: "The Hot Boys' joyous sound provides its strongest draw. The group makes a typically Southern brand of hip hop, complete with humid horns and heavy use of the 'bounce' beat, marked by a faster rhythm and a richer, friendlier bass sound." New Orleans's distinctive local style of rap was conflated with southern rap in general, as a New York–based writer explained that Mannie Fresh "calls his sound 'bounce,' a common Southern term for dance music."[103]

Another critic linked Cash Money's local musical identity to Mannie Fresh's recording practices: "[He] uses his drum machines and keyboards to give the Cash Money–label records he produces that Southern 'bounce' or party feel."[104] Simon Reynolds, writing in the *Village Voice,* offered a more sophisticated interpretation of the relationship: "The bounce element is what gives Fresh's drum programming its hop, skip, and bump—those rat-a-tat-tat snare rolls and double-time/triple-time hi-hats that feel simultaneously frisky and martial."[105] Still, few critics understood that the almost exclusive use of originally composed music in Mannie Fresh's late 1990s productions represented a departure from the conventions of the early 1990s bounce scene, in which sampled recordings provided a significant portion of the musical content of local rap.

Nevertheless, Mannie Fresh and his Cash Money Records associates rejected the idea of transcending New Orleans, for reasons related as much to their business strategy as to their own sense of identity and place. With regard to his own decision to embrace rather than shun New Orleans's distinctive preferences, the producer recalled a conversation with his father, who had urged him, "Don't change your stuff. Show them what your town sounds like," during a period in which New Orleans was uncharted territory on the national rap map. He explained his motivation as "[wanting] to be able to go home when all this is over and still have New Orleans behind me. That's the thing you keep—not the money."[106] Baby Williams expressed the importance of a generative (and gendered) connection between place, culture, and identity more forcefully: "In this (rap) game, you've got to be true to your culture. Once you lose your culture . . . it's like losing your manhood. I could never see that happening to me. You've got niggas who do that, and fall short."[107]

While the fortunes of individual performers and companies rose and fell, the events covered in this chapter, taken together, constituted a dramatic reversal of the situation prevailing in the earlier part of the decade with regard to New Orleans's profile in the national rap music landscape. Often framed in opposition to the bounce era, these achievements nevertheless built on the preexisting New Orleans scene and local style in important ways, and bounce remained a basic frame of reference for aspiring artists, producers, and record label owners, whatever their relationship to or opinion of it. To a large extent, the isolation of New Orleans from national companies and audiences in the early 1990s set the stage for the subsequent success of Big Boy, No Limit, and Cash Money later in the decade. These three labels benefited from the absence of outside competitors in their efforts to exploit the vast and untapped talent pool of rappers and producers in the city.

In a general sense, the stories of Mystikal, Cash Money, and No Limit exist within a trajectory of expanding access to national companies and artists on the part of New Orleans–based artists and companies and a progressive movement toward more explicit and substantive associations with locally oriented lyrical and musical content. But while they share many similarities, Mystikal and the two record labels are also distinguished by important differences. They diverged both in the ways they connected to the prior or contemporaneous New Orleans rap scene and in the ways they represented this connection in discourse. Each of these intersections between the New Orleans rap scene and the wider, national-level music industry happened at a particular point in time and according to particular (and culturally influenced) values. For this reason, in each case the relationship between New Orleans's grassroots rap scene and national audiences had its own stylistic and thematic particularities.

Mystikal's creative and biographical relationship to the local scene and the bounce style was complex and conflicted. While he rejected local conventions and challenged prior assumptions about what a New Orleans rapper could sound like, his inclusion of local legend T. Tucker as the protagonist in the lyrics of a song set in the context of the burgeoning bounce scene spoke to his own formative engagement with and participation in the phenomenon. Still, his successful deal with Jive hinged on his status as a somewhat anomalous performer rather than as a representative of an underappreciated local scene or style. For this reason, his development of a national career failed to carry Big Boy Records along with it, and the company was increasingly sidelined by other New Orleans–based labels.

While Mystikal tried to escape from the limiting aspects of bounce and local style, Master P found ways to exploit New Orleans's wealth of raw musical material. He drew heavily on the New Orleans scene for recording talent; the voluminous output of No Limit between 1995 and 2000 included many memorable and influential songs and performances, by artists and producers who had deep roots in New Orleans and who drew inspiration from the local musical and cultural vernacular. Still, the defining quality of No Limit's relationship to the local context was its contingent nature, as it formed merely one prong of an ambitious strategy based on branding and identity marketing that aimed to transcend local culture and markets and, eventually, the music business itself.

Over time, Master P continued to plot a course away from locally themed expressions, as the number of producers and rappers on the label with meaningful connections to the New Orleans rap scene dwindled. Outside of the profit motive, a commitment to helping his immediate family members was his only strategic constant; creative relationships and artistic quality both suffered from Master P's disinterest in music as a central focus. No Limit soon ceased to be relevant, and whatever success the many side ventures had enjoyed evaporated as the company's musical output went into a creative tailspin.

Cash Money shared many similarities with No Limit. Both companies were founded by individuals whose perspective was shaped by a childhood spent in the housing projects and poor neighborhoods of New Orleans, and both produced music that often exploited that outlook and setting. Both signed lucrative contracts with major entertainment companies, and did so at a point when they were sufficiently capitalized to be able to prioritize a long-term strategy based on retaining ownership and control of their master recordings. This in turn solidified their status as the conduits connecting New Orleans–based artists to national audiences and defining the city's image for rap audiences at the national level. Both propagated metaphors of "family" to describe their highly centralized and hierarchical business models and enforced an insular and isolationist approach to collaboration with other local companies.

But Cash Money maintained a much narrower focus on music than did No Limit, supporting rappers' development over the course of multiple albums and allowing them a significant degree of creative freedom.[108] The result was a much more substantive engagement with the local in terms of style and content. No Limit made millions for Master P and his associates, but the rise to popularity of Cash Money artists B.G. and Juvenile in 1998 and 1999 represented an unprecedented breakthrough in terms of achieving chart success with dynamic, participatory ideas drawn from the local vernacular music sensibility. In contrast to No Limit, Cash Money "went national" after years as a central player in the local bounce scene, a background that influenced their creative and marketing decisions later in the decade. As we will see in the next chapter, this put Cash Money in a better position to continue its success into the next millennium, while No Limit abruptly dropped off the map.

The success of Mystikal, No Limit, and Cash Money ended a long period of isolation for the city's rap music scene, but the associated profits and networking opportunities were concentrated in the hands of a few individuals who were strategically positioned to mediate the dynamic and idiosyncratic New Orleans rap scene and style for wider audiences. These labels (and by extension, their partners at the national level) operated according to an extractive model, in which the New Orleans scene was exploited for its resources but did not benefit from any significant investments in longer-term infrastructure. As with earlier genres like jazz, R&B, rock 'n' roll, and soul, the big companies stayed around only as long as the hits were coming. When the boom years of the late 1990s were over, the likelihood of a New Orleans–based rapper breaking into the national mainstream was not much increased from a decade earlier.

5

"Lights Out"

Stagnation, Decline, and the Resurgence of the Local, 2001–2005

Thanks to the lucrative partnerships between major music corporations and local independent record labels, the exposure of New Orleans–based artists and labels within the national rap music industry reached its zenith in the years from 1996 to 1999. The achievements of No Limit and Cash Money were the stuff of legend, fueling the aspirations of artists and entrepreneurs in New Orleans and elsewhere. Between 2000 and 2005, however, the city's standing with national rap audiences and companies suffered a precipitous decline. Both No Limit and Cash Money retreated further from the grassroots New Orleans scene on which they had built their early successes, but, as we will see, important differences marked their relationship to the local; these differences were produced by distinct long-term business strategies that influenced musical style and content.

No Limit's gangsta rap empire collapsed by 2002, a result of market saturation, a dwindling roster of talent, and the overweening ambitions of Master P, among other problems. Ultimately, family ties and a relentless entrepreneurial drive trumped any commitment to the "street" or to New Orleans's distinctive cultural orientation, forces that Master P had fully and profitably exploited during No Limit's commercial heyday in the late 1990s. Cash Money's position also began to slip beginning in 2000, as the label scored fewer hits and lost many of its star rappers. Unlike No Limit, however, Cash Money managed to retain a presence in rap at the national level through the meteoric career of Lil Wayne. Not only were Cash Money and No Limit becoming increasingly detached and isolated from the grassroots rap scene that nourished them in the mid-1990s, but other New Orleans–based companies were also having more difficulty connecting to the national mainstream. Among them were Take Fo' Records, an important player in the local market since 1993, which tried to replicate the success that No Limit and Cash Money had enjoyed using artists and producers extracted from the local scene, but with disappointing results. Take Fo' artists such as DJ Jubilee, Choppa, and Katey Red remained too idiosyncratically local to win over national audiences.

The years 2000–2005 were marked by important shifts in the organization of the New Orleans rap scene and the ways in which its possible connections to national companies and audiences were imagined. With the important exception of Lil Wayne, New Orleans–based artists largely disappeared from the national rap consciousness and charts after 2000, providing a stark contrast with the preceding half-decade. The rap music scene in the city became reoriented toward local audiences in nightclubs and block parties, who shared many of the central concerns and preferences that had defined bounce. The diminished national profile of New Orleans rap on the eve of Hurricane Katrina is evidenced by the list of finalists in the 2005 *Billboard*/American Urban Radio Networks R&B/Hip-Hop Awards, which "honor the genres' most popular albums, songs, artists and contributors, as determined by actual sales and radio airplay data." The increasingly dominant Atlanta scene contributed three artists (Lil' Jon & the East Side Boyz, T.I., and Ying Yang Twins), who among them garnered nearly a third of the twenty-nine nominations for rap. In contrast, Juvenile was the sole representative from New Orleans, and he was nominated in only one category.[1]

Multiple factors contributed to the decline of New Orleans's profile in the rap world between 2000 and 2005. Some of the most popular new arrivals on the local rap scene were "sissy rappers," openly gay men who were more or less accepted in New Orleans but unable to extend their careers outside of the city. A deal fell through between the bounce label Take Fo' Records and Tommy Boy Records (based in Washington, D.C.), which would have given national distribution for their premiere artist, Jerome "DJ Jubilee" Temple. James "Soulja Slim" Tapp, a legendary local gangsta rapper who seemed to be on the verge of breaking nationally, was shot to death in late 2003, an event that still haunted the city's rap scene in the summer of 2005, when Hurrricane Katrina unleashed a wave of devastation and displacement in the low-lying areas of New Orleans, historically associated with impoverished black populations.

No Limit Records: Decline

It may have been inevitable that the No Limit juggernaut would start to slow after several years of record-breaking success, but the label's steep decline after 1998 seems to have several root causes. In the late 1990s many of its rappers and producers departed under a cloud of dissatisfaction; according to a former artist, Master P "started concentrating on himself" and his immediate family, allowing No Limit's promising roster to disintegrate: "It stopped being about [the artists] and started being about the Millers."[2] While he insisted that family ties were irrelevant in his calculations ("If you're not qualified, I don't care if you're my cousin, my sister, my mama, my brother—if you can't keep up, I'm getting rid of you"), he and his brothers enjoyed the longest careers at the label, despite a pronounced lack of critical enthusiasm for their work (with the possible exception of that of Corey "C-Murder" Miller), and Master P's son Lil' Romeo was more and more at the center of the label's efforts to develop new artists. Outside of his family, the most enduring relationships within the company linked Miller to a "core of trusted friends and business associates" largely made up of people he had known for decades.[3]

No Limit suffered "a mass exodus" over the course of the late 1990s, as rappers including Fiend, Mystikal, and Skull Dugrey and the production team Beats by the Pound all left the label.[4] The company lost market share quickly from 1999 onward: "Of No Limit's 15 releases in 1999, only half reportedly sold 500,000 or more copies; in previous years, anything No Limit touched was almost guaranteed to break the half-million barrier." The rise of Cash Money Records—an established and dominant presence in the local market—to national prominence challenged No Limit's monopoly on New Orleans–based rap music. In 2000 a *Times-Picayune* writer observed, "The brisk pace of No Limit CD releases slowed to a trickle while Cash Money Records . . . stole the national spotlight."[5]

No Limit's inability to reverse its declining trajectory related in some measure to the rigid vertical organization of the company, with its CEO exercising tight control over nearly all creative and business decisions. The autocratic, military-inspired approach that had helped the label conquer the heights of the music industry in the mid-1990s became a liability in later years, as Master P's instincts fell out of sync with the tastes of national rap audiences. Rappers suffered from his failure to build relationships with other rap companies (both inside and outside of New Orleans), evidenced by his insistence that No Limit's recordings should promote and feature only artists associated with the label, rather than the guest appearances and other collaborative efforts that were becoming central to rap at the wider, national level.

Miller, however, still had a few aces up his sleeve. In 2000 he formed 504 Boyz, a trio consisting of himself, Mystikal, and Silkk the Shocker, modeled after Cash Money's successful Hot Boys. As the group's name (based on the New Orleans telephone area code) suggests, the music of 504 Boyz as featured on the album *Goodfellas* and the chart-topping single "Wobble Wobble" was more explicitly linked to the local rap style—as one critic observed, "The 504 Boyz CD, . . . tellingly, has more 'bounce' influences than past No Limit releases."[6] Soulja Slim's last album for the company, *The Streets Made Me* (released in 2001 on the short-lived sublabel No Limit South), was also distinguished by a closer connection to local values and preferences, especially in songs such as "Make It Bounce" and "Get Cha Mind Right."

As No Limit lost ground in the rap marketplace, corporate restructuring prompted an end to its mutually beneficial relationship with Priority Records in 2001, as "parent company EMI folded Priority into Capitol and released most of the former label's staff," who departed along with CEO and founder Bryan Turner.[7] Master P incorporated the New No Limit label and secured a partnership with Cash Money's longtime partner Universal/Motown (also known as Universal Music and Video Distribution, or UMVD). Hardcore rap releases, like the 2002 album *Ballers* by 504 Boyz, formed an increasingly minor part of the label's output, as Miller concentrated his efforts on conquering the pop charts with expressions devoid of regional identity. These bore fruit in 2001, when his eleven-year-old son, Percy Romeo Miller, debuted as a solo artist under the name Lil' Romeo and reached the top of the charts with the single "My Baby," which relied heavily on a Jackson Five sample in its backing music. Having sold almost a million records in 2001, Lil' Romeo continued to release albums and (like his father) branched out into acting, appearing in several feature films and a television series, *Romeo!*, on the children's network Nickelodeon. Other teen-oriented acts in development at the New No Limit in 2002 included "6-Piece, an all-white boy band modeled after 'Nsync, and Sera-Lynn, a blond, blue-eyed singer and dancer" who Miller hoped would be "the next Britney Spears."[8]

By early 2001, the journalist Brett Pulley wrote, the "No Limit empire was a shell of its former self, undone almost as rapidly as it was built. Outsize ambition, irrational growth and poor management caused several of the No Limit ventures to either stall or fail."[9] Still, Master P forged ahead with an ambitious strategy of brand-driven diversification, with projects including "more films, two clothing lines, . . . No Limit Wireless and two books—*How to Win,* a business book, and *Father and Son,* co-written by Lil' Romeo."[10] The Miller family was also distracted by the ongoing legal problems facing Master P's brother Corey "C-Murder" Miller, who in 2003 was convicted of fatally shooting a sixteen-year-old at a local nightclub.

Granted a retrial because of prosecutorial irregularities, he was convicted a second time in April 2009 and sentenced to life imprisonment.[11]

Master P moved closer to New Orleans's grassroots local rap scene in an effort to slow the decline in his company's market share. In 2003 the New No Limit label acquired rising star Choppa (Darwin Turner) from Take Fo' and released a remade version of his local hit "Choppa Style," with an added guest appearance by Master P. The song charted in *Billboard*'s "Hot R&B/Hip-Hop Singles & Tracks," and the label released a full-length album, *Straight from the N.O.*—a title that further demonstrates No Limit's embrace of more explicitly local sounds and imagery. But Choppa's career failed to take root at the national level, despite concert appearances with 504 Boyz and New York rapper 50 Cent. By 2004 he had moved to boxer Roy Jones Jr.'s Body Head Entertainment label, leaving Master P and his relatives as the New No Limit's only artists.

In early 2004 the New No Limit label moved from Universal to Koch Entertainment, an up-and-coming independent distributor known for its "ability to make profits in specific niche-oriented genres that are too small for the majors," according to the label's president, Bob Frank.[12] Under the new arrangement, Master P continued to promote a roster consisting of himself (the first release under the deal was his tenth solo album, the double CD *Good Side/Bad Side*) as well as family members Lil' Romeo and Silkk the Shocker. In spite of Master P's impressive track record, however, New No Limit fell short of the success attained by other Koch properties, including former Cash Money artist B.G.'s Choppa City label.[13]

Miller obviously underestimated the extent to which the decline of audience interest in his label's music had affected his company's ability to cross-market and spin off side ventures. With sales of more than 50 million albums, No Limit had grown to become one of the biggest independent companies in the history of the music business, but after 2000 it quickly descended to a state of complete irrelevance in both the local and national rap music scene.[14] In 2007 Master P had little to lose when he appeared before a House Energy and Commerce subcommittee hearing and renounced gangsta rap and his label's contributions to the genre. He testified to the music's dangerous effects and accused those in the rap industry of "inflaming [social problems] by not being responsible," offering his apologies to "all the women out there" for his own role in the genre's popularization: "I was honestly wrong."[15]

Cash Money Records, 2000–2005

While the No Limit bubble burst relatively quickly, Cash Money lost momentum but managed to retain some degree of relevance and profitability in the wider rap market. The label enjoyed a respectable level of chart success in from 2000 to 2005 and survived the departure of several of its most popular rappers during these years. The exodus began with Christopher "B.G." Dorsey, who left after his sixth solo album, *Checkmate* (2000). As Keith Spera reported, "By the end of 2002, three of the four Hot Boys—Juvenile, Turk and B.G.—were no longer actively recording for Cash Money," and the label's efforts to develop other popular artists had met with little success.[16]

The unraveling of Cash Money's relationship with Terius "Juvenile" Gray was one of the more challenging developments after the millennium. Juvenile's 2000 album *Tha G-Code* had failed to capture the imagination of the rap-buying public to the same extent as his quadruple-platinum smash *400 Degreez*, and the rapper claimed that he "didn't really play a big role" in the 2001 album *Project English*, which he described as a collection of "songs they scraped up." His complaints about Cash Money (which eventually formed the basis of a lawsuit) included failure to pay royalties and tour revenue and the related issue of a disadvantageous contract that "essentially made the Williams brothers his managers as well as the heads of the record label."[17]

As their relationship with Juvenile faltered, Cash Money's owners focused on the handful of artists who remained with the label. Efforts to reinforce the dwindling roster by signing emerging rappers were unsuccessful. In 2002 the duo Big Tymers (Bryan "Baby" Williams and producer/rapper Mannie Fresh) released their fourth album, *Hood Rich*, which like its predecessor, *Got That Work* (2000), sold over a million copies; it was the first rap album of the year to reach the top of the *Billboard* 200 albums chart. Baby's limited abilities as a rapper and lyricist likely contributed to the label's decision to break with its "closed-shop" strategy for his 2002 solo debut, *Birdman*, which boasted appearances by prominent producers, rappers, and vocalists from outside the Cash Money stable. Riding this wave of success, the Williams brothers "inked [a] second deal with Universal Records for an undisclosed amount" in the spring of 2003.[18] That year saw the release of the final Big Tymers album, *Big Money Heavyweight*. In early 2005 Mannie Fresh released his first album as a solo rapper, *The Mind of Mannie Fresh*, but he parted ways with Cash Money later that year.

Given Baby's and Mannie Fresh's limited abilities in writing and performing raps, the level of commercial success that these efforts achieved can in large measure be attributed to Cash Money's successful branding efforts in the late 1990s in the hands of rappers such as Juvenile and B.G. A more future-oriented line of artist development was embodied by Dwayne "Lil Wayne" Carter Jr., the only performer from Cash Money's late 1990s peak to remain on its roster after 2002. While the teenaged rapper had largely stayed in the background during the late 1990s, he grew to become the label's top-selling act after 2000. His albums *Lights Out* (2000) and *500 Degreez* (2002) failed to match the sales of his platinum-selling 1999 debut, *Tha Block Is Hot,* but he regained his momentum with the 2004 release *Tha Carter.* The album sold over a million copies, driven by the single "Go D.J."

With the exception of a brief foray into feature film with *Baller Blockin'* in 2000, the Williams brothers wisely avoided diversifying their efforts beyond music, and they managed to retain a presence on the national scene through the success of one or two highly successful artists. Both the style of music on the label and its approach to artist development have changed substantially since the early 1990s, when Cash Money was strongly connected to the thriving local scene. In the years leading up to Katrina, the label moved further away from the locally keyed sounds and themes that had been its bread and butter during the mid-1990s and closer to the development of star artists with little or no explicit connections to New Orleans. Despite signing a handful of aspiring rappers (including Boo & Gotti, Mikkey, and TQ), Cash Money disconnected not only from the local scene but from rap generally; in late 2004 the label's owners initiated a "new full-service label, Roun'Table Entertainment . . . [which will work] with Cash Money to develop artists beyond the rap realm," with a concentration on "R&B and urban/pop."[19] The most successful of these ventures outside of rap has been 1980s R&B diva Teena Marie, who released two albums for the Cash Money Classics sublabel in 2004 and 2006.

Juvenile returned to the label in 2003, releasing another album as part of the terms reached to settle a lawsuit he had filed against the company. *Juve the Great* was his sixth solo album and produced the hit single "Slow Motion," a collaborative effort with Soulja Slim. The song reached number 1 on the "Hot Rap Tracks" chart, helping make distributor UMVD the top-selling company of the year in the genre.[20] As the album's sales approached the one million mark, Juvenile enjoyed more chart success as part of a trio that also included unknown local rappers Skip and Wacko. The group released a successful single, "Nolia Clap," and an album called *The Beginning of the End. . .* on UTP/Rap-A-Lot 4 Life, which featured guest appearances by New Orleans local favorites Kango Slim (of the group Partners-N-Crime) and Ms. Tee. Around the same time, Juvenile finalized a deal as a solo artist with Atlantic Records, as well as a separately negotiated agreement for distribution of his UTP Records label.

The astounding profits generated by No Limit and Cash Money remained concentrated in the hands of a few individuals. Although the wealth enjoyed by the Millers and the Williams brothers exercised a powerful inspirational effect on aspiring artists and companies, little of it ultimately trickled down to the grassroots local rap scene from which No Limit and Cash Money had extracted much of their talent. Both labels have undertaken a variety of charitable initiatives over the years, however, including Cash Money's annual Thanksgiving turkey giveaway (a tradition since 1999) and Master P's substantial donations to two Catholic churches and to the Catholic elementary school that he attended.[21] These efforts, though commendable, have done little to span the chasm that separates the lifestyle and economic situation of these individuals from those of the vast majority of African Americans in New Orleans, and in some ways merely serve to put the bleakness of the latter's situation into starker relief. That No Limit and Cash Money built their fortunes by selling narratives and imagery of ghetto violence, poverty, crime, and excess further complicates the relationship between for-profit expressive culture and the day-to-day experiences of New Orleans's black poor.

The success of No Limit and Cash Money had diverse effects on the local New Orleans scene between 2000 and 2005. Whether or not they remained on the label in the long term, artists and producers associated with these two companies gained valuable experience and often forged productive contacts in the wider music industry. Some of the rappers who achieved national exposure between 1996 and 1999 built on their success by forming record labels to release their own music as well as that of their protégés. They included former Cash Money artists B.G. and Juvenile (who founded Choppa City Records and UTP Records, respectively), as well as No Limit alumni Soulja Slim (Cutthroat Committy), Magic (The Vault), and Mystikal (Big Truck Records). Several of these labels secured distribution from Koch Entertainment. Yet none of them succeeded in developing any new national artists between 2000 and 2005, and several became inactive as a result of the death or incarceration of their anchoring star rapper.

Smaller labels catering to local preferences continued to emerge in the post-2000 period. Releasing music by artists including Gotti Boi Chris,

Déjà Vu, 10th Ward Buck, Hot Boy Ronald, and others, labels such as Black House, Bigg Face, Kings Entertainment, Money Rules, and Ditty Boo maintained a much closer connection to the preferences of New Orleans audiences. Like the independent bounce labels of the early 1990s, they produced music that was distinctive in its adherence to local aesthetic and thematic preferences. Among the local trends that these labels exploited was "remix bounce," in which well-known songs (from a variety of eras and genres) were overlaid with a beat and samples characteristic of the local New Orleans sound. Locally oriented releases by producers including Money Fresh and DJ Chicken featured songs by Janet Jackson, Phil Collins, and Kenny Rogers remixed with a bounce beat.

Soulja Slim

Small independent labels such as Black House or Ditty Boo, like the music they released, remained a strictly local phenomenon. But other participants in the post-2000 rap music scene in the city found ways to harness the energy, authenticity, and context provided by the local while minimizing its constraining, idiosyncratic qualities. With a decade of experience in the local scene, James "Soulja Slim" Tapp was poised to become the next New Orleans–based artist likely to cross over to national audiences. His career came to an abrupt end in late November 2003, when he was gunned down in the front yard of a house he had just purchased for his mother.

Tapp grew up in the Magnolia/C. J. Peete housing projects, and began his career under the name "Magnolia Slim," releasing an album-length cassette on the local Parkway Pumpin Records in 1994 and an EP on the short-lived Hype Enough label in 1995. He appeared on Master P's *Down South Hustlers* compilation, but he was locked up for much of the second half of the 1990s, serving time for armed robbery beginning in 1995 and returning to prison for parole violation on the eve of his solo debut on No Limit. Prior to the release of *Give It 2 'Em Raw* in 1998, he changed his stage name from Magnolia Slim to Soulja Slim "in a conscious effort to 'go national.' "[22] The album's sales fell just short of gold-record status (500,000 copies sold) despite minimal promotion. After a final album with No Limit South in 2001, he released *Years Later* independently in 2002 before signing with Koch, which distributed his Cutthroat Committy Records label. A song he recorded with Juvenile, "Slow Motion," became a number-one hit after his death.

Like Juvenile, Soulja Slim had cultivated an approach to performance and composition that presented complex, rhythmically imaginative lyrical constructions grounded in a persona and narrative perspective linked to the vernacular culture of New Orleans's housing projects and black neighborhoods. Tapp had family ties to the "second line" subculture; his mother, Linda Porter, was president of the Original Lady Buck Jumpers club (one of many "social and pleasure" organizations founded since the 1970s), and her husband, Philip Frazier, was the longtime tuba player for the renowned Rebirth Brass Band.[23] Tapp rapped on a song ("You Don't Wanna Go To War") included in Rebirth's 2001 release, *Hot Venom;* the recording exemplifies the tightly intertwined nature of New Orleans's rap scene and style with the city's other African American expressive cultural forms. Tapp's own funeral was marked by a rowdy wintertime second line.

Tapp was a victim of New Orleans's violence-plagued street culture, within which he served as both chronicler and participant. The rapper had a fairly extensive criminal record and had survived two previous shootings, both occurring in the Magnolia Projects.[24] Ultimately, no charges were filed in Tapp's murder, despite suggestions that a twenty-two-year-old career criminal and alleged hitman (who was himself shot to death in August 2011) had killed the rapper for $10,000 over a dispute having "something to do with the record industry and a rival record label."[25] That the police implicated Tapp himself in another, unrelated murder two months prior to his own did not diminish his reputation as a fallen hero among young rap fans in New Orleans.

Take Fo' Records & DJ Jubilee

Founded in 1993 by Earl Mackie and Henry Holden, Take Fo' and was one of the few labels from the early days of bounce to survive past 2000. The label outlasted competitors like Big Boy, Tombstone, and Mobo Records, eventually rising to become "New Orleans' third place rap label," although its profits and profile fell far short of those of No Limit and Cash Money.[26] Its owners harbored aspirations of national success, but the company remained a local or, at best, regional phenomenon. Limited distribution and promotion outside of New Orleans made the likelihood of one of Take Fo's artists breaking through to national audiences remote, which encouraged the company to cater more specifically and exclusively to local audiences in their recordings.

Mackie, who helped run a family roofing business, was inspired to start a record label after staging a rap-oriented benefit party to raise money for *Positive Black Talk,* a public access cable television show that he and Holden produced. The event was so successful that Mackie signed up his cousin and his niece, Danielle Eugene and Rene Porche, to record under the name Da' Sha Ra'. Their 1993 single "Bootin' Up" was the first release on Take Fo' Records. Produced by Henry Holden (who would continue as Mackie's partner in the label), the catchy dance number was driven by a propulsive horn sample from Rebirth Brass Band's "Feel Like Funkin' It Up." Da' Sha Ra' never succeeded in matching the success they enjoyed with their first single, however, and after several more releases the duo dropped out of the scene around 1995 or 1996.

Take Fo' found its next prospect in Jerome "DJ Jubilee" Temple, who had been introduced to the music business by his older brother Shawn "Lil' Nerve" Temple when they were growing up in the St. Thomas housing project, and who had family connections to the Mardi Gras Indian subculture through his father.[27] Jerome DJed parties while a student at Grambling State University, a historically black institution located in northern Louisiana. His involvement with music continued after he returned to New Orleans to work as a special education teacher. Impressed by the enthusiastic crowd response to Temple's DJ sets, Mackie signed him to his fledgling label. DJ Jubilee's first single, "Stop, Pause (Do the Jubilee All)," released in 1994, sold thirty thousand copies locally.[28] Jubilee continued to be the label's best-selling artist throughout the late 1990s and into the new century.

DJ Jubilee's performance style was rooted in the core values of bounce, relying on chanted, repeated phrases designed to inspire dancing and audience participation. These themes, along with "shout-outs" to projects, neighborhoods, and schools, also predominated in his lyrics and imagery, which were devoid of references to violence and criminal activities, helping cement his reputation as one of the "cleanest" rappers in the New Orleans rap scene and in the bounce genre. While his friendly and upstanding demeanor made him a favorite among younger listeners, however, he did not entirely avoid the erotic dimension. This was put more clearly into relief during his live performances, where he was often supported by a group of male back-up dancers performing athletic and highly suggestive moves.

Mackie's vision for Take Fo' was profit-driven but was constrained by his financial realities. Nik Cohn's assertion that the company was "a rarity among Southern rap labels" because it was "not funded by drug money" and therefore "couldn't afford major promotion or the hefty bribes to radio DJs that were needed for widespread exposure" requires further evaluation, but the claim nonetheless points to another way in which the label may have been strategically disadvantaged within the local rap scene.[29] Mackie's religious values led him to avoid associating Take Fo' with "songs that

Jerome "DJ Jubilee" Temple (right) with friends at a block party at the
Melpomene housing project in 2003. Catch the Wall Productions.

advocated killing or violence to women," and, with a few notable exceptions, the label released music that was oriented toward a more celebratory
perspective than that of most of its local competitors.[30]

The tendency to foreground dancing, partying, and sex over "gangsta"
themes had important consequences. Take Fo' served as a platform for a
large number of women rappers (including Da' Sha Ra', 2-Sweet, Junie B,
and K.C. Redd), in contrast to labels like No Limit, Cash Money, and Big
Boy, all of which were moving toward more exclusively male-dominated
rosters. DJ Jubilee's clean-living image, combined with the generally up-
beat tenor of the music and lyrical perspective of other Take Fo' artists,
had the potential to alienate fans of hardcore rap, but these dimensions
also helped open other doors in terms of press coverage and performance
opportunities.

Mackie was not above releasing music with sexually explicit and demeaning lyrics (as in Big Al & Lil' Tee's "Another Story to Tell," released in 1994), and his opposition to violent lyrics did not completely exclude gangsta themes and imagery from the Take Fo' catalog. Exceptions to the label's generally "family friendly" image include the 1994 Flesh-N-Blood song "Mob on a Mission" (laden with lyrical descriptions and sampled sounds of gun violence), or the material on the Tec-9 CD *Ready 4 War* (2000). Take Fo' frequently borrowed ideas or strategies from No Limit and (especially) Cash Money over the years. The influence of the city's top independents can be seen in the way Mackie and Holden managed and controlled collaborations and guest appearances, as well as in the marketing of rapper Willie Puckett as "the million dollar hot boy" (a persona likely inspired by the groups Cash Money Millionaires and Hot Boys). The success of label "supergroups" like Cash Money's Hot Boys or No Limit's 504 Boyz inspired the release of various artist compilations on Take Fo' under group names like "The Bounce Squad" and "The Take Fo' Superstars."

In early 1996 Take Fo' was in an expansive mode, and Mackie was sanguine about the future. He told a local music journalist that the label had "six new artists" and was stylistically branching out from bounce into hip-hop and R&B.[31] Mackie spoke of a possible distribution deal with Solar Records and his intention to open his own record store locally, although neither of these ideas panned out. Later in the decade, however, as two New Orleans–based record labels rose to dominate the national rap industry, Mackie and Holden felt that their own time was at hand, and were "poised to follow No Limit and Cash Money in graduating from the local to national ranks." In 1999 DJ Jubilee and Take Fo' secured "a multi-album deal with urban music powerhouse Tommy Boy Records" (owned by Capitol Records).[32] But despite his aspirations to MC Hammer–level success, Jubilee's national career never materialized. Instead, it stalled when Tommy Boy balked and released him from his contract in 2000, quashing Take Fo's hopes for wider exposure.[33]

The disappointment that resulted after the unraveling of the deal with Tommy Boy was compounded by the fact that, according to Jubilee and his record company, million-selling rappers Juvenile and 504 Boyz had made hits ("Back That Azz Up" and "Wobble, Wobble," respectively) from catchphrases he had introduced.[34] A federal jury decided in 2003 that the similarities between Juvenile's 1998 song, "Back That Azz Up" ("among the most popular singles of 1999") and a similarly titled song by DJ Jubilee released earlier in the same year were insufficient to require compensation, a decision upheld in early 2005 by the U.S. Circuit Court of Appeals for the Fifth Circuit.[35] Nevertheless, the case highlighted the problematic effects of differential access to national audiences and channels of distribution, which allows well-connected artists or companies to profitably exploit elements drawn from the local music culture. At the grassroots level, these ideas are routinely borrowed and adapted within a network of mutual influence and significance, a fact that complicates legal notions of authorship and intellectual property.

With its anticipated access to national audiences stymied, Take Fo' still occupied a distinct niche in the New Orleans scene, producing a steady stream of music that was strongly oriented toward local preferences and perspectives. Following the collapse of DJ Jubilee's deal with Tommy Boy, Mackie developed another artist with the potential to cross over from the local scene to wider, national rap audiences. Darwin "Choppa" Turner, a teenager from the West Bank, had made a name for himself by competing in WQUE's call-in rap contests, the "Nine O'Clock Props."[36] In 2001 Take Fo' released his single, "Choppa Style," and the following year put out a full-length CD of the same name. The label also signed his younger brother, who performed under the name Baby Boy and who led Choppa's team of male backup dancers.

Driven by chanted, melodically inflected refrains, the uptempo and dance-oriented "Choppa Style" became a local hit, enabling Take Fo' to broker a deal for national exposure with the New No Limit label. But Master P's fading influence was insufficient to attract a national audience for Choppa's music. After more than a decade in the record business, Mackie and his partner, Henry Holden, stepped down from the leadership roles at Take Fo', passing the reins to younger protégés Eldon Anderson and Terrance "Terry" Wilburn in 2004.[37]

Sissy Rappers

Take Fo' ultimately failed in its drive to reach a national audience, but the label played a pioneering role in one of the most remarkable trends of the early 2000s in New Orleans when it signed an openly gay male rapper, the first of several such artists to emerge from the local scene after the millennium. These artists, most of whom grew up in the city's housing projects, identify themselves as "sissies" or "punks" through their lyrics and self-presentation. The distinctive and historically rooted cultural values of New Orleans encouraged receptiveness to the work of this cohort of gay rappers, who rose to widespread local popularity at the center of a new wave of grassroots activity in the bounce scene. Their ultra-local perspective and style was intertwined with the limitations imposed by biases against their sexuality—sissy rappers had difficulty being accepted by audiences in other places.

Born around 1980, Kenyon "Katey Red" Carter had been rapping for fun with friends in the hallways of the Melpomene (later Guste) housing project, eventually making a spontaneous public debut at a 1998 block party.[38] The positive response to this initial foray led to further performances, including one at a 1999 block party where she was "discovered" by DJ Ron, a Take Fo' Records associate. The packaging of Katey Red's debut EP *Melpomene Block Party*, released by Take Fo' in 1999, did not feature any pictures of the rapper, but her sexual identity was clearly manifest in the lyrics of the title track, which revolve around the subject of male prostitution. The EP was followed in 2000 by a full-length release titled *Y2Katey: The Millennium Sissy*, which featured pictures of Katey Red in feminine garb (on the front cover she appears costumed as the Statue of Liberty in front of the New York skyline), at times surrounded by her female backup group, Dem Hoes. The CD was the first full-length rap release by an openly gay or transgender performer in New Orleans, and one of the first in the larger national and international rap music field.

In the years between 2000 and 2003, other sissy rappers made their recorded debuts through small, independent record companies and built their local careers through performances at clubs and block parties and on public access cable television programs like *It's All Good in the Hood*. The notoriety and local success that Katey Red enjoyed fueled an intense and often vitriolic sense of rivalry that permeated several of these releases. Coming fast on the heels of *Y2Katey* and bristling with personal attacks on Katey Red, Vockah Redu & Tha Cru's CD *Can't Be Stopped* was released by the Tampa-based C2K label in 2000. While Katey Red and Vockah Redu (born Javocca Davis) began their careers performing in drag, most of the sissy rappers that followed them were not cross-dressers but rather out, effeminate gay men (although many prefer to use the female pronoun). In 2002 King's Entertainment released Chev's album *Straight Off the Ave*, while the fly-by-night Too Cold Records released two volumes of the *Battle of the Sissies* CD compilations, which featured all of the previously mentioned rappers as well as Sissy Jay, Sissy Nobby, and the group S.W.A. (a play on the name of gangsta rap group N.W.A., "niggas with attitude"). Signed to the local independent Money Rules label, Big Freedia released a double CD titled *Queen Diva* in 2003, which included local hits "Gin in My System" and "A'han, Oh Yeah."

The character of the "sissy" has a long and rich history within African American vernacular culture, and the participation of gay performers in

New Orleans rap builds on similar efforts in the city's popular music scene dating back to the early twentieth century, if not earlier.[39] Jazz legend Jelly Roll Morton held the musical abilities of Tony Jackson (1876–1921) in the highest esteem, despite the fact that the pianist "happened to be one of those gentlemens that a lot of people call them lady or sissy."[40] Guitarist Danny Barker, who played in Storyville during the early decades of the twentieth century, recalled the diversity of the gay crowd at a bar called Beansy's Boudoir, where "each night there were present about two hundred sissies, faggots, punks, moffydice [i.e., hermaphrodites], she-men and she-boys—all colors, all sizes and all ages (from sixteen to sixty.) They were high-class, low-class, well-dressed, ragged, dignified, loud-mouthed."[41] The sexual experimentation and boundary crossing that took place in Storyville was often commodified, heteronormative, and structured by ideas of racial hierarchy, but the infamous district nonetheless held out possibilities (albeit limited) of social and sexual freedom for gay men and lesbians that did not exist elsewhere in the U.S. South.

In the 1940s and 1950s, New Orleans's R&B scene also saw important participation by gay performers. Drummer Earl Palmer, born in 1924 and raised by a lesbian or bisexual single mother who performed on the vaudeville circuit, grew up surrounded by individuals such as "Van Epps, . . . a gay dancer I called my Uncle Van, and Clifton Phelps . . . [who] was what you might call Van's old lady. When I was coming up, I didn't know nothing about no closet gays."[42] Palmer remembered several gay or bisexual male performers—including Bobby Marchan, Patsy Valdalia, Chalida, Esquerita, and Larry Darnell—who performed at the Dew Drop Inn and similar clubs, often in the role of emcee and usually in drag. The mostly instrumental quartet The Meters included several references to the sissy concept in their late 1960s catalogue, which included the singles "Sophisticated Cissy" and "Cissy Strut," titles that speak to the participation of sissies in the New Orleans R&B and soul music scenes.

Whether in the jazz age or the 1950s and '60s, the acceptance of openly gay performers was always qualified; even in the sheltered world of segregated black show business, gays' ability to openly express their sexuality was constrained within particular stereotypes. In the wider social context of New Orleans, as Palmer observed, "running gay was [not] a popular thing . . . the only place you'd see three or four gays going down the street together was the French Quarter and they were white."[43] But working-class and poor African American gay men have always been among those who sold their bodies for sex in New Orleans. Barker remembered "Titanic, the District's most famous homosexual. He had a whole lot of homosexual friends who dressed as women and hustled as women, even back in the twenties."[44]

Sissy rappers' participation in the local scene has always been somewhat controversial, but their adherence to local preferences and perspectives helped them attain a substantial level of general popularity in the city. Their performance style and the production values that underlie their raps represent in many ways a return to the core values of bounce, with lyrics structured by call-and-response rather than by extended narrative, and musical accompaniment that is marked as local by tempo and samples, including those drawn from "Drag Rap." Rather than remaining constrained to "an openly gay hip hop world," sissy rappers in New Orleans are, to a large extent, able to participate in creative and commercial relationships—with producers, record label owners, other artists, and audiences—that are not limited to people who self-identify as gay.[45]

The audience for sissy rappers is often imagined in gendered terms, with women as the primary, driving force; as Katey Red observed, "The guys come by because they want to see the girls bend over and shake their behinds. And the girls come by just so they can shake their behinds."[46] Whether true or not, such claims provide an excuse of sorts for straight men to listen to sissy rappers' music. Straight-identified men often hesitate to express the same enthusiasm as women for the sissies' music, and homophobia drives some to shun or denigrate them. Still, the central connections between sissy rappers' music and the wider cultural environment of New Orleans have made them largely unavoidable for those wishing to participate in the social events around rap music and dancing in the city.

In their lyrics, sissy performers adhere to many of the established conventions of bounce, including prominent call-and-response, references to neighborhoods, housing projects, or wards, and a lyrical emphasis on dancing, pleasure, and commodified sexual relations. Some themes and strategies, however, stand out as relatively unique to sissy rappers as a group. References to the public antagonism toward gay men, jargon derived from "hustling" male prostitution, and acrimonious attacks on other sissy rappers all serve to distinguish the work of these rappers within the local context.[47] In their lyrics, some use humor and irony to counter anti-gay attitudes present in their social environment, ridiculing the secrecy and denial that often characterize gay identity in working-class African American communities through lyrics that express pleasure in "having" or "breaking" men who present themselves as not gay (such as "A'Han, Oh Yeah" and "Stupid"). With a small number of exceptions (such as Sissy Nobby's "Dat Boi Is Special"), the sissy rappers express a deep and abiding cynicism with regard to matters of sex and intimacy that generally resembles the heterosexual perspective expressed in many bounce songs from the early 1990s.

Though the sissies' appeal would be limited to the New Orleans area, Katey Red's releases generated a significant amount of national publicity. The sheer novelty of an openly gay performer in a notoriously anti-gay genre of popular music helped drive coverage in the *New York Times, Entertainment Weekly,* and the *Village Voice,* which, although fleeting, represented a new peak of exposure for Take Fo' and its artists.[48] Neil Strauss, a music critic for the *New York Times,* attended a concert by Katey Red in New Orleans and penned an article in May 2000 that is notable for its treatment of the rapper as a freakish anomaly. Strauss's insistence on using the male pronoun in reference to Katey Red would be less offensive if the article itself did not explicitly mention "his wish to be referred to as 'she,' " which was respected by the various rappers and New Orleans music scene participants whose comments were quoted.[49] The article was the subject of irate commentary in *PlanetOut,* which excoriated the writer for the pronoun misuse and for his conflation of "homosexual" with "cross-dresser" or "drag queen."[50]

After the brief sensation caused by Katey Red's debut, the goings-on in New Orleans once again sank below the radar of national critics as well as, to a large extent, local music journalists. Before Katrina, the emergence of sissy rappers and their continuing popularity received scant comment in the New Orleans press, which is usually eager to celebrate local musical achievements and evidence of cultural distinctiveness. Katey Red was the subject of a 2000 article in the free monthly *Offbeat* magazine, but the New Orleans *Times-Picayune* did not carry a single article profiling a sissy rapper or discussing the general phenomenon until 2009.[51]

Notwithstanding the importance of the successes of artists like Lil Wayne, Soulja Slim, and Juvenile, in general the New Orleans rap scene was rapidly losing ground to regional competitors such as Houston, Miami, and especially Atlanta in its ability to maintain a consistent and diversified (i.e., involving more than one artist or label) presence within the national market. In the late 1990s major labels had relied on intermediaries like Master P or the Williams brothers for their access to local talent and had never established any presence of their own in the city. Consequently, as Cash Money and No Limit disconnected from New Orleans's vital grassroots rap music scene, so did the national music industry, and, by extension, national audiences. Like the early years of jazz or the "golden age of New

Orleans R&B," the late 1990s rap boom was an intense, profitable, and ultimately fleeting event within the city's history of popular music. As the new millennium dawned, New Orleans rap in general returned to a state of isolation similar to that of the early 1990s: a rich, dynamic, but largely self-contained universe of small record labels and aspiring rappers who made music that was unmistakably marked by local values and preferences.

In spite of New Orleans's position at the forefront of the "Dirty South" movement in the late 1990s, the connections between the city's rap scene and the national-level rap industry and audience remained tenuous and underdeveloped. That New Orleans had been home to the two most successful independent rap labels of the late 1990s did not change the basic fact of its geographic isolation within the U.S. music industry, a handicap that continued to work against aspiring rappers, producers, and record label owners based in the city. Its historically rooted cultural distinctiveness, kept alive through ongoing traditions of music, dance, and public spectacle, represented a vast and vital resource for inspiration, adaptation, and appropriation, but this uniqueness could also contribute to a sense of provincialism, an undesirable distance between local tastes and values and those of wider, mainstream rap audiences.

6
Bouncing Back

After Katrina, Toward an Uncertain Future

Over the twenty-five years leading up to Hurricane Katrina, bleak socio-economic conditions in New Orleans took their toll on participants in the local music scene, as rappers, producers, DJs, and record label owners were among those affected by violent crime and economic marginalization. Long before Katrina made landfall in September 2005, New Orleans was experiencing a slow-motion social disaster defined by hopelessness and unfulfilled potential, factors that multiplied the destructive power of the storm and its aftermath; as Kelefa Sanneh writes, "The story of Katrina is in large part a story of poverty and neglect."[1] Still, it's hard to imagine a more disruptive or traumatic event within the realm of contemporary urban life in the United States.

Katrina's devastation disproportionately affected the low-lying neighborhoods to which the city's black poor and working class had been relegated. With the projects evacuated after the storm, city planners and politicians took advantage of the unique circumstances around the disaster and moved forward with the already-planned demolition of most of the city's remaining public housing units. At the same time, the loss of housing stock in storm-ravaged neighborhoods pushed rental prices upward, making it all the more difficult for poor and working-class residents to return to the city. In combination with the bungled response in the direct aftermath of the storm, the morally bankrupt neoliberal ideology that predominated before, during, and after Katrina left tens of thousands of the city's poorest residents permanently stranded, providing them with the equivalent of a one-way bus ticket out of New Orleans. The Katrina disaster intensified a racially inflected process of population decline in the city that was already under way before the storm. The 2010 census revealed that New Orleans had lost 118,000 black residents in the preceding decade, compared with a decline of 24,000 white residents.[2]

Katrina may have been a defining event in the lives of those associated with the rap scene, but its effects were diverse, complex, and long-lasting. The disaster irrevocably changed their perspective on the place they grew up in and increased their awareness of both negative and positive aspects of their lives before the storm. The resilience, creativity, and collective cultural practices that helped to make life bearable in the pre-Katrina years also helped them cope with displacement and the challenge of reestablishing themselves in New Orleans or elsewhere. Exiled and returning rappers used the storm and its implications as subject matter for songs; some channeled their efforts into protest and political activism. For young black New Orleanians generally, bounce and local rap connoted a home place and familiar cultural and spatial environment, serving as resources that helped them find meaning in life despite Katrina's heavy toll. In the years after the storm, local rap served many of the same functions for inner-city New Orleanians as it had previously: as an expression of cultural identity, a tool for making the surrounding environment and one's experience within it more pleasurable and humane, and a set of open-ended economic possibilities.

There were several important developments in the world of New Orleans rap in the six years after Katrina. The so-called sissy rappers continued to occupy a prominent place in the local scene, drawing the attention of music journalists and fans inside and outside of the city. Press coverage of New Orleans rap was more frequent and positive than in the years before the storm, reflecting an increased sense of urgency with regard to the documentation and promotion of distinctive local culture. In contrast to the sissy rappers, lauded by those seeking an "alternative" to commercial, heteronormative rap music, one New Orleans–based artist, Dwayne "Lil Wayne" Carter, rose to become one of the most popular and profitable commodities within the industry at a national and global level. As with Mystikal, Lil Wayne's relationship to New Orleans is not central to his self-presentation, and his music contains few aesthetic or thematic ties to bounce or local culture. If the persistence of "that beat" in New Orleans clubs and parties speaks to the ways in which the city's rap draws from long-standing and deeply rooted traditions and cultural history, Lil Wayne's work represents the possibilities for a small number of individual artists to transcend the local or regional context.

Katrina affected every individual and small business associated with the New Orleans rap scene, regardless of whether they were already famous or virtually unknown before the storm. How much individual artists' careers suffered depended on their economic resources and connections to the national music industry. Those who had already achieved commercial success—including Lil Wayne, Baby, Mannie Fresh, and B.G.—were able to relocate to other major cities such as Miami, Los Angeles, or Detroit without interrupting their careers. Less established artists found themselves struggling to maintain momentum without the concentrated support of local audiences.

Many of the artists displaced from New Orleans did not end up in major cities, but those who did tried to take advantage of the comparatively more robust connections that existed between regional hubs like Atlanta, Dallas, or Houston and the national music industry. They were disadvantaged by the fact that these places lacked the cultural center of gravity that had grounded locally produced popular music from New Orleans in a distinctive and remarkably consistent musical sensibility throughout the twentieth century. While some individual rappers or producers were, to varying extents, able to relocate without disrupting their careers and earning potential, the collective energy that had infused New Orleans's vernacular traditions and served as a vital spark to the city's popular music production was diffused and dissipated in the post-Katrina diaspora. The individuals associated with the city's rap scene who did eventually return found themselves in a city that had undergone substantial changes in the interim, many of which, like the storm itself, affected the black and poor more than other groups.

For some Katrina survivors, the rupture of the storm and its aftermath was a necessary if painful intervention into the pathological social ecology and culture of dependence in pre-Katrina New Orleans. Slab-One, a DJ who performs with Juvenile, lauded "the culture, the musical culture and the camaraderie that came with it" in the years before the storm, but suggested that the accompanying "drug culture and . . . jail culture" were "nothing we need to be teaching the kids."[3] Melvina Crawford, a resident of the Calliope/B. W. Cooper housing project, reflected on her forced displacement from the project as "a blessing" that allowed her to gain perspective on the cycles of poverty and dependency that kept families in the projects for generations: "Being on the inside, I don't think I would ever notice, but being on the outside I could see pretty much what it is—drugs, violence, all in this little square."[4] On the other hand, for some the loss of community and a sense of place that the projects had provided was a traumatic experience on par with Katrina. Janice Taylor, a former resident of the Desire Projects who was "forced" to leave the project in the years before the storm, lamented, "I was sorry they tore it down. I just was used to that place and wanted to be there. That was a total loss right there, so Katrina wasn't too much. Oh, it was a loss, but Desire was the biggest loss to me."[5]

Local Rap and the Response to Katrina

In terms of musical production and related activities, participants in New Orleans's rap scene responded to the Katrina disaster and its aftermath in many different ways. In the immediate aftermath of the storm, displaced New Orleanians found ways to keep a local perspective alive while in exile. In Houston and Dallas, clubs hosted "New Orleans" nights, when local fare was replaced by rap music from the Crescent City. Kenneth "DJ Chicken" Williams Jr. and radio host Wayne "Wild Wayne" Benjamin started "504 Radio," an internet-based mixtape project oriented toward those who wanted to hear the distinctive New Orleans rap sound.

Many artists who lived through the storm wrote songs about their experience, giving voice to the wider struggles of their ravaged communities. Terius "Juvenile" Gray was almost finished recording *Reality Check,* his first post–Cash Money solo album, when Katrina and the related flooding turned his life upside down, "destroying his newly constructed mansion on the shore of Lake Pontchartrain."[6] He recorded a new song for the album, "Get Ya Hustle On," in which he responded to the hurricane and the political and economic circumstances that worsened its devastating effects. The song's lyrics offered sharp criticism of New Orleans mayor Ray Nagin, and the accompanying music video drew widespread commentary for its depiction of figures wearing masks of Nagin, Vice President Cheney, and President Bush picking through the rubble of the flood-ravaged Lower Ninth Ward, formerly a stronghold of black working-class culture in the city.

The substantial corpus of Katrina-related rap songs from both inside and outside New Orleans in the year immediately after the storm encompasses both resistance and accommodation to neoliberal ideologies.[7] Many of these songs exist within the historical trajectory of the protest ethic in African American music and culture; as Zenia Kish notes in a study of post-Katrina hip-hop, New Orleans–based artists such as Mia X and Fifth Ward Weebie used rap to express their anger, grief, and loss, as well as their resolute perseverance in the face of disaster.[8] On the other hand, rap songs about Katrina and its aftermath have the potential to operate as a musical version of disaster tourism, continuing efforts under way before Katrina to market the image of a dystopic, corrupt, racist, and violent city and to sensationalize the struggles of its poor and working-class black residents.

While some artists focused on keeping their careers moving forward, others associated with the New Orleans rap scene took up the challenge of representing and advocating for their dispersed and traumatized communities. Katrina served as an artistic muse and subject matter for rappers; it also inspired increased political consciousness and activism, both in New Orleans and elsewhere. Rappers from other locales, including Atlanta's T.I. and Mississippi's David Banner, used their wealth and media profile to bring aid to desperate New Orleanians and call attention to their suffering in the immediate aftermath of the storm. Outspoken rapper Kanye West hit a nerve when he held up the inadequate government response to Katrina as evidence that "George Bush doesn't care about black people."[9]

The Katrina debacle also politicized participants in New Orleans's rap scene. With a career spanning twenty years, Mia "Mia X" Young—who lost five family members in the flood, as well as her home in Slidell (a suburb located across Lake Pontchartrain)—was one of the most prominent individuals associated with local rap to take up the gauntlet of activism in the aftermath of Katrina. In March 2006 she traveled from her temporary home in Dallas to Washington, D.C., where she joined fellow New Orleans rapper Joseph "Joe Blakk" Francois in a protest and press conference organized by the Hip Hop Caucus to draw attention to the plight of displaced New Orleanians. Flanked by prominent political figures and civil rights icons, including the Reverend Jesse Jackson and Congressman John Lewis, Mia X delivered a passionate plea on behalf of Katrina evacuees whose housing vouchers were about to expire. She then marched to a nearby park where she performed an a capella rap based on her experience of the storm's devastation. Back in New Orleans, she spoke at an event held in the storied Congo Square to commemorate the one-year anniversary of the disaster. In the summer of 2009 she pitched in to help other hip-hop artists in a volunteer effort to refurbish a baseball field and playground in St. Roch, a "neighborhood pock-marked with empty lots and boarded or burned houses." But even four years after the storm, Mia X conceded, "the stress level has been unbelievable."[10]

Rapper Darell "Sess 4-5" Warren also returned to New Orleans with a determination to channel his anger and frustration into political activism. Raised in the Desire Projects, he was at the forefront of spirited protests over the fate of the city's remaining public housing buildings after Katrina. At a time when elevated rents were making it difficult for poor and working-class African Americans to reestablish residence, plans to raze nearly all of the project complexes in the city (many of which remained relatively undamaged) were pushed through at a City Council meeting in late December 2007. Sess 4-5 and other protesters were arrested, and the city government voted to close all the city's public housing complexes and replace them with "mixed-use" developments that would house only a fraction of the previous residents.[11]

Along with many other small businesses in New Orleans, the commercial establishments connected to the local rap scene suffered setbacks as a result of Katrina. Several independent record stores closed after the storm, although the historic Peaches Records relocated from suburban Gentilly to the French Quarter, expanding into a two-story space once occupied by Tower Records. The influence of local independent record labels declined sharply, a trend already under way before Katrina as a result of the emergence of new media (including easily pirated compact discs) and internet-based distribution and promotion.

A number of clubs continued to serve the hip-hop clientele, including a few (such as Ceasar's and the now defunct Club Sam's) that existed before the storm and a larger group of newer establishments including the Venue, the Chat Room, Club 50/50, Club Youngin, the Shake Box, the Duck Off, the Bottom Line, and the Chocolate Bar. Despite a significant decline in the size of New Orleans's media market after Katrina, local radio helped bounce and New Orleans rap retain a strong presence in the city.[12] The efforts of veteran "mixologist" Roland "DJ Ro" Watson and others continued to put a local stamp on the music played on WQUE (also known as Q93), which is owned by Clear Channel. More recently, KKND, known as Power 102.9 and owned by Citadel, rose to challenge Q93's hold on the area's rap listeners, employing veteran bounce DJ and producer DJ Chicken as the host of a morning show and playing significantly more local music than its competitor.

As in the years before the storm, some participants in New Orleans's hip-hop scene relied on independent entrepreneurial activities to make a living in the post-Katrina environment, following in the tradition of local R&B and soul performers (such as Irma Thomas and Ernie K-Doe) who supplemented their music-related earnings with investments in small-scale operations including lounges, restaurants, and record stores. Both Mia X and Sess 4-5 were among those who started or revived retail or service-oriented businesses. Sess 4-5 is one of the co-owners of Nuthin But Fire Records on North Claiborne Avenue, which became a hub of the local scene. Mia X was among several New Orleans hip-hop luminaries to try their hands at the restaurant business, opening an establishment called True Friends. Rapper 10th Ward Buck, who operated a mobile snack truck and helped run the Bigg Face Records label before the storm, opened Finger Lick'n Wings in the spring of 2010; a year later the business had expanded to a second location. Earl Mackie and Henry Holden, partners in the operation of Take Fo' Records label between 1993 and 2004, launched Big Mama's Chicken and Waffles in eastern New Orleans.

In addition to restaurants, local rappers pursued and initiated a range of other entrepreneurial projects and crossover creative ventures. Big Freedia kept running her decorating business during the day while maintaining an active weekly schedule of performances. Joe Blakk's business, Joe Blakk Income Tax Service, continued to operate in multiple locations. In addition to his work as a restaurateur, 10th Ward Buck published a memoir that chronicles his career as a bounce artist and his experiences during Katrina, when he and his neighbors watched the waters rise around their apartment complex. In collaboration with Lucky Johnson, he also wrote a stage play about New Orleans bounce, appropriately titled "Dat Beat." In February 2011 tickets were on sale for performances of "Dat Beat," part two.

In sharp contrast to these uplifting examples of resourcefulness and creativity in the face of obstacles, others associated with the city's rap scene were dragged down by undercurrents of poverty, violence, and despair in the post-Katrina era. Karen Cortello, an advocate of local rap in the late 1980s and early '90s from her positions as radio program director and music journalist, committed suicide shortly after the storm, one of an increasing number of New Orleanians who chose to end their own lives in the years following Katrina. As in the decade before the storm, the appallingly high numbers of young black New Orleanians dying from gun violence included many individuals associated with the city's rap scene. Kasey "K.C. Redd" Segue, who recorded for Take Fo' Records in the late 1990s, was killed in 2006 in Houston. Terence "Sporty T" Vine, who released a single in 1986 as a member of Ninja Crew and produced a handful of local hits in the bounce era, was shot to death in a FEMA trailer in Gentilly in July 2008.

The following year, Cicely "Ju' C" Crawford McCallon, one of several female rappers to release "answer records" to "Where Dey At" in the early 1990s, was shot and killed at the age of thirty-six. Kevin "T. Tucker" Ventry, the charismatic bounce pioneer whose career was hobbled by repeated periods of incarceration, was arrested in late 2009 in connection with large-scale thefts of cigarettes and liquor. Henry "DJ Red Neck" Adams, a longtime fixture on the local scene, died after being caught in the crossfire at a block party in July 2010 along with 10th Ward Buck, who survived his injuries. Anthony "Messy Mya" Barre, an aspiring bounce performer who gained notoriety by posting acerbic monologues on YouTube, was shot to death in November 2010 after attending a baby shower. Twenty-eight-year-old Renetta "Magnolia Shorty" Lowe, who recorded with Cash

Money Records in the mid-'90s and had enjoyed several club hits after Katrina, died the following month in a hail of bullets directed at her acquaintance Jerome "Man Man" Hampton.

Lil Wayne

One of the most dramatic developments in the world of New Orleans rap during the post-Katrina period was the remarkable success of Cash Money Records artist Dwayne "Lil Wayne" Carter Jr. in the national (and global) entertainment market. While the number of New Orleans–based rappers to achieve mainstream success declined after its late 1990s peak, Lil Wayne built a career that places him in the top tier of New Orleans musical celebrities, alongside Louis Armstrong and Fats Domino. In many ways, Lil Wayne's phenomenal success is a validation of Cash Money Records' strategy of long-term investment in young artists. A one-man money-making machine who has been called "the psychic center of hip-hop," Lil Wayne allowed Cash Money to remain profitable despite a dwindling roster of artists.[13]

Born in 1982 to a teenaged mother, and with his biological father more or less out of the picture, Lil Wayne (like Master P) spent his early years mostly in the care of his grandmother, in the Uptown neighborhood of Hollygrove. As an intellectually gifted child living in an environment marked by deprivation and lack of opportunity, he withdrew from peers and family, living a relatively isolated existence. "I was raised in my room by myself with a television and a radio," he told an interviewer in 2007.[14] Though hardly ideal, this arrangement was apparently conducive to the development of the precocious youngster's rapping abilities. He connected with Cash Money Records after meeting Baby Williams at an event at Odyssey Records, and at the age of eleven became the junior partner in the "B.G.'z" duo alongside Christopher Dorsey.

Lil Wayne's blossoming relationship with the Williams brothers was a source of friction with his mother. As he recalled, "She went to school with Slim, Baby's older brother. She didn't like Baby. She knew Baby was wild, he went to jail for five years." Angered by his mother's insistence that he leave the record label, the despondent preteen shot himself in the chest with his stepfather's pistol, a nearly fatal experience that put him on a ventilator for two weeks.[15] When he was fourteen, his mother insisted that he drop out of school (despite being an honor student) when she realized that he was carrying a pistol for protection. In light of the shortcomings of the public school system, Baby did not seem like such a bad influence after all; his mother changed her mind about Cash Money and encouraged Lil Wayne to devote his time and energy to pursuing a rap career under the guidance of Baby and Slim, whose role as father figures became even more significant after his stepfather was shot to death in 1997.

In the late 1990s Lil Wayne resumed his work with Cash Money as a member of the group Hot Boys, where he took a back seat to older members Juvenile and B.G. The relatively modest success that he enjoyed over the few years that followed did not hint at his future superstar status. In terms of sales, none of his three albums released between 2001 and 2005 (*Lights Out, 500 Degreez,* and *Tha Carter*) matched his platinum-selling 1999 solo debut, *Tha Block Is Hot.* But the hit single "Go DJ," from his 2004 album *Tha Carter,* sparked wider interest in his work.[16] After Katrina, he relocated to Miami, as did Cash Money CEO Baby Williams. The storm figured in several of his songs, most notably "Georgia Bush" (released on the mixtape *Dedication 2* with Atlanta-based DJ Drama), in which he drew attention to the plight of displaced New Orleanians and documented his own loss of two Jaguar automobiles, one of several rappers to "situate themselves within the matrix of loss by enumerating their personal property losses."[17] Ultimately, however, Lil Wayne's response to Katrina suggests that he resists being too closely tied to place. He seemed to resent the expectation that he would use his prominent position in the music industry to speak for the dispossessed and displaced of his hometown: "Nobody from my city wants to hear about my city," he remarked to an Associated Press reporter in late 2006.[18]

Lil Wayne's career picked up speed a time when most of the other artists on Cash Money's roster were leaving the label. Fueled by the hit single "Fireman," sales of the late 2005 sequel *Tha Carter II* (the second in a planned five-album *Carter* series) reached double platinum status. Still in his early twenties, he was named president of Cash Money in 2005 and founded the sublabel Young Money Entertainment (he later removed himself from the executive functions of both companies). In late 2006 he and Baby collaborated on the album *Like Father, Like Son.* His 2008 album *Tha Carter III* sold over a million copies in its first week on the market, driven by singles including the danceable "Lollipop" and the idiosyncratic "A Milli." The album, certified triple platinum in 2009, was the best-selling release of 2008. Nominated for eight Grammy awards (including Album of the Year), Lil Wayne won four, including Best Rap Album.

In the years after Katrina, Lil Wayne accelerated his creative output, releasing not only a string of hit albums but also numerous "mixtapes" (unofficial albums often made in collaboration with another rapper or producer) and making dozens of guest appearances on other artists' recordings. A top earner at arena shows, he toured constantly, living, recording, and conducting business in his tricked-out bus. This relentless schedule of performance and recording was accompanied by heavy use of intoxicants, including marijuana, cocaine, and cough syrup. His distinctive lifestyle was interrupted in 2010, when he served eight months in jail in New York after conviction on charges stemming from a 2007 incident in which a loaded handgun was found on his tour bus. His album *I Am Not a Human Being*, recorded before he went to jail, reached the top of the *Billboard* album charts in late 2010.

Lil Wayne's emergence as a global entertainment superstar made him a favorite son in New Orleans, but his relationship to the local scene and his identification with the city have always been qualified and ambiguous. Although several of the rappers on his Young Money label—including Jermaine "Mack Maine" Preyan, Carl "Gudda Gudda" Lilly, and the teen-aged Rashad "Lil Chuckee" Ballard—hail from New Orleans, none have managed to match the success of the label's top-drawer artists, such Onika "Nicki Minaj" Maraj (born in the Caribbean and raised in Queens) and the Canadian Aubrey "Drake" Graham.

As an artist, Lil Wayne's relationship to New Orleans has generally stayed in the background of his wide-ranging, idiosyncratic, and imaginative lyrical vision. Still, he has occasionally appropriated phrases, hooks, or ideas from songs in the New Orleans environment. His 2004 hit single "Go DJ," from the breakthrough album *Tha Carter*, used "a hook jacked from UNLV's 'Don't U Be Greedy,'" which was released on Cash Money Records in the late 1990s.[19] Similar practices—whether characterized as borrowing, stealing, adapting, or imitating—are essential to the creative evolution of the local scene, but they become more complicated and controversial in the context of Lil Wayne's superstar status, which produces a stark divide in the areas of exposure, credit, and profit. Lil Wayne's outlook, attitudes, and creative abilities were doubtlessly shaped by his experiences as a child in 1990s New Orleans, but his ties to the city and its local rap scene remain tenuous and qualified. In fact, his "outsider" status (within his own family and cultural milieu as well as within the world of local rap music) is central to his ability to reach audiences beyond the local market. His music and lyrics often reflect the ideas and values of globally mediated popular culture rather than the local, neighborhood culture of New Orleans.

Sissy Rappers

With the transformation of New Orleans into a smaller, whiter city with fewer areas of concentrated black poverty, the core audience for bounce artists was dispersed and diminished to an important extent. But the sissy rappers were better positioned than most to carve out a viable career in the years after Katrina, largely because of their crossover appeal with a mostly white, middle-class audience base. Sissy rappers continued to perform regularly at clubs, block parties, and music festivals around the city, and they benefited from a growing level of exposure in the local and national press. The increase in coverage at the local level (which began in 2009) was matched by national magazines and newspapers, including the *New York Times Magazine* and *Bust*. In addition to performing at clubs in New York and a variety of other cities in the Northeast and West, sissy rappers appeared at music festivals, such as South by Southwest, and gay pride events, including Atlanta's Mondo Homo, along with brief appearances on television shows such as *Treme* and the *Carson Daly Show*.

As with other local expressive cultural traditions such as brass bands or Mardi Gras Indians, the audience for sissy rappers within New Orleans differs substantially from its external, national-level counterpart; as the *New York Times* writer Jonathan Dee remarked, "Inside New Orleans, the genius of sissy bounce is how perfectly mainstream it is; in the world beyond, the genius of sissy bounce is how incredibly alternative it is."[20] In the city, sissy rappers remained at the forefront of the rap scene thanks to the intensely local nature of their music and lyrical perspective. Through live performances and the playing of recordings within club or block party settings in the city, their audience crosses lines of gender and sexuality. Outside of New Orleans, their appeal is narrower and more politicized, as they connect with audiences dominated by white, middle-class hipsters who wish to support expressions that counter the regressive sexual politics that are thought to characterize mainstream rap music.

Within New Orleans, the music of the sissy rappers was central to the continuation of (and continued evolution of) the grassroots local preferences that emerged during the early 1990s. While their sexual orientation or preference exercises a profound influence on their sense of identity and artistic personae, the sissy rappers resist separation from the context of the wider local community of poor and working-class African Americans in New Orleans. In 2010, responding to questions about the existence of a subgenre labeled "sissy bounce," Katey Red averred, "Ain't no such thing as 'sissy bounce' . . . It's bounce music. It's just sissies that are doing it."[21] Similarly, Big Freedia insisted, "We're basically just bounce rappers. Bounce has artists from all walks of life."[22] That these comments can be understood as defensive responses to prevailing anti-gay attitudes should not diminish their expression of a positive connection to the values and cultural practices of New Orleans.

In the years after Katrina, the stylistic evolution of bounce and local rap, for the most part, continued in the same basic direction as before the storm. With regard to their vocal performance and lyrics, artists popular with New Orleans audiences continued to move away from extended narrative, instead relying almost exclusively on rapid-fire repetition of call-and-response phrases. Rap continued to serve as a vehicle for expressions of local identity at the neighborhood level, as in the eponymous song by female rapper Sixth Ward Dumaine, while songs such as "Drop It like a Hot Potato" carried forward bounce's central focus on dance. The production of rap at the local level grew increasingly less specialized, as advances in computer-based music recording and editing technology lowered the barriers to participation. Newer DJs such as Flipset Fred continued the pre-Katrina "remix bounce" trend, adding the signature New Orleans rhythmic elements to nationally popular rap and R&B recordings.

In general, rap produced for local audiences is becoming faster and more rhythmically intense, with frenetic, layered rhythm parts contributing to music that drives high-energy, intense shaking dances. Notwithstanding the significant impact that bounce and other 1990s local styles exercised on the conventions of commercial rap at the national level, the New Orleans scene has continued to operate according to its own priorities and preferences. In many ways, the local scene has more in common with other regional or local styles of African American dance music (like Chicago's juke or "Baltimore Club") than it does with mainstream hip-hop.

New Orleans–based rappers have increasingly participated in collaborative projects that cross lines of genre, race, class, and sexuality in the name of expressing and marketing the idea of local musical distinctiveness. The 2010 release *Ya-Ka-May* by nationally popular white funk band Galactic featured appearances by rappers Big Freedia, Katey Red, Sissy Nobby, and Cheeky Blakk, who joined other representatives of New Orleans's rich musical heritage, including producer Allen Toussaint and Bo Dollis, a performer of Mardi Gras Indian music. In late 2010 bandleader Trombone Shorty (Troy Andrews) included local rap duo Partners-N-Crime and legendary producer Byron "Mannie Fresh" Thomas alongside stars from older genres in his second line–themed Red Hot + New Orleans AIDS benefit concert in New York.

The trauma of Katrina intensified an already high level of awareness and appreciation of New Orleans's cultural distinctiveness, but, as Kelefa Sanneh observes, those who are concerned with restoring the cultural patrimony of New Orleans often focus on musicians and performers who are "old, poor and humble," rather than participants in more recently introduced and more explicitly commercial genres like rap.[23] Local rap's connections to the city's rich history of African American expressive culture were too strong to ignore, however, and since Katrina it has increasingly drawn the interest of journalists, scholars, filmmakers, musicians, and other motivated allies who wish to document and preserve the city's distinctive cultural practices and traditions and call attention to the challenges faced by its poor and working-class residents.

Katrina accelerated the movement of local rap into the pantheon of New Orleans Traditional Music, a process that was already under way before the storm. The HBO dramatic series *Treme,* which began in the summer of 2010 and was renewed for a third season in May 2011, has included rap alongside older and more "traditional" forms in its portrayal of the city's rich musical scene and neighborhood culture. The series has featured the music of local rappers, including Mystikal and Juvenile, and walk-on appearances by Katey Red, Big Freedia, Sissy Nobby, Truth Universal, and Don B (son of the legendary trumpeter and arranger Dave Bartholomew). The award-winning film *Trouble the Water* (2008) chronicled the toll that the experiences of exile and return exacted on members of the hip-hop generation, as represented by the film's central character, aspiring rapper Kimberly Roberts. The high-profile producer DJ Diplo has drawn attention to New Orleans's local rap style in the Mad Decent Radio mixtape/podcast series, while national R&B star Beyoncé used vocal and musical elements drawn from bounce in the song "Get Me Bodied" (2007).

In the arena of music journalism, the coverage of local rap increased with the hiring of Alison Fensterstock (a graduate of Tulane with roots in New York City) as contributing writer to the *Times-Picayune.* While earlier critics such as Scott Aiges and Keith Spera were generally annoyed by the pervasiveness of a retrograde local rap sensibility, Fensterstock places more value on the identifiably local aspects of rap music from the city. Her sympathetic and frequent coverage of local stalwarts such as Cheeky Blakk and DJ Jubilee and her articles on "sissy" rappers like Katey Red and Big Freedia has helped drive the national exposure of these artists—and, to some extent, the local scene they represent—in subsequent articles in the *New York Times Magazine, Bust,* and elsewhere. In collaboration with photographer Aubrey Edwards, Fensterstock organized the "Where They At" project, which involved the collection of oral history interviews and portrait photographs of over forty individuals associated with bounce and local rap. The materials were on exhibit at the University of New Orleans's Ogden Museum of Southern Art in 2010 for a month, augmented by archival items such as cassettes, promotional photographs, and snapshots. The grant-funded (and ongoing) project produced a website where photographs and portions of the oral histories are accessible.

The Neighborhood Story Project, directed by husband and wife Abram Himelstein and Rachel Breunlin, aims to empower residents of inner-city neighborhoods through self-ethnography, helping them collect, edit, and publish their own oral histories. In this way the initiative has made important contributions to efforts to document the distinctive rap music culture of New Orleans. *Coming Out the Door for the Ninth Ward* (2006), a book compiled by members of the Nine Times Social and Pleasure Club, features firsthand descriptions of block parties, DJs, and dance crews from the pre-bounce era. In *Signed, The President* (2009), Kenneth Phillips recorded family memories of his murdered uncle, bounce pioneer Irvin "DJ Irv" Phillips, and interviewed his aunt Lorén Phillips Fouroux about the emergence of the local scene in the early 1990s. *Beyond the Bricks* (2009), a book resulting from a collaborative effort between Daron Crawford and Pernell Russell, illuminates the more recent history and future directions of the local scene and the bounce genre, offering insight into the ways in which participation (especially in the form of dancing) creates gendered and sexualized subjects.

For residents of New Orleans, these efforts and others like them have helped to document and preserve the distinctive cultural practices and traditions of New Orleans. But perhaps the strongest impulse in this area has emerged from the exile experience itself. For individuals, families, or communities with long-standing ties to a particular location, the experience of spending an extended amount of time away from home can transform their perspective on the wider world as well as the place and circumstances from which they came. After moving to Las Vegas, one resident returned because he missed the "second lines on Sundays . . . DJs in the street," the backyard barbecues and the "family aspect" of New Orleans life: "You really begin to understand the culture of New Orleans and what you're missing once you leave it."[24] After Katrina, the collective experience of forced migration and exile on the part of inner-city black New Orleanians

As a crowd of children looks on, a man and a young boy try to outdo each other dancing at a 2005 block party in Annunciation Park. Catch the Wall Productions.

changed their understanding of and attitudes toward the city and the cultural and social values that it represents. As Rebirth Brass Band leader and tuba player Phil Frazier remarked, "It took Katrina for everybody to realize what we really got."[25]

Katrina contributed a new sense of urgency to projects related to popular music and the expression of a local cultural identity and perspective. Part of the reason that the local rap music culture has been able to reestablish itself is that displaced New Orleanians relied on their hometown music to get through the exile experience after Katrina. Distinctive musical values that had been absorbed and imprinted over generations helped preserve and recreate a sense of place that added meaning to their experience. Barbara Bush's glib assertion that the Katrina evacuees she met "all want to stay in Texas" and that it was "working very well for them" because they "were underprivileged anyway" shows her ignorance of the cultural and social resources that existed in New Orleans in spite of increasingly bleak economic conditions.[26] The residents of New Orleans's poor and working-class black neighborhoods supported a vital culture of day-to-day entertainment and occasional celebration that provided a reservoir of direct and indirect inspiration for creative artists within and beyond that world.

Despite the massive changes in the physical and political landscape of New Orleans since Katrina, many of the conditions and forces that shaped bounce and other engaging forms of local expressive culture remain. The local scene and the musical and social values it embodies still set New Orleans apart from the rest of the country, contributing a sense of distinctiveness and collective identity while at the same time working against the possibility of artists from the city connecting with national audiences. Local popular music will continue to serve as an outlet for the creativity and economic aspirations of the city's poor and working-class African American residents. Whether or not bounce persists as a local subgenre marked by particular musical and lyrical preferences and values, the more abstract notions that informed it—collective celebration and a spirit of resilience and creativity—will continue to be crucial tools for the psychic survival of African Americans in New Orleans and will doubtlessly produce innovative and influential musical expressions in the process.

Notes

Introduction

1. Dolamite, "3rd Ward on My Mind." oral history excerpt, Where They At, 2010, www.wheretheyatnola.com/artists.php?id=89.

2. Bakari Kitwana, *The Hip-Hop Generation: Young Blacks and the Crisis in African American Culture* (New York: Basic Civitas Books, 2002), 9.

3. New Orleans rapper Kilo calls bounce "project music" in the documentary film *Ya Heard Me?* (2008), directed by Matt Miller and Stephen Thomas.

4. Alexander Stewart, "'Funky Drummer': New Orleans, James Brown and the Rhythmic Transformation of American Music," *Popular Music* 19.3 (Oct. 2000), 293, 296, 306.

5. Ned Sublette, *The Year Before the Flood: A Story of New Orleans* (Chicago: Lawrence Hill, 2009), 186.

6. Louis Armstrong, *Satchmo: My Life in New Orleans* (New York: Prentice-Hall, 1954), 101. It is unknown whether this is the same person as Elmer "Cheeky Black" Brown, who stabbed a saloon keeper with a pocket knife in 1936. "Saloon Proprietor Is Stabbed in Back," *Times-Picayune,* 11 July 1936, 7.

7. Ingrid Monson, "Riffs, Repetition, and Theories of Globalization," *Ethnomusicology* 43.1 (Winter 1999), 33.

8. Mick Burns, *Keeping the Beat on the Street: The New Orleans Brass Band Renaissance* (Baton Rouge: Louisiana State University Press, 2006), 8.

9. Stephen Verderber, *Delirious New Orleans: Manifesto for an Extraordinary American City* (Austin: University of Texas, Press, 2009), 160.

10. Adam Krims, *Music and Urban Geography* (New York: Routledge, 2007), 105.

11. Sara Cohen, "Sounding Out the City: Music and the Sensuous Production of Place," in *The Place of Music,* ed. Andrew Leyshon, David Matless, and George Revill (New York: Guilford Press, 1998), 287.

12. Tia Denora, *Music in Everyday Life* (Cambridge: Cambridge University Press, 2000), xi.

13. Charles Keil and Steven Feld, *Music Grooves: Essays & Dialogues* (Chicago: University of Chicago Press, 1994), 20.

14. Roger D. Abrahams, *Deep Down in the Jungle: Negro Narrative Folklore from the Streets of Philadelphia,* rev. ed. (New York: Aldine, 1970), 2.

15. Martin Stokes, "Introduction: Ethnicity, Identity and Music," in *Ethnicity, Identity, and Music: The Musical Construction of Place,* ed. Stokes (Oxford: Berg, 1994), 4.

16. Quoted in Nine Times Social and Pleasure Club, *Coming Out the Door for the Ninth Ward* (New Orleans: Neighborhood Story Project, 2006), 65, 67.

17. Kelly M. Askew, *Performing the Nation: Swahili Music and Cultural Politics in Tanzania* (Chicago: University of Chicago Press, 2002), 281.

18. Curtis D. Jerde, "Black Music in New Orleans: A Historical Overview," *Black Music Research Journal* 10.1 (Spring 1990), 18.

19. Richard A. Peterson and Andy Bennett, "Introducing Music Scenes" in *Music Scenes: Local, Translocal, and Virtual,* ed. Bennett and Peterson (Nashville: Vanderbilt University Press, 2004), 7–8.

20. Michael P. Smith, *Spirit World: Pattern in the Expressive Folk Culture of African American New Orleans* (Gretna, La.: Pelican Publishing, 1992), 27.

1. African American Life and Culture in New Orleans: From Congo Square to Katrina and Beyond

1. Nicholas R. Spitzer, "Monde Créole: The Cultural World of French Louisiana Creoles and the Creolization of World Cultures," *Journal of American Folklore* 116.459 (1 Jan. 2003), 58.

2. Ben Sandmel, "The Treasured Traditions of Louisiana Music," 2003, www.louisianafolklife. org/LT/Articles_Essays/treas_trad_la_music.html.

3. Michael P. Smith, *Spirit World: Pattern in the Expressive Folk Culture of African American New Orleans* (Gretna, La.: Pelican Publishing, 1992), 27.

4. Gwendolyn Midlo Hall, *Africans in Colonial Louisiana: The Development of Afro-Creole Culture in the Eighteenth Century* (Baton Rouge: Louisiana State University Press, 1992), 161.

5. Gwendolyn Midlo Hall, "The Formation of Afro-Creole Culture," in *Creole New Orleans: Race and Americanization,* ed. Arnold R. Hirsch and Joseph Logsdon (Baton Rouge: Louisiana State University Press, 1992), 66, 68.

6. Curtis D. Jerde, "Black Music in New Orleans: A Historical Overview," *Black Music Research Journal* 10.1 (Spring 1990), 18.

7. Ira Berlin, *Many Thousands Gone: The First Two Centuries of Slavery in America* (Cambridge: Belknap Press of Harvard University Press, 1998), 206; Jerah Johnson, "New Orleans' Congo Square: An Urban Setting for Early Afro-American Culture Formation," *Louisiana History* 32.2 (Spring 1991), 122.

8. Peter Manuel with Kenneth Bilby and Michael Largey, *Caribbean Currents: Caribbean Music from Rumba to Reggae,* rev. and expanded ed. (Philadelphia: Temple University Press, 2006), 11.

9. Sandmel, "Treasured Traditions of Louisiana Music."

10. Ibid.; Eileen Southern, *The Music of Black Americans: A History,* 3rd ed. (New York: Norton, 1997), 44–46.

11. Mary Frances Berry and John W. Blassingame, *Long Memory: The Black Experience in America* (New York: Oxford University Press, 1982), 36; Jason Berry, "African Cultural Memory in New Orleans Music," *Black Music Research Journal* 8.1 (Spring 1988), 5.

12. Arnold R. Hirsch and Joseph Logsdon, "Introduction to Part III," in *Creole New Orleans: Race and Americanization,* ed. Hirsch and Logsdon (Baton Rouge: Louisiana State University Press, 1992), 189.

13. Hall, *Africans in Colonial Louisiana,* 157.

14. Spitzer, "Monde Créole," 59; see also Richard Campanella, *Geographies of New Orleans: Urban Fabrics before the Storm* (Lafayette: Center for Louisiana Studies, 2006), 205–8, for discussion of the meaning of the world *creole.*

15. Johnson, "New Orleans' Congo Square," 135.

16. Ibid., 140.

17. Berry and Blassingame, *Long Memory,* 298.

18. John W. Blassingame, *Black New Orleans, 1860–1880* (Chicago: University of Chicago Press, 1973), 15.

19. Campanella, *Geographies of New Orleans,* 12; Pierce F. Lewis, *New Orleans: The Making of an Urban Landscape* (Santa Fe, N.M.: Center for American Places, in association with the University of Virginia Press, 2003), 45; Daphne Spain, "Race Relations and Residential Segregation in New Orleans: Two Centuries of Paradox," *Annals of the American Academy of Political and Social Science* 441 (Jan. 1979), 87.

20. Hirsch and Logsdon, "Introduction to Part II," in *Creole New Orleans*, 98; William Ivy Hair, *Carnival of Fury: Robert Charles and the New Orleans Race Riot of 1900* (Baton Rouge: Louisiana State University Press, 1976), 71.

21. Jerah Johnson, "Jim Crow Laws of the 1890s and the Origins of New Orleans Jazz: Correction of an Error," *Popular Music* 19.2 (Apr. 2000), 243.

22. Blassingame, *Black New Orleans,* 17; Gwendolyn Midlo Hall, "Gwendolyn Midlo Hall with Charles Henry Rowell," *Callaloo* 29.4 (Fall 2006), 1053; James G. Hollandsworth, *The Louisiana Native Guards: The Black Military Experience during the Civil War* (Baton Rouge: Louisiana State University Press, 1995), 4–5.

23. Johnson, "New Orleans' Congo Square," 139.

24. Hall, "Formation of Afro-Creole Culture," 60.

25. Hollandsworth, *Louisiana Native Guards,* 5.

26. Blassingame, *Black New Orleans,* 173.

27. Johnson, "Jim Crow Laws of the 1890s," 243, 248.

28. Charles Hersch, *Subversive Sounds: Race and the Birth of Jazz in New Orleans* (Chicago: University of Chicago Press, 2007), 10.

29. Campanella, *Geographies of New Orleans,* 14; Johnson, "Jim Crow Laws of the 1890s," 249.

30. Johnson, "Jim Crow Laws of the 1890s," 247.

31. Blassingame, *Black New Orleans,* 140.

32. Thomas Brothers, *Louis Armstrong's New Orleans* (New York: Norton, 2006), 159.

33. Brothers, *Louis Armstrong's New Orleans,* 159–60.

34. Hersch, *Subversive Sounds,* 160.

35. Jerde, "Black Music in New Orleans," 22.

36. Alan Lomax, *Mister Jelly Roll: The Fortunes of Jelly Roll Morton, New Orleans Creole and "Inventor of Jazz,"* 2nd ed. (Berkeley: University of California Press, 1973), 50–51.

37. Danny Barker, *Buddy Bolden and the Last Days of Storyville,* ed. Alyn Shipton (London: Cassell, 1998), 6–23.

38. Jason Berry, Jonathan Foose, and Tad Jones, *Up from the Cradle of Jazz: New Orleans Music since World War II* (Athens: University of Georgia Press, 1986), 4; Armstrong, *Satchmo,* 97–98.

39. "Jass and Jassism" [editorial], *Times-Picayune,* 20 June 1918, 4.

40. Bruce Boyd Raeburn, *New Orleans Style and the Writing of American Jazz History* (Ann Arbor: University of Michigan Press, 2009), 19.

41. Lomax, *Mister Jelly Roll,* 84.

42. Brothers, *Louis Armstrong's New Orleans,* 182.

43. Raeburn, *New Orleans Style and the Writing of American Jazz History,* 9.

44. Baby Dodds, *The Baby Dodds Story: As Told to Larry Gara,* rev. ed. (Baton Rouge: Louisiana State University Press, 1992), 25–29.

45. Hersch, *Subversive Sounds,* 11–12, 8.

46. Ibid., 12; Johnson, "Jim Crow Laws of the 1890s," 249.

47. Johnson, "Jim Crow Laws of the 1890s," 249.

48. Armstrong, *Satchmo,* 128, 180.

49. Brothers, *Louis Armstrong's New Orleans,* 112.

50. William Russell and Stephen W. Smith, "New Orleans Music," in *Jazzmen,* ed. Frederic Ramsey Jr. and Charles Edward Smith (New York: Harcourt, Brace, 1939), 10; Larry Gara in Dodds, *The Baby Dodds Story,* xvi.

51. Lyle Saxon, Edward Dreyer, and Robert Tallant. eds., *Gumbo Ya Ya: A Collection of Louisiana Folk Tales* (Boston: Houghton Mifflin, 1945), 5; Shane White and Graham White, *Stylin': African-American Expressive Culture from Its Beginnings to the Zoot Suit* (Ithaca: Cornell University Press, 1998), 144.

52. George Lipsitz, *Time Passages: Collective Memory and American Popular Culture* (Minneapolis: University of Minnesota Press, 1990), 235–37.

53. Robert Palmer, *A Tale of Two Cities: Memphis Rock and New Orleans Roll* (Brooklyn: Institute for Studies in American Music, Brooklyn College of the City University of New York), 1979, 7.

54. Michael P. Smith, "Behind the Lines: the Black Mardi Gras Indians and the New Orleans Second Line," *Black Music Research Journal* 14.1 (Spring 1994), 66; Palmer, *A Tale of Two Cities*, 7.

55. Helen A. Regis, "Second Lines, Minstrelsy, and the Contested Landscapes of New Orleans Afro-Creole Festivals," *Cultural Anthropology* 14.4 (Nov. 1999), 473.

56. Armstrong, *Satchmo*, 143.

57. Burns, *Keeping the Beat on the Street*, 2; John Broven, *Rhythm & Blues in New Orleans* (Gretna, La.: Pelican Publishing, 1988), xx; Mark McKnight, "Researching New Orleans Rhythm and Blues," *Black Music Research Journal* 8.1 (Spring 1988), 115.

58. Andrew Young, *An Easy Burden: The Civil Rights Movement and the Transformation of America* (New York: HarperCollins, 1996), 21.

59. Larry Wilson quoted in Nine Times Social and Pleasure Club, *Coming Out the Door for the Ninth Ward* (New Orleans: Neighborhood Story Project, 2006), 45.

60. Linda Porter, ibid., 217; Scott Aiges, "Dancing in the Streets," *Times-Picayune*, 12 Oct. 1990, L19.

61. Burns, *Keeping the Beat on the Street*, 8; Vincent Fumar, "Brass Band Revival," *Times-Picayune*, 16 Mar. 1986, Dixie section, 11, 15.

62. Campanella, *Geographies of New Orleans*, 21; Aiges, "Dancing in the Streets."

63. Joseph Logsdon with Lawrence Powell, "Rodolphe Lucien Desdunes: Forgotten Organizer of the *Plessy* Protest," in *Sunbelt Revolution: The Historical Progression of the Civil Rights Struggle in the Gulf South, 1866–2000*, ed. Samuel C. Hyde Jr. (Gainesville: University Press of Florida, 2003), 59.

64. Claudrena N. Harold, *The Rise and Fall of the Garvey Movement in the Urban South, 1918–1942* (New York: Routledge, 2007), 29; Tony Martin, *Race First: The Ideological and Organizational Struggles of Marcus Garvey and the Universal Negro Improvement Association* (Dover, Mass.: New Press, 1976), 16.

65. Lewis, *New Orleans*, 52; Campanella, *Geographies of New Orleans*, 9, 308.

66. Lewis, *New Orleans*, 66.

67. Campanella, *Geographies of New Orleans*, 18.

68. Ibid., 19.

69. Berry, Foose, and Jones, *Up from the Cradle of Jazz*, 8.

70. Lomax, *Mister Jelly Roll*, 181.

71. Broven, *Rhythm & Blues in New Orleans*, 4.

72. Jeff Hannusch, *I Hear You Knockin': The Sound of New Orleans Rhythm and Blues* (Ville Platte, La.: Swallow Publ., 1985), 3.

73. Alexander Stewart, "'Funky Drummer': New Orleans, James Brown and the Rhythmic Transformation of American Music," *Popular Music* 19.3 (Oct. 2000), 294.

74. Tony Scherman, *Backbeat: Earl Palmer's Story* (New York: Da Capo, 1999), 63.

75. Hannusch, *I Hear You Knockin'*, 119–23; Bill Grady, "Radio Pioneer Recalls the Birth of 'Mr. Cool': Black DJ Broke Mold Chunkin' Hip Lingo," *Times-Picayune*, 9 Sept. 2001, B1.

76. Sandmel, "Treasured Traditions of Louisiana Music."

77. Broven, *Rhythm & Blues in New Orleans*, 14, 17, 86.

78. Ibid., 2.

79. Hannusch, *I Hear You Knockin'*, 109, 111–12.

80. Broven, *Rhythm & Blues in New Orleans*, 113.

81. Hannusch, *I Hear You Knockin'*, 107.

82. Stewart, "'Funky Drummer,'" 293, 300, 302; Jim Payne, *Give the Drummers Some! The Great Drummers of R&B, Funk and Soul*, ed. Harry Weinger (Katonah, N.Y.: Face the Music Prod.; Miami: Manhattan Music, 1996), 5.

83. Scherman, *Backbeat*, 63, 69–70, 94; Broven, *Rhythm & Blues in New Orleans*, 96–97; Berry, Foose, and Jones, *Up from the Cradle of Jazz*, 59–60.

84. Earl Palmer in Scherman, *Backbeat*, 80; Berry, Foose, and Jones, *Up from the Cradle of Jazz*, 58–59.

85. Hannusch, *I Hear You Knockin'*, 151.

86. Jim Bessman, "Big Easy: the Sounds of New Orleans," *Billboard*, 28 Oct. 1995, 69; Hannusch, *I Hear You Knockin'*, 105, 115.

87. Smith, "Behind the Lines," 66.

88. Lewis, *New Orleans*, 133.

89. Martha Mahoney, "Law and Racial Geography: Public Housing and the Economy in New Orleans," *Stanford Law Review* 42.5 (May 1990), 1268; Larry Wilson in Nine Times Social and Pleasure Club, *Coming Out the Door for the Ninth Ward*, 22.

90. Lewis, *New Orleans*, 98; Campanella, *Geographies of New Orleans*, 19; Burns, *Keeping the Beat on the Street*, 125.

91. Campanella, *Geographies of New Orleans*, 23.

92. Ibid., 24; Lewis, *New Orleans*, 127.

93. John E. Rousseau, "Louisiana History Repeats Itself over School Mixing Fight," *New Pittsburgh Courier*, 18 Mar. 1961, 16.

94. Lewis, *New Orleans*, 99, 124.

95. Jason DeParle, "Ignorance Has a High Price," *Times-Picayune*, 27 Oct. 1985, A1; Lewis, *New Orleans*, 131; Aesha Rasheed, "La. Schools' Racial Gap Widens: Tammany at Top; Orleans at Bottom," *Times-Picayune*, 21 Apr. 2004, A1.

96. Coleman Warner and Matt Scallan, "Minority Income Gap Narrowing, Census Shows," *Times-Picayune*, 24 Sept. 2002, A1.

97. Campanella, *Geographies of New Orleans*, 24.

98. "New Orleans after the Storm: Lessons from the Past, a Plan for the Future," report by the Brookings Institution Metropolitan Policy Program (2005), 5.

99. Steve Ritea and Tara Young, "Cycle of Death: Violence Thrives on Lack of Jobs, Wealth of Drugs," *Times-Picayune*, 8 Feb. 2004, A1.

100. Ed Anderson, "Bill Would Ban Wearing Loose Pants in School," *Times-Picayune*, 29 Mar. 1999, A4; Lynne Jensen, "Latest Teen Style Relies on a Tight Belt, Clean Undies and a Pledge to Stroll," *Times-Picayune*, 14 May 2000, B1; Rob Nelson, "Low-Riders Must Go, Says Councilman," *Times-Picayune*, 16 Oct. 2002, A1; Michelle Krupa, "Waist Case," *Times-Picayune*, 22 Apr. 2004, A1.

101. Campbell Robertson, "Smaller New Orleans after Katrina, Census Shows," *New York Times*, 3 Feb. 2011, A11.

2. "The City That Is Overlooked": Rap Beginnings, 1980–1991

1. Ruth Finnegan, *The Hidden Musicians: Music-Making in an English Town* (Cambridge: Cambridge University Press, 1989), 341.

2. Murray Forman, *The 'Hood Comes First: Race, Space, and Place in Rap and Hip-Hop* (Middletown, Conn.: Wesleyan University Press, 2002), 137.

3. Jim Fricke and Charlie Ahearn, *Yes Yes Y'all: The Experience Music Project Oral History of Hip-Hop's First Decade* (Cambridge, Mass.: Da Capo, 2002); Forman, *The 'Hood Comes First*; Steven Hager, *Hip Hop: The Illustrated History of Break Dancing, Rap Music, and Graffiti* (New York: St. Martin's, 1984); Cheryl Keyes, *Rap Music and Street Consciousness* (Urbana: University of Illinois Press, 2002); Tricia Rose, *Black Noise: Rap Music and Black Culture in Contemporary America* (Middletown, Conn.: Wesleyan University Press, 1994); David Toop, *Rap Attack 3: African Rap to Global Hip Hop*, expanded 3rd ed. (London: Serpent's Tail, 2000).

4. Dick Hebdige, *Cut 'n' Mix: Culture, Identity, and Caribbean Music* (New York: Methuen, 1987), 136–41; Keyes, *Rap Music and Street Consciousness*, 1, 66; Toop, *Rap Attack 3*, 12, 18–19,

28–53; Fricke and Ahearn, *Yes Yes Y'all,* 23–65; William Eric Perkins, "The Rap Attack: An Introduction," in *Droppin' Science: Critical Essays on Rap Music and Hip Hop Culture,* ed. Perkins (Philadelphia: Temple University Press, 1996), 5–6.

5. Keyes, *Rap Music and Street Consciousness,* 59; Robert Palmer, "Funk Takes a Provocative Turn," *New York Times,* 21 Nov. 1982, sec. 2, 19; Perkins, "Rap Attack," 7–9; Toop, *Rap Attack 3,* 26.

6. Forman, *The 'Hood Comes First,* 69; Toop, *Rap Attack 3,* 132–33.

7. Toop, *Rap Attack 3,* 16.

8. Ibid., 158; Forman, *The 'Hood Comes First,* 136.

9. Adler quoted in Robert Palmer, "Street-Smart Rapping Is Innovative Art Form," *New York Times,* 4 Feb. 1985, C-13.

10. Forman, *The 'Hood Comes First,* 138; Peter Watrous, "It's Official: Rap Music Is in the Mainstream," *New York Times,* 16 May 1988, C11; Palmer, "Street-Smart Rapping."

11. Dartanian "MC Dart" Stovall (Philadelphia), telephone interview by author, 12 Jan. 2008.

12. Forman, *The 'Hood Comes First,* 148, 161, xvii.

13. Ibid., 169, 194.

14. Ibid., 198.

15. Toop, *Rap Attack 3,* xi; Forman, *The 'Hood Comes First,* 193.

16. Adam Krims, *Rap Music and the Poetics of Identity* (New York: Cambridge University Press, 2000), 74, 78.

17. Forman, *The 'Hood Comes First,* 179, xvii.

18. Krims, *Rap Music and the Poetics of Identity,* 124.

19. Forman, *The 'Hood Comes First,* 170.

20. Shea Dixon, "Future of Music Industry Here Looks Promising," *Times-Picayune,* 7 Feb. 1990, B8.

21. Plotnicki quoted in Watrous, "It's Official," C11.

22. Janine McAdams and Deborah Russell, "Rap Rates with Adults, Say Radio, Retail," *Billboard,* 21 Sept. 1991, 91.

23. Forman, *The 'Hood Comes First,* 330.

24. N. Anand and Richard A. Peterson, "When Market Information Constitutes Fields: Sensemaking of Markets in the Commecial Music Industry," *Organization Science* 11.3 (May–June 2000), 276.

25. Herbert Michael "Ice Mike" Scott, interview by author, New Orleans, 18 July 2005; Forman, *The 'Hood Comes First,* xvii.

26. Petula Dvorak, "Bounce: Rap Music Meant for Dancing Fuels the Phenomenon of New Orleans Block Parties," *Times-Picayune,* 25 Oct. 1998, E1.

27. Eric Barra quoted in Nine Times Social and Pleasure Club, *Coming Out the Door for the Ninth Ward* (New Orleans: Neighborhood Story Project, 2006), 72.

28. Roni Sarig, *Third Coast: OutKast, Timbaland, and How Hip-Hop Became a Southern Thing* (New York: Da Capo, 2007), 251; Charlie Braxton, "Magic" [interview], *Murder Dog,* 2003, www.murderdog.com (no longer available); Charlie Braxton, [Interview with Sporty T], DownSouth.com, 2002 (no longer available).

29. Eric Barra quoted in Nine Times Social and Pleasure Club, *Coming Out the Door for the Ninth Ward,* 72.

30. Sarig, *Third Coast,* 251.

31. "Joe Blakk: Blood Sweat & Tears." Oral history excerpt, Where They At, 2010, www.wheretheyatnola.com/artists.php?id=95.

32. Joseph Baker quoted in Nine Times Social and Pleasure Club, *Coming Out the Door for the Ninth Ward,* 71.

33. Dvorak, "Bounce"; Yolanda Marrero quoted ibid.

34. Quoted in Nine Times Social and Pleasure Club, *Coming Out the Door for the Ninth Ward,* 75.

35. Perry McDonald quoted ibid., 65.

36. Troy Materre quoted ibid., 74.

37. Platenburg quoted ibid., 76.

38. Joseph Baker quoted ibid., 72.

39. Dvorak, "Bounce."

40. Raymond Williams quoted in Nine Times Social and Pleasure Club, *Coming Out the Door for the Ninth Ward*, 75.

41. Karen Cortello, "Street," *OffBeat*, Dec. 1997, 17.

42. Platenburg quoted in Nine Times Social and Pleasure Club, *Coming Out the Door for the Ninth Ward*, 103.

43. John Burke, "Going Going Gong! The Talent Show Is Alive and Well in New Orleans," *Times-Picayune*, 2 June 1989, L18.

44. Jill Anding, "Talent Show Gives Local Performers Shot at Big Time," *Times-Picayune*, 20 Nov. 1990, C6; Jean A. Williams, "WYLD Comes through Loud, Clear in Efforts," *Times-Picayune*, 14 Jan. 1990, A17.

45. "Bust Down, Pop that Thang." Oral history excerpt, Where They At, 2010, www.wheretheyatnola.com/artists.php?id=81.

46. Jeff Hannusch, *I Hear You Knockin': The Sound of New Orleans Rhythm and Blues* (Ville Platte, La.: Swallow Publ., 1985), 301.

47. Jeff Hannusch, "Bobby Marchan, 69, Noted N.O. R&B Artist," *Times-Picayune*, 15 Dec. 1999, B4; Bill Grady, "Singer Gave Voice to an R&B Original," *Times-Picayune*, 5 May 1995, B1.

48. Hannusch, *I Hear You Knockin'*, 306; Karen Cortello, "Street," *OffBeat*, Sept. 1993, 22.

49. Charles "Captain Charles" Leach, interview by author, New Orleans, 16 July 2005.

50. Hannusch, "Bobby Marchan, 69, Noted N.O. R&B Artist."

51. Bill Grady, "Singer Gave Voice to an R&B Original," *Times-Picayune*, 5 May 1995, B1.

52. Quoted in Jeff Hannusch, "Backtalk: DJ Jubilee," *OffBeat*, Sept. 2000, 93.

53. Aiges, "The '80s," L7.

54. Ben Sandmel, "Offbeat Sensations." *Times-Picayune*, 28 Apr. 1989, J4.

55. "Louisiana Heritage Fair," *Times-Picayune*, 26 Apr. 1985, L18; Keith Spera, "Second-Line Time Line," *Times-Picayune*, 23 Apr. 1993, L7.

56. Calvin Gilbert, "Get Ready for New Orleans and All That Jazz," *Baton Rouge Advocate*, 25 Apr. 1986, 28-Fun; Calvin Gilbert, "N.O. Jazz & Heritage Festival Schedule," *Baton Rouge Advocate*, 24 Apr. 1987, 34-Fun; Calvin Gilbert, "New Orleans & All That Jazz," *Baton Rouge Advocate*, 22 Apr. 1988, 30-Fun; Ben Sandmel, "Offbeat Sensations." *Times-Picayune*, 28 Apr. 1989, J4; Scott Aiges, "Making Tracks: Hot Tix Hot Pix," *Times-Picayune*, 6 Apr. 1990, L6; Scott Aiges, "Week One at the Fair Grounds," *Times-Picayune*, 26 Apr. 1991, L21; Scott Aiges, "Best Bets," *Times-Picayune*, 2 May 1991, J1.

57. "Concerts," *Times-Picayune*, 28 Mar. 1986, L19; Scott Aiges, "Ice Cube's Rap Boils with Rage," *Times-Picayune*, 21 Dec. 1990, L6.

58. "N.O. Tourists Robbed after Rap Concert," *Baton Rouge Sunday Advocate*, 28 Dec. 1986, 4-B; "Teens Go on Rampage in N.O. on July 4th," *Baton Rouge Advocate*, 7 July 1987, 4-B; Jon Pareles, "Have Rap Concerts Become Inextricably Linked to Violence?," *New York Times*, 13 Sept. 1988, C13.

59. Forman, *The 'Hood Comes First*, xvii.

60. Bill Grady, "Turn-Down-the-Volume Pleas Sometimes Fall on Deaf Ears," *Times-Picayune*, 26 Feb. 1985, A13, A14; "Letters," *Times-Picayune*, 13 Mar. 1985, A14; "Letters," *Times-Picayune*, 16 Mar. 1985, A22.

61. Cindy Hebert, "Lunch Music Is Food for Students' Soul," *Times-Picayune*, 3 Oct. 1985, F1.

62. Gerald Platenburg quoted in Nine Times Social and Pleasure Club, *Coming Out the Door for the Ninth Ward*, 76; Raymond Williams quoted ibid., 75.

63. Platenburg quoted ibid., 76, 75, 103.

64. "Bust Down, Pop That Thang."

65. Scott Aiges, "A Hard-Hitting Rap Evening," *Times-Picayune,* 29 May 1992, L7.

66. Sarig, *Third Coast,* 251; Braxton, [Interview with Sporty T].

67. Bill Murphy, "Bounce on the Brain," *Remix,* 1 Mar. 2005, 34; "Concerts," *Times-Picayune,* 28 Mar. 1986, L19.

68. Aiges, "A Hard-Hitting Rap Evening"; Scott Aiges, "The Local Scene Explodes," *Times-Picayune,* 14 Aug. 1992, L6.

69. Mariel Concepcion, "A Bad Rap? Facing Declining Sales and Limited Opportunities, the Female Hip-Hop Industry Ponders Its Future," *Billboard,* 9 June 2007, 25.

70. Sarig, *Third Coast,* 252.

71. Ibid., 252–53.

72. "Nardwuar vs. Lil Wayne," www.youtube.com/watch?v=wgMUhI_SN68.

73. Sarig, *Third Coast,* 253.

74. "Ain't My Vault: Mannie Fresh Interview pt. 1," Cocaine Blunts, 29 Apr. 2009, www.cocaineblunts.com/blunts/?p=2510.

75. Abdul Malik, interview by author, Atlanta, Georgia, 22 Mar. 2011.

76. Ben Sandmel, liner notes on Rebirth Brass Band, *Feel like Funkin' It Up* (Rounder Records, 1989).

77. Richard Follett, *The Sugar Masters: Planters and Slaves in Louisiana's Cane World, 1820–1860* (Baton Rouge: Louisiana State University Press, 2005), 222.

78. Shane White and Graham White, *The Sounds of Slavery: Discovering African American History through Songs, Sermons, and Speech* (Boston: Beacon Press, 2005), 50.

79. Charles Hersch, *Subversive Sounds: Race and the Birth of Jazz in New Orleans* (Chicago: University of Chicago Press, 2007), 81.

80. Jason Berry, Jonathan Foose, and Tad Jones, *Up from the Cradle of Jazz: New Orleans Music since World War II* (Athens: University of Georgia Press, 1986), 5.

81. Jabo Starks in Jim Payne, *Give the Drummers Some! The Great Drummers of R&B, Funk and Soul,* ed. Harry Weinger (Katonah, N.Y.: Face the Music Prod.; Miami: Manhattan Music, 1996), 53.

82. ":Gregory D: Buck Jump Time," Where They At, 2010, www.wheretheyatnola.com/artists.php?id=92.

83. "Mannie Fresh: That's My DJ," Where They At, 2010, www.wheretheyatnola.com/artists.php?id=77.

84. "Gregory D: Buck Jump Time"; Leach, interview by author.

85. Leach, interview by author; Dan Bennett, "Teen Birthday Party Ends in Fatal Shots," *Times-Picayune,* 16 Oct. 1990, B1; Christopher Cooper, "Rap Chant Led to Killing, Both Sides Agree," *Times-Picayune,* 11 Mar. 1993; Bill Walsh, "After the Gunshots: Fear Meets a $50 Gun, and a Life Is Gone," *Times-Picayune,* 25 July 1993, A14.

86. Scott Aiges, "This Weekend's JazzFest," *Times-Picayune,* 27 Apr. 1990, J1.

87. Simon Reynolds, "For the Love of Money," *Village Voice,* 30 Nov. 1999, 123.

88. Scott Aiges, "Rappin' Up the Big Easy," *Times-Picayune,* 23 Mar. 1990, L6; Bob Davis, "Tuning Out: Black Radio Stations Face Balky Advertisers as Competition Rises," *Wall Street Journal,* 23 Sept. 1987, 1.

89. Scott Aiges, "Gold Records (Big Easy-Style)," *Times-Picayune,* 21 Dec. 1990, L23.

90. Karen Cortello, "Street," *OffBeat,* Nov. 1992, 16.

91. "Ain't My Vault: Mannie Fresh Interview pt. 1."

92. Leslie Williams, "Radio Anthem Raps Life in Marrero," *Times-Picayune,* 19 Aug. 1991, B1.

93. Ibid.

94. Scott Aiges, "West Bank Rapper Wraps Up a Deal," *Times-Picayune,* 25 Oct. 1991, L7.

95. Williams, "Radio Anthem Raps Life in Marrero."

96. Scott Aiges, "Jazz Fest '92: Best Bets at the Fest," *Times-Picayune,* 24 Apr. 1992, J1.

97. Ice Mike (Herbert Michael Scott), interview by author.

98. Travis "T-Hustler" Lyons, interview by author, New Orleans, 18 July 2005.

99. Carlton Wade and Charlie Braxton, "Wobble, Wobble, Shake It!," *Source,* Apr. 2001, 136.

100. George "DJ Duck" Thomas quoted in Wade and Braxton, "Wobble, Wobble, Shake It!," 137.

101. "Warren Henry 'Stone' Mayes III," *Times-Picayune,* 5 Aug. 1999, B4; Walt Philbin, "Suspect Surrenders in Shooting of Rap Artist," *Times-Picayune,* 5 Aug. 1999, B8.

3. "Where They At": Bounce, 1992–1994

1. Murray Forman, *The 'Hood Comes First: Race, Space, and Place in Rap and Hip-Hop* (Middletown, Conn.: Wesleyan University Press, 2002), 334.

2. Scott Aiges, "The Sound and the Fury: Not Everyone Loves New Orleans Bounce," *Times-Picayune,* 18 Feb. 1994, L18 ("cookie-cutter"); Keith Spera, "Whither Rap?," *OffBeat,* July 1993, 32 (Spera: "the lightweight 'bounce' artists whose repetitive, crowd-pleasing cheers are the most successful at winning local airplay and generating local sales"; Aiges: "It's a completely separate style of music that I find completely unpalatable"). Spera used the term "rap-lite" in the following articles: "The Mind of Mystikal," *OffBeat,* June 1995, 32; "Rapper Lives Up to Name," *Times-Picayune,* 5 May 1996, A1; "The Master Plan," *Times-Picayune,* 15 Aug. 1997, L18.

3. Aiges, "The '80s"; Scott Aiges, "Rap Fans Follow the Bouncing Beat of a Home-Grown Style," *Times-Picayune,* 18 Feb. 1994, L19.

4. Scott Aiges, "Hot Wax in New Orleans," *Times-Picayune,* 18 Sept. 1992, L7.

5. Aiges, "Rap Fans Follow the Bouncing Beat"; Scott Aiges, "Home-Grown Bounce Music Rules Big Easy's Rap Roost," *Billboard,* 19 Mar. 1994, 26; Karen Cortello, "Street," *OffBeat,* Aug. 1993, 21; Charles "Captain Charles" Leach, interview by author, New Orleans, 16 July 2005; Tim Smooth quoted in Spera, "Whither Rap?," 35.

6. Ned Sublette, *The Year Before the Flood: A Story of New Orleans* (Chicago: Lawrence Hill, 2009), 212.

7. J-Dogg [John Shaw], "Parallels in the Development of Memphis and New Orleans Rap," originally posted in Usenet newsgroups rec.music.hip-hop, neworleans.general, 9 Dec. 1997; archived at https://groups.google.com/forum/#!topic/neworleans.general/TO3V25bTL6I.

8. "DJ Jimi: The J, the I, the M, the I . . . it's Jimi," Where They At, www.wheretheyatnola.com/artists.php?id=94.

9. Roni Sarig, *Third Coast: OutKast, Timbaland, and How Hip-Hop Became a Southern Thing* (New York: Da Capo Press, 2007), 257.

10. Phillip Price quoted in Pig Balls, "Show Boys: Bugs Can Can/Triggaman: Interview," *Murder Dog* 7.4 (2000), 90.

11. "Ain't My Vault: Mannie Fresh Interview Pt. 2," *Cocaine Blunts,* Apr. 30, 2009, www.cocaineblunts.com/blunts/?p=2526.

12. Orville Hall quoted in Pig Balls, "Show Boys," 90.

13. Tony Green, "Bounce ta This," *XXL,* 1999, 129.

14. Orville Hall quoted in Pig Balls, "Show Boys," 90.

15. Aiges, "Sound and the Fury."

16. Sublette, *Year Before the Flood,* 213.

17. "Nardwuar vs. Lil Wayne," www.youtube.com/watch?v=wgMUhI_SN68.

18. Leach, interview by author.

19. Aiges, "Home-Grown Bounce Music," 30.

20. "Ain't My Vault: Mannie Fresh Interview Pt. 2."; Andrew Noz, "The Big Bang," *Scratch,* Sept.–Oct. 2007, 80.

21. "Nardwuar vs. Lil Wayne."

22. Lorén K. Phillips Fouroux quoted in Carlton Wade and Charlie Braxton, "Wobble, Wobble, Shake It!," *Source,* Apr. 2001, 137; Scott, interview by author.

23. Leach, interview by author.

24. Aiges, "Sound and the Fury"; Petula Dvorak, "Bounce: Rap Music Meant for Dancing Fuels the Phenomenon of New Orleans Block Parties," *Times-Picayune,* 25 Oct. 1998, E1.

25. Aiges, "Rap Fans Follow the Bouncing Beat."

26. Aiges, "Home-Grown Bounce Music," 26; "Wild Wayne: Ya Boy," Oral history excerpt, Where They At, 2010, www.wheretheyatnola.com/artists.php?id=121.

27. Gary Holzenthal quoted in Aiges, "Home-Grown Bounce Music," 26.

28. Aiges, "Sound and the Fury"; Tucker quoted in Aiges, "Rap Fans Follow the Bouncing Beat."

29. Aiges, "Home-Grown Bounce Music," 26.

30. Norman C. Stolzoff, *Wake the Town & Tell the People: Dancehall Culture in Jamaica* (Durham: Duke University Press, 2000), 19.

31. Peter Manuel with Kenneth Bilby and Michael Largey, *Caribbean Currents: Caribbean Music from Rumba to Reggae,* rev. and expanded ed. (Philadelphia: Temple University Press, 2006), 9.

32. William Russell and Stephen W. Smith, "New Orleans Music," in *Jazzmen,* ed. Frederic Ramsey Jr. and Charles Edward Smith (New York: Harcourt, Brace, 1939), 10.

33. Chadwick Hansen, "Jenny's Toe: Negro Shaking Dances in America," *American Quarterly* 19.3 (Autumn 1967), 555.

34. Aiges, "Rap Fans Follow the Bouncing Beat."

35. Ibid.

36. Sarig, *Third Coast,* 258.

37. Lorén K. Phillips Fouroux quoted in Kenneth Phillips, *Signed, The President* (New Orleans: Neighborhood Story Project, 2009), 85.

38. Aiges, "Home-Grown Bounce Music" 26; Aiges, "Rap Fans Follow the Bouncing Beat."

39. Aiges, "Home-Grown Bounce Music," 26.

40. Leach, interview by author. .

41. Karen Cortello, "Street," *OffBeat,* Dec. 1992, 10.

42. Larry Flick, ed., "Single Reviews," *Billboard,* 3 Oct. 1992, 72; Cortello, "Street," Dec. 1992, 10.

43. Isaac Bolden, interview by author, Atlanta, Georgia, 25 Feb. 2006.

44. Ibid.

45. Green, "Bounce ta This," 129.

46. Bolden, interview by author.

47. Ibid.

48. Bruce Westbrook, "New Rating System Measures Houston's Taste in Music," *Houston Chronicle,* 16 Aug. 1992, Zest section, 12.

49. DJ Jimi quoted in Aiges, "Rap Fans Follow the Bouncing Beat."

50. Larry Flick, ed., "Single Reviews," *Billboard,* 10 Apr. 1993, 72.

51. Karen Cortello, "Street," *OffBeat,* Feb. 1993, 22.

52. Terius "Juvenile" Gray quoted ibid.

53. Ibid.

54. Scott Aiges, "He's Superman of the Keyboard Set," *Times-Picayune,* 5 Mar 1993, L7; Aiges, "Rap Fans Follow the Bouncing Beat."

55. Terius "Juvenile" Grayquoted in Cynthia Fuchs, "Interview with Juvenile: Hip Hop artist," Pop Matters, 2000, www.popmatters.com/music/interviews/juvenile.html.

56. Keith Spera, "La. Artists Top the Charts for 2 Weeks in a Row," *Times-Picayune,* 5 Feb. 1999, L8.

57. "SoundScan: Best-Sellers," *Cincinnati Post,* 13 Feb. 1993, 4B.

58. Aiges, "Local Scene Explodes."

59. Aiges, "Home-Grown Bounce Music," 30.

60. Aiges, "Local Scene Explodes"; Holzenthal quoted ibid.

61. Holzenthal quoted in Aiges, "Home-Grown Bounce Music," 26.

62. Scott Aiges, "Sounds of the City," *Times-Picayune,* 10 July 1992, L14.

63. Jason Patterson quoted in Charles Henry Rowell, "Jason Patterson & Andrea DuPlessis with Charles Henry Rowell." *Callaloo* 29:4 (2007), 1291.

64. Scott Aiges, "A Home for Hip-Hop?," *Times-Picayune,* 9 July 1993, L6; Scott Aiges, "Rap is Lukewarm Even for Granny," *Times-Picayune,* 27 Aug. 1993, L7; Aiges, "Rap Fans Follow the Bouncing Beat"; Spera, "Rapper Lives Up to Name"; Keith Spera, "400 Degreez Puts Juvenile in Hot Spot," *Times-Picayune* 19 Mar. 1999, L8; Keith Spera, "Bouncing Back," *Times-Picayune,* 7 Jan. 2004, L1; Keith Spera, "Pushing the Limit," *Times-Picayune,* 11 June 2000, A1; Keith Spera, "Spare Notes," *Times-Picayune,* 23 Mar. 2007, L26.

65. Aiges, "The Sound and the Fury."

66. Tricia Rose, *Black Noise: Rap Music and Black Culture in Contemporary America* (Middletown, Conn.: Wesleyan University Press, 1994), 169.

67. Alecia P. Long, *The Great Southern Babylon: Sex, Race, and Respectability in New Orleans, 1865–1920* (Baton Rouge: Louisiana State University Press, 2004), 1–9.

68. Roger D. Abrahams, *Deep Down in the Jungle: Negro Narrative Folklore from the Streets of Philadelphia,* rev. ed. (New York: Aldine, 1970), 19.

69. Aiges, "Rap Fans Follow the Bouncing Beat."

70. Aiges, "Sound and the Fury."

71. Aiges, "Home-Grown Bounce Music," 26.

72. Dewey Doo (Lendar Dent III) quoted in Aiges, "Home-Grown Bounce Music," 26.

73. Aiges, "Sound and the Fury."

74. Quoted in Karen Cortello, "Street," *OffBeat,* Oct. 1993, 22.

75. Quoted in Aiges, "Sound and the Fury."

76. Aiges, "Rap Fans Follow the Bouncing Beat."

77. Cortello, "Street," Aug. 1993, 21.

78. Aiges, "The Local Scene Explodes"; Cortello quoted ibid.

79. Spera, "Whither Rap?," 34.

80. Aiges, "Local Scene Explodes."

81. Peter Stallybrass and Allon White, *The Politics and Poetics of Transgression* (London: Methuen, 1986), 2.

82. Spera, "Whither Rap?," 34; Tim Smooth and Gregory D quoted ibid.

83. Quoted ibid., 35.

84. Quoted in Aiges, "Sound and the Fury."

85. Quoted in Aiges, "Home-Grown Bounce Music," 26; Aiges, "Sound and the Fury."

86. Quoted in Aiges, "Rap Fans Follow the Bouncing Beat."

87. Quoted in Aiges, "Sound and the Fury."

88. Ibid.

89. Quoted in Aiges, "Home-Grown Bounce Music," 26; Karen Cortello, "Backtalk with Precise," *Offbeat,* June 1996, 85.

90. Quoted in Aiges, "Rap Fans Follow the Bouncing Beat."

91. Quoted in Aiges, "Home-Grown Bounce Music," 26; quoted in Aiges, "Sound and the Fury."

92. Quoted in Daron Crawford and Pernell Russell, *Beyond the Bricks* (New Orleans: Neighborhood Story Project, 2009), 123.

93. Quoted ibid., 134.

94. Greg Baker, "Crew You, Too," *Miami New Times,* 31 July 1991, www.miaminewtimes.com/1991-07-31/music/crew-you-too/.

95. Melville J. Herskovits, *The Myth of the Negro Past* (1941; repr., Boston: Beacon, 1958), 271; Hansen, "Jenny's Toe," 561.

96. Quoted in Phillips, *Signed, The President,* 84.

97. Jackson, Mia X, and Yolanda Marrero quoted in Dvorak, "Bounce."

98. "Josephine Johnny: Workin With Sumthin," *Where They At,* 2010, www.wheretheyat-nola.com/artists.php?id=97.

99. Crawford and Russell, *Beyond the Bricks,* 122, 117.

100. "Gary Holzenthal and Father: Mister Odyssey," Where They At, 2010, www.wheretheyat-nola.com/artists.php?id=91.

101. Aiges, "Home-Grown Bounce Music," 30.

102. Cortello, "Street," Oct. 1993, 22.

103. Cortello, "Backtalk with Precise," 85.

104. Aiges, "Home-Grown Bounce Music," 26.

105. Eileen Hudson, "Market Profile: New Orleans," *Mediaweek,* 7 May 2001.

106. Aiges, "Home-Grown Bounce Music," 26.

107. Scott Aiges, "Rap Takes a Bounce in N.O.," *Times-Picayune,* 24 Dec. 1993, L8; Aiges, "Rap Fans Follow the Bouncing Beat"; Aiges, "Home-Grown Bounce Music," 26; Spera, "Whither Rap?," 32.

108. Quoted in Aiges, "Home-Grown Bounce Music," 26.

109. Ibid., 1.

110. Aiges, "Rap Fans Follow the Bouncing Beat"; Lorén K. Phillips Fouroux quoted in Phillips, *Signed, The President,* 83.

111. Aiges, "Home-Grown Bounce Music," 1.

112. Scott Aiges, "Locals Have It Rapped Up," *Times-Picayune,* 7 Aug. 1992, L7.

113. Aiges, "Rap Takes a Bounce in N.O."

114. Gionne Jourdan, "The Party's Over," *Times-Picayune,* 14 Aug. 1992, L17.

115. Scott Aiges, "This Weekend's JazzFest," *Times-Picayune,* 27 Apr. 1990, J1; Scott Aiges, "Jazz Fest '92: Best Bets at the Fest," *Times-Picayune,* 24 Apr. 1992, J1; "1993 Jazz & Heritage Festival: Weekend Schedule," *Times-Picayune,* 30 Apr. 1993, J2. Michael Tisserand, "The 1st Unofficial OffBeat Jazz Fest Awards," *OffBeat,* June 1994, 29, 31; "Saturday," *Times-Picayune,* 28 Apr. 1995, L26.

116. Aiges, "Rap Fans Follow the Bouncing Beat"; Aiges, "Home-Grown Bounce Music," 26.

117. Aiges, "Home-Grown Bounce Music," 26.

118. Leach, interview by author; Aiges, "Home-Grown Bounce Music," 26.

119. Scott, interview by author.

120. J-Dogg [John Shaw], "Parallels in the Development of Memphis and New Orleans Rap."

121. Spera, "Whither Rap?," 33.

122. Scott Aiges, "Local Albums Take the Rap," *Times-Picayune,* 26 Nov. 1993, L9; Aiges, "Sounds of the City"; Aiges, "Sound and the Fury."

123. Aiges, "A Home for Hip-Hop?"; Aiges, "Sounds of the City."

124. Scott Aiges, "Big Easy Is Ready for Rap," *Times-Picayune,* 5 June 1992, L7; Aiges, "Local Scene Explodes."

125. Aiges, "Local Scene Explodes."

126. Aiges, "Local Albums Take the Rap"; Aiges, "Sound and the Fury."

127. Aiges, "Local Scene Explodes."

128. Aiges, "Rap Takes a Bounce in N.O."

129. Aiges quoted in Spera, "Whither Rap?," 33; Aiges, "Sound and the Fury."

130. Spera, "Whither Rap?," 32.

131. Ibid.; Spera, "Mind of Mystikal," 32; Spera, "Rapper Lives Up to Name"; Spera, "Master Plan."

132. Karen Cortello, "Street," Nov. 1992, 16.

133. "Reeling In a 'Fresh Catch': New CD Touts Local Artists," *Times-Picayune,* 25 Feb. 1994, L7.

134. John Soeder, "Juvenile Puts Bounce in Tour of Hip-Hop Superstars," *Cleveland Plain Dealer,* 31 Mar. 2000, Friday section, 16.

135. Bolden, interview by author.

136. Scott, interview by author.

4. "Bout It": New Orleans Breaking Through, 1995–2000

1. Neil Strauss, "A Trendsetter on Rap's Fringe," *New York Times,* 28 May 2000, section 2, 23.

2. Keith Negus, *Music Genres and Corporate Cultures* (London: Routledge, 1999), 90; Scott Aiges, "Home-Grown Bounce Music Rules Big Easy's Rap Roost," *Billboard,* 19 Mar. 1994, 1; Scott Aiges, "Rap Fans Follow the Bouncing Beat of a Home-Grown Style," *Times-Picayune,* 18 Feb. 1994, L19; Karen Cortello, "Street," *OffBeat,* July 1996, 13–14.

3. Negus, *Music Genres and Corporate Cultures,* 96.

4. Aiges, "Home-Grown Bounce Music," 1, 26.

5. Karen Cortello, "Street," *OffBeat,* Jan. 1997, 20.

6. Karen Cortello, "Street," *OffBeat,* Jan. 1996, 24.

7. Keith Spera, "The Mind of Mystikal," *OffBeat,* June 1995, 34, 35.

8. Ibid., 35; Karen Cortello, "Street," *OffBeat,* Apr. 1995, 24.

9. Mystikal quoted in Matt Diehl, "Q&A: Mystikal," *Rolling Stone,* 26 Oct. 2000, 36.

10. Karen Cortello, "Street," *OffBeat,* Aug. 1995, 31.

11. "Mystikal profile," BBC Radio 1, 2000, www.bbc.co.uk (no longer available).

12. Havelock Nelson, "Mergers, Money & Marketing: With the Help of Former Indie Powerhouses the Majors Get In on the Rap Boom," *Billboard,* 23 Nov. 1991, R-18.

13. *Offbeat* staff, "The Best of 1996," *Offbeat,* Jan. 1997, 51.

14. Quoted in Spera, "The Mind of Mystikal," 32.

15. Ibid., 35.

16. Spera, "The Mind of Mystikal," 35, 32; quotations on 35.

17. Karen Cortello, "Street," *OffBeat,* July 1994, 5.

18. Herbert Michael "Ice Mike" Scott, interview by author, New Orleans, 18 July 2005.

19. Scott Aiges, "A Heavy Rap Debut," *Times-Picayune,* 9 Sept. 1994, L8.

20. Cortello, "Street," Jan. 1996, 24.

21. Charlie Braxton, [Interview with Sporty T], Down-South.com, 2002 (no longer available).

22. Fred Schruers, "Survival of the Illest," *Rolling Stone,* 27 Nov. 1997, 19.

23. See Roy S. Johnson, "Diamond in the Rough," *Fortune,* 27 Sept. 1999, 166–80.

24. Miller quoted in Schruers, "Survival of the Illest," 22.

25. Johnson, "Diamond in the Rough"; Tariq K. Muhammad, "Hip-Hop Moguls: Beyond the Hype," *Black Enterprise,* Dec. 1999, 79.

26. Roni Sarig, *Third Coast: OutKast, Timbaland, and How Hip-Hop Became a Southern Thing* (New York: Da Capo Press, 2007), 82.

27. Charlie Braxton, "Master P's Theater," *XXL,* [Sept.] 1997, 95; Cheryl Keyes, *Rap Music and Street Consciousness* (Urbana: University of Illinois Press, 2002), 90.

28. Susan H. Gordon, "New Orleans Musicians Get Sound New Housing," *Architectural Record* 195.6 (1 June 2007), 42.

29. Matt Miller, "Rap's Dirty South: From Subculture to Pop Culture," *Journal of Popular Music Studies* 16.2 (Aug. 2004), 182–89; Matt Miller, "Dirty Decade: Rap Music and the U.S. South, 1997–2007," *Southern Spaces,* 10 June 2008, www.southernspaces.org/2008/dirty-decade-rap-music-and-us-south-1997-2007.

30. Craig Rosen, "After 10 Years, Priority Proves It's More Than Rap," *Billboard,* 10 June 1995, 10, 18.

31. Negus, *Music Genres and Corporate Cultures,* 99.

32. Jay W. Babcock, "Master P, Hip & Hoppin': For Rap Entrepreneur, No Limit Is Pure Gold," *Washington Post,* 25 Sept. 1997, C14.

33. Muhammad, "Hip-Hop Moguls."

34. Johnson, "Diamond in the Rough,"

35. Keith Spera, "Local Rapper Master P Bumps the Big Guys with No. 1 Album," *Times-Picayune,* 20 Sept. 1997, A1; Keith Spera, "Rising Star Exits Center Stage to Rap up Entertainment Deals," *Times-Picayune,* 14 Nov. 1997, A1.

36. Spera, "Local Rapper Master P."
37. Spera, "Master Plan."
38. Johnson, "Diamond in the Rough."
39. Keith Spera, "Pop Master," *Times-Picayune,* 20 June 1998, A1; Barry Michael Cooper, "Dope Tapes, No Limit," *Village Voice,* 5 May 1998, 69–71.
40. Kwaku, "Virgin Makes Global No Limit Deal," *Billboard,* 18 July 1998, 53, 58.
41. Master P quoted in Spera, "Pushing the Limit."
42. Sarig, *Third Coast,* 81.
43. Quoted in Johnson, "Diamond in the Rough."
44. Spera, "Master Plan;" Master P quoted ibid.
45. Miller quoted in Rhonda Baraka, "Q&A with 'P,'" *Billboard,* 16 Mar. 2002, 50.
46. Cooper, "Dope Tapes, No Limit."
47. Ibid.
48. Latrice Goss, "Joe Blakk: New Orleans' Best Kept Secret," *New York Beacon,* 10 July 2002, 27; Joe Blakk quoted ibid.
49. "BR-based rapper Master P ranks 10th on *Forbes* money list," *Baton Rouge Advocate,* 8 Sept. 1998, 1A; Keith Spera, "The Midas Touch," *Times-Picayune,* 11 Oct. 1998, A1.
50. Scott Stossel, "Baton Rouge Dispatch: Gate Crashers," *New Republic,* 30 Aug. 1999, 18–22.
51. Quoted in Rashaun Hall, "Master Builder: Creating an Empire the Old-Fashioned Way," *Billboard,* 16 Mar. 2002, 38.
52. Quoted in Schruers, "Survival of the Illest," 22.
53. Quoted in Muhammad, "Hip-Hop Moguls."; Baraka, "Q&A with 'P,'" 52.
54. Quoted in Baraka, "Q&A with 'P,'" 50.
55. Schruers, "Survival of the Illest," 22, 34.
56. Quoted in Spera, "Pushing the Limit."
57. Brett Pulley, "Soldier under $iege," *Savoy,* June–July 2002, 77.
58. Soulja Slim quoted in Black Dog Bone, "Soulja Slim" [interview]. *Murder Dog,* 2003, http://murderdog.com/archives/2003/soulja_slim.html.
59. Magic quoted in Charlie Braxton, "Magic" [interview], *Murder Dog,* 2003, http://murderdog.com (no longer available).
60. Quoted in Spera, "Pushing the Limit."
61. Miller quoted in Baraka, "Q&A with 'P,'" 50.
62. Marci Kenon, "To Keep It Real or Make a Deal?," *Billboard,* 7 Apr. 2001, 26.
63. Jason Fine, "Cash Money's Midnight Ride," *Rolling Stone,* 8 June 2000, 82; Slim quoted ibid.,; Sarig, *Third Coast,* 262.
64. Slim quoted in Jim Farber, "Home-Grown Rap Pays Off for Cash Money," *New York Daily News,* 28 Feb. 2000, 40; Slim quoted in Fine, "Cash Money's Midnight Ride," 83.
65. Slim quoted in Tony Green, "Money Changes Everything," *XXL,* Apr. 1999, 70.
66. Quoted in Fine, "Cash Money's Midnight Ride," 82.
67. Alona Wartofsky, "Watching 'Baby' Grow: The Hip-Hop Mogul, Finding Rhyme & Reason to Succeed," *Washington Post,* 13 Apr. 2003, G1.
68. Green, "Money Changes Everything," 67.
69. Jeff Hannusch, "Bobby Marchan, 69, Noted N.O. R&B Artist," *Times-Picayune,* 15 Dec. 1999, B4.
70. Fine, "Cash Money's Midnight Ride," 82.
71. Ibid., 85; Green, "Money Changes Everything," 70.
72. Quoted in Braxton, [Interview with Sporty T].
73. Green, "Money Changes Everything," 67.
74. Aiges, "Home-Grown Bounce Music," 30.
75. Green, "Money Changes Everything," 67.
76. Quoted in Cortello, "Street," Jan. 1996, 24.

77. Farber, "Home-Grown Rap Pays Off."

78. Hillary Crosley, "Wayne's World," *Billboard*, 4 Nov. 2006, 86.

79. Fine, "Cash Money's Midnight Ride," 84.

80. Keith Spera, "Raps to Riches," *Times-Picayune*, 5 Nov. 1999, L24; Keith Spera, "Local Focus: Cash Money Stable 'Bounces' Up the Charts," *Billboard*, 15 Apr. 2000, 40; Fine, "Cash Money's Midnight Ride," 81.

81. "Interview with BG," Murder Dog, [2000?], www.murderdog.com (no longer available).

82. Quoted in Wartofsky, "Watching 'Baby' Grow," G1.

83. Quoted in Farber, "Home-Grown Rap Pays Off."

84. Havelock Nelson, "After Chronic Growing Pains, Hardcore Gains Acceptance," *Billboard*, 27 Nov. 1993, 32.

85. John Soeder, "Juvenile Puts Bounce in Tour of Hip-Hop Superstars," *Cleveland Plain Dealer*, 31 Mar. 2000, Friday section, 16.

86. Quoted in Spera, "Raps to Riches"; quoted in Fine 2000, 87.

87. Quoted in Steve Jones, "Juvenile Spreads His 'Slanguage,'" *USA Today*, 18 Feb. 2000, 2E.

88. Quoted in Fine, "Cash Money's Midnight Ride," 88.

89. Jon Pareles, "Gangsta Rap's Choices in Life, Death and Love," *New York Times*, 29 Feb. 2000, E5.

90. Murray Forman, *The 'Hood Comes First: Race, Space, and Place in Rap and Hip-Hop* (Middletown, Conn.: Wesleyan University Press, 2002), 335.

91. Muhammad, "Hip-Hop Moguls."

92. Quoted in Gail Mitchell, "Six Questions: Universal's Dino Delvaille Discusses the A&R Knack, the Next Big Thing," *Billboard*, 23 Sept. 2000, 38.

93. Keith Spera, "Juvenile Raps About His Storm-Damaged Hometown," Associated Press State & Local Wire, 21 Jan. 2006.

94. Kelefa Sanneh, "Loving, Rapping, Snuggling and. . . ," *New York Times*, 3 Jan. 2005, E1.

95. Fine, "Cash Money's Midnight Ride," 85; Mannie Fresh quoted ibid.

96. Simon Reynolds, "For the Love of Money," *Village Voice*, 30 Nov. 1999, 133; Fine, "Cash Money's Midnight Ride," 88.

97. Mannie Fresh interview by Rap Basement, *Rap News Direct*, www.rapnews.net/0-202-257919-00.html.

98. Sarig, *Third Coast*, 250; Keith Spera, "La. Artists Top the Charts for 2 Weeks in a Row," *Times-Picayune*, 5 Feb. 1999, L8.

99. Quoted in Spera, "La. Artists Top the Charts."

100. Quoted in Green, "Money Changes Everything," 68.

101. Spera, "Raps to Riches," emphasis added.

102. Spera, "La. Artists Top the Charts."

103. Farber, "Home-Grown Rap Pays Off."

104. Steve Jones, "Architects of Today's Sound: Music Producers Are Superstars behind the Scenes, Designing the High-Rise Hits," *USA Today*, 22 Oct. 1999, 1E.

105. Reynolds, "For the Love of Money."

106. Quoted in Fine, "Cash Money's Midnight Ride," 88.

107. Quoted in Spera, "La. Artists Top the Charts."

108. Gail Mitchell, "Change Works at Cash Money," *Billboard*, 21 Aug. 2004, 17.

5. "Lights Out": Stagnation, Decline, and the Resurgence of the Local, 2001–2005

1. Ivory M. Jones, "Lil Jon, 50 Cent, Keys Leads Finalists," *Billboard*, 6 Aug. 2005, 22, 24–25.

2. Magic quoted in Charlie Braxton, "Magic" [interview], *Murder Dog*, 2003, www.murderdog.com (no longer available).

3. Keith Spera, "Pushing the Limit," *Times-Picayune,* 11 June 2000, A1.

4. Braxton, "Magic" [interview].

5. Spera, "Pushing the Limit."

6. Ibid.

7. Mina Patel with Gail Mitchell, "Analysis: What the Charts Say," *Billboard,* 7 Dec. 2002, 54.

8. Miller quoted in Brett Pulley, "Soldier under $iege," *Savoy,* June–July 2002, 78.

9. Pulley, "Soldier under $iege," 75.

10. Rashaun Hall, "Master Builder: Creating an Empire the Old-Fashioned Way," *Billboard,* 16 Mar. 2002, 50.

11. Paul Purpura, "Judge: Remove Cordless Phones: Troubles Have Plagued Rapper's Home Arrest," *Times-Picayune,* 3 Apr. 2009, B2.

12. Quoted in Todd Martens, Phyllis Stark, Hilary Crosley, Leila Cobo, and Jim Bessman, "2006 Power Players," *Billboard,* 5 Aug. 2006, 43.

13. Chris Morris, "Breakthroughs and Swan Songs," *Billboard,* 27 Dec. 2003/3 Jan. 2004, YE58.

14. "No Limit Ends Its Six-Year Distribution Deal with Priority Records," *Business Wire,* 1 Oct. 2001, 1.

15. Quoted in Jeff Leeds, "Hearing Focuses on Language and Violence in Rap Music," *New York Times,* 26 Sept. 2007, A24.

16. Keith Spera, "Bouncing Back," *Times-Picayune,* 7 Jan. 2004, L1.

17. Ibid.

18. Alona Wartofsky, "Watching 'Baby' Grow: The Hip-Hop Mogul, Finding Rhyme & Reason to Succeed," *Washington Post,* 13 Apr. 2003, G1.

19. Gail Mitchell, "Cash Money Sets Up a 'Roun' Table,'" *Billboard,* 2 Oct. 2004, 19–20.

20. Gail Mitchell, "UMVD Stays Ahead," *Billboard,* 17 July 2004, 20.

21. Margena A. Christian, "The Man with the Half-Million Dollar Smile," *Jet,* 28 Aug. 2006, 63; Keith Spera, "Rapper's Gift Saves Troubled School," *Times-Picayune,* 19 Mar. 1999, A1.

22. Michael Perlstein, "Rapper Kept It Real, to His Death," *Times-Picayune,* 22 Mar. 2004, A1.

23. Nine Times Social and Pleasure Club, *Coming Out the Door for the Ninth Ward* (New Orleans: Neighborhood Story Project, 2006), 212–17.

24. Perlstein, "Rapper Kept It Real, to His Death."

25. Michael Perlstein, "DA's Decision Shocks Family of Slain Rapper," *Times-Picayune,* 22 Mar. 2004, A1.

26. Keith Spera, "Take Fo' Turnover," *Times-Picayune,* 18 June 2004, L29.

27. Roni Sarig, *Third Coast: OutKast, Timbaland, and How Hip-Hop Became a Southern Thing* (New York: Da Capo, 2007). 251.

28. Scott Aiges, "Home-Grown Bounce Music Rules Big Easy's Rap Roost," *Billboard,* 19 Mar. 1994, 26.

29. Quoted in Chris Floyd, "Mista Triksta," *Guardian,* 6 Dec. 2003, Weekend Pages, 32.

30. Mackie quoted in Nik Cohn, *Triksta: Life and Death and New Orleans Rap* (New York: Alfred A. Knopf, 2005), 74.

31. Karen Cortello, "Street," *OffBeat,* Jan. 1996, 24.

32. Keith Spera, "Jubilee on Brink of Making It Big," *Times-Picayune,* 7 May 1999, L9.

33. Neil Strauss, "A Trendsetter on Rap's Fringe," *New York Times,* 28 May 2000, section 2, 23.

34. Ibid.

35. Keith Spera, "Up From the Street," *Times-Picayune,* 22 Dec. 2002, L1; John Council, "Fifth Circuit Rules in Battle over Rap Phrase," *Entertainment Law & Finance* 20.11 (2 Feb. 2005), 3.

36. Jessica Koslow, "Choppa: the Hot, New No Limit Soldier," *Rap-Up,* 2003, www.rap-up.com (no longer available).

37. Spera, "Bouncing Back."

38. Elizabeth Wolfson, "Katey Red," *OffBeat*, Sept. 2000, 64.

39. Paul Garon, *Blues & the Poetic Spirit* (New York: Da Capo, 1975), 71; Charles White, *The Life and Times of Little Richard, the Quasar of Rock* (New York: Harmony Books, 1984), 10.

40. Quoted in Alan Lomax, *Mister Jelly Roll: The Fortunes of Jelly Roll Morton, New Orleans Creole and "Inventor of Jazz,"* 2nd ed. (Berkeley: University of California Press, 1973), 45.

41. Danny Barker, *Buddy Bolden and the Last Days of Storyville,* ed. Alyn Shipton (London: Cassell, 1998), 110.

42. Quoted in Tony Scherman, *Backbeat: Earl Palmer's Story* (New York: Da Capo, 1999), 12, 24.

43. Quoted ibid., 94.

44. Barker, *Buddy Bolden,* 107.

45. Touré, "Gay Rappers: Too Real for Hip-Hop?," *New York Times,* 20 Apr. 2003, Section 2, 1.

46. Quoted in Neil Strauss, "A Most Unlikely Star," *New York Times,* 28 May 2000, Section 2, 24.

47. Andy Hopkins, "Katey Red: Punk Under Pressure," *Rocktober,* Winter 2002, 9.

48. Strauss, "A Most Unlikely Star," 24; Craig Seymour, "Yep, They're Gay," *Entertainment Weekly,* 6 Oct. 2000, 44; Liz Armstrong, "The Last Mardi Gras," *Village Voice,* 23 Oct. 2001, 149.

49. Strauss, "A Most Unlikely Star."

50. Matt Alsdorf, "Straight Talk: Sunday, Tranny Sunday." *PlanetOut,* 31 May 2000, www.planetout.com (no longer available).

51. Elizabeth Wolfson, "Katey Red," *OffBeat,* Sept. 2000, 64.

6. Bouncing Back: After Katrina, Toward an Uncertain Future

1. Kelefa Sanneh, "Gangsta Gumbo," *New York Times,* 23 Apr. 2006, Music 1.

2. Campbell Robertson, "Smaller New Orleans after Katrina, Census Shows," *New York Times,* 3 Feb. 2011, A11.

3. Stated in "Rapper Juvenile Returns to New Orleans," *Weekend Edition,* NPR, 6 May 2006, available at http://m.npr.org/news/front/5388518?page=2.

4. Quoted in Daron Crawford and Pernell Russell, *Beyond the Bricks* (New Orleans: Neighborhood Story Project, 2009), 75.

5. Quoted in Nine Times Social and Pleasure Club, *Coming Out the Door for the Ninth Ward* (New Orleans: Neighborhood Story Project, 2006), 183.

6. Keith Spera, "Juvenile Raps About His Storm-Damaged Hometown," Associated Press State & Local Wire, 21 Jan. 2006.

7. Raju Mudhar, "The Katrina Files." *Toronto Star,* 17 Sept. 2005, J3; Zenia Kish, "'My FEMA People': Hip-Hop as Disaster Recovery in the Katrina Diaspora," *American Quarterly* 61.3 (Sept. 2009), 671–92.

8. Kish, "'My FEMA People,'" 676–77.

9. Quoted in Gail Mitchell and Bill Werde, "An Urban Music Industry Ponders a Rapper's Words." *Billboard,* 17 Sept. 2005.

10. Lynne Jensen, "In Tune with Their Community: Local Hip-Hop Artists Help Out, Musicians Gather to Clean St. Roch." *Times-Picayune,* 30 July 2009, B1.

11. Susan Finch and Katy Reckdahl, "Five Are Guilty in Council Protest: They Rallied at N.O. Housing Meeting," *Times-Picayune,* 27 Mar. 2008, B1; Coleman Warner and Gwen Filosa, "Unanimous: Council Votes to Raze 4,500 Units; Old Housing Model to Give Way to Mixed-Income Developments," *Times-Picayune,* 21 Dec. 2007, A1.

12. Dave Walker, "Big Fish in a Smaller Pond: WQUE Is Still No. 1 Local Radio Station, but Just Barely," *Times-Picayune,* 15 Aug. 2006, L1.

13. Laura Checkoway, "The Art of Storytelling," *Vibe Magazine,* Nov. 2007, 116–23, quotation on 118.

14. Quoted ibid.

15. Benjamin Meadows-Ingram, "Touch the Sky." *Vibe Magazine,* May 2008, 87.

16. Ibid., 80.

17. Kish, "'My FEMA People,'" 682.

18. Quoted in Jake Coyle, "Lil Wayne's School of Hard Knocks," *South Florida Sun-Sentinel,* 29 Dec. 2006, Showtime 25.

19. Ned Sublette, *The Year Before the Flood: A Story of New Orleans* (Chicago: Lawrence Hill, 2009), 222.

20. Jonathan Dee, "Neither Straight nor Out of Compton," *New York Times Magazine,* 25 July 2010, 27.

21. Quoted ibid., 28.

22. Quoted in Callie Watts, "Sissy Act," *Bust,* Apr.–May 2010, 67.

23. Sanneh, "Gangsta Gumbo."

24. Roderick Gordon quoted in Crawford and Russell, *Beyond the Bricks,* 29.

25. Quoted in Nine Times Social and Pleasure Club, *Coming Out the Door for the Ninth Ward,* 157.

26. "Barbara Bush Calls Evacuees Better Off," *New York Times,* 7 Sept. 2005, A22.

New Orleans Rap

A Selected Discography

1st Amendment. *1st Amendment.* Ready-Or-Not Records (RON2011), 1992.

2 Blakk. *The Game.* TTH Marketing (41764), 1995.

———. *Represent 4 Life.* Tombstone Records (TR-0006), 1996.

II Marx of Terra. "Take It Off" / "Make My Day." Lamina Records (LR2001), 1992.

———. *Witness the Strength.* Rap Dis! Records (RDR 911), 1993.

2-Sweet. *Ready to Rumble.* Take Fo' Records (701), 1997.

———. *Actin Bad.* Take Fo' Records (702), 1997.

3 N's from the 9th. "Punk Ass Nigga." Totally Dope Records (1718), 1993.

10th Ward Buck. *It's Ya Birthday.* Bigg Face Records, 2003.

———. *A True Bounce Artist.* Bigg Face Records, 2005.

39 Posse. *39 Posse.* Parkway Pumpin Records (PKY-1001), 1991.

———. *39 Automatic.* Parkway Pumpin Records (PKY-1021), 1993.

69 Boyz. "Don't Start No Shh." Home Bass Entertainment (ATT-12036), 1999.

187 Featuring Childs Play. "Hoes Ain't Nuttin But Hoes." Emoja Records (PSY00744), 1993.

Da 187 Klick. *Whoz-N-da House?* Terrible T. Records (TST103), 1994.

B-32 & DJ Crackout. *I Need a Bag of Dope.* Cash Money Records, 1993.

B.G. *Chopper City.* Cash Money Records (CMR-9610), 1997.

———. *It's All On U.* Cash Money Records (CMR-9613), 1997.

———. *It's All On U Vol. 2.* Cash Money Records (CMR-9616), 1997.

———. "Cash Money Is an Army." Cash Money Records (U8P 1354), 1998.

———. "Bling Bling." Cash Money Records (0121156483-1), 1999.

———. *Chopper City in the Ghetto.* Cash Money Records (UD-53265), 1999.

B.G.'z. *True Story.* Cash Money Records (CSH-9503), 1995.

Baby Boy. *Like Dat.* The New Take Fo' Records (TFM-2101), 2003.

Baby T. & Devious D. *Down with the Program.* Soulin' Records, 1989.

———. "Miss Priscilla" / "Street Life." Brutal Records (DJ 1003), 1992.

Bally-B. *Gotta Be Greedy.* Hit 'Em Up Records (HUMR-4441), 1998.

Bally Boyz with Fila Phil. *Bally Boyz.* Slaughterhouse Records (PSY0003CA), 1995.

Battle of the Sissys: Round 1. Too Cold Records, 2002.

Battle of the Sissys: Round 2. Too Cold Records, 2002.

Big Al & Lil Tee. *B***h You Know Who I Am!* Take Fo' Records (TFP-302), 1996.

Big Heavy (as "M.C. Heavy"). "Gangster Walk." Cash Money Records, 1992?

————. *Doggin Em.* RedRum Records (RR112), 1996.

Big Tymers. *Big Tymers.* Cash Money Records (U8P 1466), 1999.

Big Freedia. *Queen Diva.* Money Rules Records (MRE-4141 741331-41412), 2003.

————. *Big Freedia.* Scion Audio/Visual, 2011.

————. "Azz Everywhere." 540 Records (540-020), 2011.

Big Slack. *Ready for Combat.* King's Entertainment, 2002.

Black Kold Madina. *Troubled the Water.* Born Hustler Records (BKM00001), 2008.

Black Menace. *Black Menace.* Prime Suspect Productions (PS 12291), 1992.

————. "Put onna Vest" / "Goin' Off." Prime Suspect Productions (PSP01), 1993.

————. *Drama Time.* Big Boy Records (BBR-0017), 1995.

Black on Track Featuring MC J. *Life in the Ghetto.* Alliv Records (JC 1594), 1991.

BlaqNMild. *Run Dat Beat.* Bigg Face Records, n.d. (2004?)

Born Suspect. *Street Life.* Street Vibe Records (SVR10012-4), 1996.

Bounce Kings: Greatest Vol. I. Sporty Records (SYU-0004), 2001.

Bounce Kings: Greatest Vol. II. Sporty Records (SYU-0005), 2001.

Brown Suga. *Female Thugs.* Street Vibe (1002), 1998.

Bruce Sampson with Chuck Turner and the Traffic Jam Band. "You're Bad." Rosemont Records, 1982.

Bust Down. "Putcha Ballys On" / "Nasty Bitch." Disotell Records (DR291), 1991.

————. *Nasty Bitch, Chapter 1.* Effect Records (E3005-2), 1991.

————. "There It Is." Sheska Records (SH20001), 1997.

By Any Means Necessary. *Take It to the Maximum.* Alliv Records (AR4404), 1992.

Cash Money Millionaires. *Baller Blockin'.* Cash Money Records (012 153 291-2), 2000.

Cheeky Blakk. *Gots 2 Be Cheeky.* Mobo Records (Mobo-16), n.d. (1994?).

————. *Let Me Get That Outcha.* Tombstone Records (0004), 1995.

————. *F**k Bein' Faithful.* Tombstone Records (0007), 1996.

————. *Whores Pimp Niggaz 2.* Total Respect Records (TRR-0409), 1997.

Chev. *Straight off the Ave.: A Sissy with Class.* King's Entertainment (821798-00052-8), 2002.

Choppa. "Choppa Style." Take Fo' Records (TFR-1901), 2001.

————. *Straight from the N.O.* The New No Limit Records (440075007-2), 2003.

————. "Hot Piece." Body Head Entertainment (BDYH 5000), 2004.

Choppa and D.J. Jubilee Present P-Popper/Club Hopper: Take Fo' Superstars Greatest Hits Plus New Songs Vol. 2. Take Fo' Records (TFR-1702), 2002.

C-Murder. *Life or Death.* No Limit Records (P2 50723), 1998.

————. *Bossalinie.* No Limit Records (P2 50035), 1999.

————. *Trapped in Crime.* TRU Records (P2 50083), 2000.

Code 6. *Let's Go Get 'Em.* Ice Mike Entertainment (IME9092), 1998.

The Compilation Album: We G's. Big Boy Records (BBR-0024), 1997.

Cool D. "What's Goin Wrong." Mugz Records (MR2729), 1992.

————. *The Unexpected.* Mr. Tee Records (TC-9401), 1994.

Da' Sha Ra'. "Bootin' Up." Take Fo' Records (TFP 102), 1993.

————. *Still Bootin Up.* Take Fo' Records (TFP 104), 1995.

Daddy Yo. "I'm Not Your Trick Daddy." Sound Express Records (SE2DYR1), 1993.

The Def Boyz. "Three the Hard Way" / "Keep Playin It." Rhythm Street Records (KMT-2), 1990.

Derek B. "Rock the Beat." Profile Records (PRO-7156), 1987.

Devious. *Picture This!* Worth the Wait Recordings (DEV1002), 1993.

Devious & Mellow-Fellow. "Work That Sucka ta Death." Worth the Wait Recordings (DEV1001LP), 1993.

D.J. Chicken. *All Your Favorite Songs Remixxed with 'Dat Beat' Vol. 1.* Arkay Music, 2004.

D.J. Duck. *Duck Remixxes.* Take Fo' Records (TFR-2001), 2001.

D.J. Jimi. "(The Original) Where They At." Soulin' Records (BM2005C), 1992.

———. "Where They At." Avenue Distribution (AVE 1208), 1992.

———. *It's Jimi.* Avenue Distribution (ACD 9105), 1992.

———. "Bounce (For the Juvenille)." Soulin Records (DJ 1213), 1993 ["Featuring D.J. Juvenille"].

———. *I'm Back! I'm Back!* Gamtown Records (CD-7001), 1994.

———. [Undated live recording from the collection of Colin Meneghini, 10:05], n.d. (1992?).

DJ Jubilee. "Stop, Pause (Do the Jubilee All)." Take Fo' Records (TFP 202), 1993.

———. *DJ Jubilee & the Cartoon Crew.* Take Fo' Records (TFP203CD), n.d. (1994).

———. *20 Years in the Jets.* Take Fo' Records, 1996.

———. "Get Ready, Ready!" Take Fo' Records (TFP-205), 1997.

———. *Take It to the St. Thomas.* Take Fo' Records (TFP-206), 1998.

———. *Do Yo Thang Girl.* Take Fo' Records (TFR 207), 2000.

———. *Walk with It.* The New Take Fo' Records (TFM-208), 2004.

DJ Jubilee Presents The Bounce Squad: Bouncing All Over the World. Take Fo' Records (TFP-1501), 2000.

D.J. Lil Daddy. *D.J. Lil Daddy Vol. 1 Featuring Tha A Team: Marked 4 Death.* Uncut Records (UN1-0001), 1997.

D.J. Money Fresh. *Follow the Leader.* Underground Attic Production (UAP-0001), 2001.

——— (as "Money Fresh"). *Triggaland.* Act Bad, 2002.

DJ Mouche: No Bounce, No Party. Ya Boy 'Nem Records (AVL96249), 1996.

DJ Precise. "Shake 'Em Up Shake 'Em." Precise Recordings (PRC1000), 1993.

DJ Ro Presents The Dirty South Boyz: From the Swamps. Don't Even Trip Entertainment (DOF-302), n.d. (1999?).

DJ Tee & Mo' Blakk. *Uptown Niggas.* Knowledge Records, n.d. (1994?).

D.O.A. Featuring the X-Conz. *Life on the Streets Ain't Easy.* Charlot Records, 1991.

Dog House Posse. *Dope Gets No Heavier.* Mobo Records (MOBO9), n.d. (1994?).

Dolemite. *3rd Ward on My Mind.* RedRum Records (RR111), 1995.

——— (as "Doleamite"). *Ruff-N-da Ghetto.* RedRum Records (RR114), 1997.

Don B. Compilation. Bang-N Records (0003), 1998.

Donkey Boyz. *Bust It Open.* Untouchable Records (EP010734), 2001.

Down South Hustlers: Bouncin' and Swingin': Tha Value Pack Compilation. No Limit Records (P2 53993), 1995.

Drama Squad. *P.N.C. Presents The Drama Squad: Chapter One.* South Coast Music Group (SCMG2CD), 1996.

———. *On Front Line: Chapter II.* South Coast Music Group (SCMG-0010), 1999.

East Bank Gangstas. *Problem Solver.* Lil Mac Records, 1995.

E.R.C. *Something for the People*. E.R.C. Records (ERC 0001), 1991.

———. *Handling Business and Then Some*. E.R.C. Records (ERC 02), 1994.

Everlasting Hitman. "Bounce! Baby, Bounce!" Mr. Tee Records (T-92001), 1992.

———. "Work that Back" / "Holla If You Hear Me." Mobo Records (MOBO3), 1995.

EWV. *True Soldiers*. Hi-Powered Records (HPR-0187), 1997.

Face Forever. *R.A.W.* RedRum Records (RR110), 1995.

The Famous Low Down Boys. "Cold Rockin' the Place: Titus Tee" / "M.C. Titus Tee." Rosemont Records (0888), 1988.

Females in Charge (Kimmy P. & Short T.). "Where's My Bitch." Pack Records (DRP-9272), 1992.

Fiend. *Won't Be Denied*. Big Boy Records (BBR-0018), 1995.

———. *There's One in Every Family*. No Limit Records (P2 50715), 1998.

———. *Street Life*. No Limit Records (P2 50107), 1999.

Fila Phil. *Da Hustla*. Slaughter House Records (PSY21117), 1994.

———. *Tha Hustla Returns*. Untouchable Records (UTC-8888), 1997.

Final Approach. *Final Approach*. Mobo Records (MOBO2), 1994.

504 Boyz. "Wobble Wobble." No Limit Records (08724-81350-15), 2000.

———. *Goodfellas*. No Limit Records (P2 50722), 2000.

———. *Ballers*. No Limit Records (440 066 372-2), 2002.

Flesh & Blood. *Flesh & Blood*. Take Fo' Records (TFP401), 1994.

FM. "Gimme What You Got! (For a Pork Chop)." Avenue Distribution (AVE 1212), 1992.

Full Blooded. *Memorial Day*. No Limit Records (P2 50027), 1998.

Full Blooded & H.O.U.N.D. Faculty. *Untamed*. Raw Dawg Entertainment (RXG-2001), 2001.

Full Pack. *9 Cuts Deep*. Pack Records, 1991.

———. "I Like to #@*§!" Brutal Records (BRU 1006), 1993.

Gangsta Boo. "Nasty Trick." Relativity (1784-1), 1999.

Gank D. *Trigga Niggaz*. Southside Records, 1996.

GBU. "Frontin' Ass Niggas." Pack Records (2124), 1993.

The Get It Girls and M.C. Donna. "Get It Boy." WMP Records (888-1), n.d. (1990?).

Ghetto Twinz. *Surrounded by Criminals*. Big Boy Records (BBR-0020), 1995.

———. *In That Water*. Rap-A-Lot Records (7243 8 44438 2 5), 1997.

Girls Talkin Shit. "Juice It" / "Skin Tight." D&D Records (DD 5248), 1988.

Gotti Boi Chris. *Bounce Down 2*. Black House Entertainment (00013), 2005.

G-Quikk. *Da Album*. Solid Entertainment (SOLID8251), 2003.

The Greatest Rap Hits from Down South New Orleans. TTH Marketing Co., n.d. (2000?).

The Greatest Rap Hits from Down South New Orleans, Volume 2. TTH Marketing Co. (700883-2000-2), n.d. (2000?).

Gregory D. *The Real Deal*. RCA (07863 66078-2), 1992.

———. *Niggaz in da Boot*. Midwest Records (MID-1020), 1994.

Gregory D & DJ Mannie Fresh. *Throw Down*. D&D Entertainment (DD5252), 1987.

——— (as "Gregory D & Mannie Fresh"). "Where You From (Party People)" / "Buck Jump Time (Project Rapp)." Uzi Records (9MM-007), 1989.

———. *"D" Rules the Nation.* Yo! Records (X-101-1), 1989.

G-Slimm. *Fours Deuces & Trays.* Big Boy Records (BB0010), 1994.

The Hideout. *War Time: The Album.* Underground Entertainment (0130), 1996.

Hollywood. "Hollywood Swingin'." Mobo Records (MOBO11), 1994.

Hot Boy Ronald. *Walk Like Ronald.* King's Entertainment, 2002.

Hot Boys. *Get It How U Live!!* Cash Money Records (CMR-9614), 1997.

———. *Guerrilla Warfare.* Cash Money Records (UD-53264), 1999.

———. *Let 'Em Burn.* Cash Money Records (422 860 966-2), 2003.

I Got the Hook-Up! No Limit Records (P2 50745), 1998.

I'm Bout It. No Limit Records (P2 50643), 1997.

Ice Mike. "Doin' My Thang" / "He Got Game." C&M Records (CMR001), 1991.

———. *Bring da Heat.* C&M Records (CMR 002), 1991.

———. *True 2 da Game!* Yo! Records (YCT-1237), 1992.

———. *Slammin' Theez Hoz.* 3rd Power Records (IW1001), 1994.

———. *Ghetto.* White Label Music (66126880092), 2001.

Illegal Justice. "6 Ft. Under" / "Drug Related." Lamina Records (LR4001), 1992.

Insane. *Camp 4 Life.* Big Boy Records (BBR-0021), 1995.

J-Dawg. *Smokin' & Rollin'.* Big Boy Records (BBR-0025), 1997.

———. *The Dawg House.* Big Boy Records (BBR-0026), 1997.

Joe Blakk. "It Ain't Where Ya From." Mercenary Records (MR01), 1993.

———. "J.B.'s Revenge." Mercenary Records (MR595181), 1994.

———. *Blood, Sweat & Tears.* Blakk Magiq Entertainment (6 60539-0009-2 8), 1998.

Joe Blakk Featuring The Rebirth Brass Band. "Caught in the Crossfire." Mercenary Records (MR59519), 1995.

The Jones and Taylor Experience. "Mardi Gras, Down in New Orleans: It's Carnival (Mardi Gras Rap)." Soulin' Records (2001), 1985.

Josephine Johnny. "Workin' wit Sumthin." Jam Tight Records (JGH-4660), 2000.

Ju'C. "P.E.B. (Eat the Cat)." Ready-Or-Not Records (RON1011), 1993.

———. *It's Gotta Be Ju'C.* Ready-Or-Not Records (RON3011), 1993.

Junie Bezel. *That's How Mess Get Started.* Take Fo' Records (TFR 1801), 2001.

Juvenile. *Being Myself.* Warlock Records (WARCD-2748), 1994.

———. *Solja Rags.* Cash Money Records (UD-53166), 1997.

———. *400 Degreez.* Cash Money Records (UD-53162), 1998.

———. "Ha." Cash Money Records (U12 56234), 1999.

———. "Follow Me Now" / "Back that Azz Up." Cash Money Records (U8P 1483), 1999.

———. *Tha G-Code.* Cash Money Records (314 542 179-2), 1999.

———. *Project English.* Cash Money Records (422 810 913 2), 2001.

———. *Juve the Great.* Cash Money Records (B0001717-02), 2003.

———. *Reality Check.* Atlantic (83790), 2006.

Katey Red. *Melpomene Block Party.* Take Fo' Records (TFP1101), 1999.

———. *Y2 Katey: The Millennium Sissy.* Take Fo' Records (TFR-1102), 2000.

K.C. Redd. *It's a G Thang.* Take Fo' Records (TFP 901), 1999.

Kilo. *Too Cold to Be a Hot Boy.* Underground Attic Records (UA-0026), 2001.

———. *Evolution.* Untouchable Records (UR-2222), 2002.

Kilo G. *The Sleepwalker.* Cash Money Records, 1992.

———. *The Bloody City.* Cash Money Records (CMR-9506), 1995.

The "L." *Black Robinhood.* Hard Head Records (BR91971), 1993.

——— (as "L The Black Robin Hood"). *True 2 Life.* Solar Music Group (SMG 35501), 1996.

——— (as "M.C. 'L.' "). *Keep Steppin 1997 Ward.* Bally Boy Records, 1997.

Lady Red. *Lady Red.* Hi Powered Records (HPR-1430), 1996.

———. *Hi A Lady.* Hi Powered Records (HPR-4301), 1998.

Lady Unique. "Froggy Style." Top Down Records (TDR 101CD), 1997.

Lil' E. *Who's Rulin'.* Slaughter House Records (PSY0002), 1995.

Lil Elt. "Get the Gat." Parkway Pumpin Records (PKY1011), 1992.

Lil Elt, DJ Tee. *Uptown.* In the House Records (ITHR98302C), 1993.

Lil Goldie. *Act a Donkey on A.* Mobo Records (MOBO 22), 1997.

Lil' Ron the Bossman. "Cold But Fair." Mugz Records (MR7001), 1993.

Lil Slim. "Bounce Slide Ride." Cash Money Records (BSR01), 1993.

———. *The Game Is Cold.* Cash Money Records, 1993.

———. *Powder Shop.* Cash Money Records (CSH-4034), 1994.

———. *Thug'n & Pluggin.* Cash Money Records (CMR0092), 1995.

Lil Soldiers. *Boot Camp.* No Limit Records (P2 50038), 1999.

Lil Wayne. *Tha Block Is Hot.* Cash Money Records (012 153 919-2), 1999.

———. *500 Degreez.* Cash Money Records (440 060 058-2), 2002.

———. *Lights Out.* Cash Money Records (422 860 911-2), 2000.

———. *Tha Carter.* Cash Money Records (B0001537-02), 2004.

———. *Tha Carter II.* Cash Money Records (B0005124-02), 2005.

———. *Tha Carter III.* Cash Money Records (B0011033-02 IN02), 2008.

———. *I Am Not a Human Being.* Young Money Entertainment (B001500202), 2010.

Lil Ya. *Another Massacre.* Hard Times Records (681507-9999-2), 1999.

L.O.G. *G's & Soldiers.* Tombstone Records (0008), 1996.

———. *Camouflaged Down.* Untouchable Records (UTC-1001), 1997.

Lokee. *I Got Dis.* Tombstone Records (0002), 1995.

———. *Voodoo Gangsta Funk.* Tombstone Records (0005), 1996.

Lower Level Organization. *Wanted by Five-O, Feared by Most.* Mobo Records (MOBO4), 1992.

Mac (as "Lil' Mac"). *Lyrical Midget.* Yo! Records (YO-1231), 1990.

———. *Shell Shocked.* No Limit Records (P2 50727), 1998.

———. *World War III.* No Limit Records (P2 50109), 1999.

Mafia Causin' Pain. *Chillin Lika Villain.* Road Dog Records (RD3358), 1994.

———. *Das' Real.* Road Dog Records (RDRC01), 1995.

Magic. *Skys the Limit.* No Limit Records (P2 50017), 1998.

———. *Thuggin'.* No Limit Records (P2 50110), 1999.

———. *White Eyes.* The New No Limit Records (422 860 993-2), 2003.

Magnolia Shorty. "Monkey on tha Dick." Cash Money Records (CMR-9611), 1996.

Marvelous & Peaches. "Wobble on da' Stick." Mobo Records (MOBO 0029), 1999.

Master P. *Get Away Clean.* No Limit Records (NLR-1001), 1991.

———. *Mama's Bad Boy.* No Limit Records (NLR 1004-2), 1992.

———. *The Ghettos Tryin to Kill Me!* No Limit Records (NLR0188), 1994.

———. *99 Ways to Die.* No Limit Records (NLR9901), 1995.

———. *Ice Cream Man.* No Limit Records (P1 53978), 1996.

————. *Ghetto D.* No Limit Records (P2 50659), 1997.

————. *MP da Last Don.* No Limit Records (P2 53538), 1998.

————. *Only God Can Judge Me.* No Limit Records (P2 50092), 1999.

————. *Ghetto Postage.* No Limit Records (P2 26008), 2000.

————. *Gameface.* The New No Limit Records (422 860 977-2), 2001.

————. *Good Side, Bad Side.* Koch Records (KOC-LP-5717), 2004.

Warren Mayes. "Get It Girl." Manicure Records (9005x10), 1989.

————. "Get It Girl (Don't Stop)." Atlantic Records (0-86049, ST-DM-60089-SP), 1991.

————. *Doin' Them Right.* Touchdown Records (DRP-9202), 1992.

———— (as "Warren Mays"). "Back for the 94" / "Represent Yourself." Party Time Records, 1994.

————. *Canivin' Boys.* Hot Crescent Records, 1995.

———— (as "Warren Mays") and Da Posse. *Ain't No Stoppin' Us Now: See Me When I Get There.* Bomb Records, n.d. (1999).

M.C. Dice & the Everloaded Posse. *M.C. Dice & the Everloaded Posse.* Mugz Records (MR4001), 1993.

M.C. Dice. "Rock City" / "Special Man." Mugz Records (MR2730), 1992.

M.C. Express. "Get Busy!!" MaDoNo Records (DRP-8810), 1987.

M.C. E. "Lick the Cat." Avenue Distribution (AVE 1214), 1993.

M.C. "J." "5.0's on My Back" / "Rest In Peace." Lamina Records (LR8001), 1992.

MC J' Ro' J. "Let's Jump." Rosemont Records (RRS 1288), 1988.

———— (as "MC JRoJ"). "Ain't Nuthin Nice." Emoja Records, n.d. (1990?).

M.C. Possie. "Chillin at the Crib" / "Drugs." Sounds Unlimited, 1988.

M.C. Spud. *Undertaker.* Triple Beam Records (TBR-0001), 1996.

————. *Gettin Blowed.* Street Playa Records (SPR-0001), 1997.

MC Spud & D.J. Def. "Holla If Ya Hear Me." Mobo Records (MOBO10), 1993.

MC Spud & the Mob. *MC Spud & the Mob.* Party Time Records, n.d. (1991?).

M.C. Thick. "What the F— Are They Yellin." Alliv Records (AR001), 1991.

————. "Marrero (What the F— They Be Yellin)." Atlantic Records (PR4310), 1991.

————. *The Show Ain't Over till the Fatman Swings.* Big Beat Records (7 14220-2), 1993.

————. "They Told Me." Boss Records (BOSS395LP), 1995.

MC T-Tucker. "Let the Booty Shake" / "Where Dey At? Part II," T-Tucker Prod. 71664TTP, 1994.

M.C. T. Tucker & DJ Irv. "Where Dey At." Charlot Records, 1991.

————. "Where Dey At." Steppin' Records (1/2), 1991.

————. [Undated live recording from the collection of Colin Meneghini, 26:25], n.d. (1992?).

Mercedes. *Rear End.* No Limit Records (P2 50085), 1999.

Mia X. "Ask Them Niggas." Lamina Records (LR9001), 1992.

————. "Da Payback." Lamina Records (LR9002), 1993.

————. *Mommie Dearest.* Emoja Records / Slaughter House Records (PSY11117), 1995.

————. *Good Girl Gone Bad.* No Limit Records (PCDS-53988), 1995.

————. *Unlady Like.* No Limit Records (P2 50705), 1997.

———. *Mama Drama*. No Limit Records (P2 53502), 1998.

Mic Fox & Ya Boy Wild Wayne. "Queing with Q93." Cash Money Record Family (AVL94076), 1994.

Mo B. Dick. *Gangsta Harmony*. No Limit Records (P2 50721), 1999.

Mobo Click. Mobo Records (MOBO-17), n.d. (1996).

Mobo Click: Brand New Funk. Mobo Joe Records (MOBO JOE-21), n.d. (1997).

Da Mobstas. *Tripple Beam*. Tombstone Records (0001), 1994.

Money Rules: The Takeover. Money Rules Records, 2003.

Most Wanted Posse. "It Was a Westbank Thing." Mugz Records (MR2728), 1992.

———. "Protect the Innocent and Punish the Guilty" / "Whatcha In For." Mugz Records (MR2731), 1992.

——— (as "Most Wanted"). *Make It Happen*. Wanted Records (AVL93134C), 1993.

Mr. Ivan. *187 In "a" Hockey Mask*. Cash Money Records (AVL-94274), 1994.

———. *Resurrection*. Bang-n Records (0005), 1999.

Mr. Marcelo. *Brick Livin*. No Limit Records (CDPTY 202), 2000.

Mr. Serv-On. *Life Insurance*. No Limit Records (P2 50717), 1997.

———. *Da Next Level*. No Limit Records (P2 50045), 1999.

Ms. Tee. "Chillin on tha Corner." Cash Money Records (MTC1993D), 1993.

———. "Hit the Road." Cash Money Records (AVL95042), 1995.

———. *Having Thing$!!* Cash Money Records (CSH-1995), 1995.

———. *Female Baller*. Cash Money Records (CMR-9608), 1996.

———. *Don't Get Mad, Get Even*. South Coast Music Group (SCMG-0018), 2001.

———. *Pimp Mama*. Big Dog / Big House Entertainment, 2003.

M.V.P. "In tha Projects." Big Boy Records (BB0005), 1994.

Mystikal. *Mystikal*. Big Boy Records (BBR0012), 1995.

———. *Mind of Mystikal*. Jive/Zomba Recording Corporation (01241-41581), 1995.

———. *Unpredictable*. Jive/Zomba Recording Corporation/No Limit Records (01241-41620-2), 1997.

———. *Ghetto Fabulous*. Jive/Zomba Recording Corporation/No Limit Records (01241-41655), 1998.

———. *Let's Get Ready*. Jive/Zomba Recording Corporation (01241-41696), 2000.

———. *Tarantula*. Jive/Zomba Recording Corporation (01241-41770), 2001.

New Jack Macks. "New Jack Summer Jam." Terrible T Records (TCP101), 1993.

Ninja Crew. "We Destroy" / "Baby T Rock." 4-Sight Records (3-86-FS-11), 1986.

Notoriou$ Nate. *A Master Mind of a Career Criminal*. Steppin' On Toes Records (6768C), n.d. (1992?).

N.P.C. "Georgia Bounce." Critique Records (EPID3478321), 1994.

Off tha Corna. *The Killing Is Real*. Hollow Point Records (UJ9963FC), 1992.

P.M.W. "The Big Man." Cash Money Records (TBM01), 1993.

——— (as "The Original P.M.W."). *Legalize "Pass tha Weed."* Cash Money Records (CSH-0464), 1993.

———. *High Life*. Cash Money Records (CSH-9420), 1994.

———. "Back Up Off Me." Cash Money Records (PMW1995), 1995.

Papadoc. "It's All About Yo Lips!" Pack Records (PAPA 1000), 1992.

Parlez. "Make It, Shake It Do It Good!" SuperDome Records (150), 1983.

Partners-N-Crime. "Pussy N a Can (Fuck U & L.V.)" / "Ride It Roll It." Big Boy Records (BB0003), n.d. (1994?).

———. *Partners-N-Crime*. Big Boy Records (BB0004), 1994.

———. *PNC3*. Big Boy Records (BB0011), 1995.

———. *Pump tha Party (Puttin' in Work)*. Big Boy Records (BB0019), 1995.

———. "N.O. Block Party (They Don't Like That)." South Coast Records (SC-MG7LP), 1998.

———. *What'cha Wanna Do?* South Coast Music Group (SCMG-0006), 1998.

———. *We Be Hound'n*. South Coast Music Group (SCMG-0012), 1999.

———. *World Premiere*. South Coast Music Group (SCMG-0019), 2001.

Partners N Crime Presents Hard Hitaz Compilation: Bases Loaded Vol. 1. Crime Labb Entertainment, 2002.

Party @ the Luau: Take Fo' Superstars Greatest Hits Plus New Songs Volume 1. Take Fo' Records (TFR1701), 2000.

Cameron Paul. *Beats & Pieces*. Mixx-it (CP-BP), 1987.

Peacachoo. *Bounce Down*. Black House Entertainment (638466), 2004.

Pimp Daddy. "Got to Be Real." Pack Records (DRP-9301), 1993.

———. *Still Pimpin'*. Cash Money Records (CSH 5000), 1994.

———. *Pimp'n Ain't E-Z*. Cash Money Records (CMR-9607), 1996.

Pimp Dogg. *Forever Loaded*. Untouchable Records (5556), 1994.

———. *Who's that Aggin*. Hollygrove Records (HGR1), 1996.

Precious T. "You Found Love" / "Diva of Rap." Jakia Productions (NR 17185), 1987.

Prime Time. *Hound Out*. South Coast Music Group (SCMG-0017), 2001.

Willie Puckett. *Doggie Hopp*. Take Fo' Records (801), 1997.

———. *Million Dollar Hotboy*. Take Fo' Records (TFP 802), 1998.

Ragtop. "Ragtime" / "The Gambler" / "F*ckin." Ready-Or-Not Records (AVL92048), 1992.

Da Rangaz. *All Night Flightaz*. Last Chance Records (LC3000), 1999.

Raw & Uncut Vol. 1. Keyz Entertaiment, 2002.

Raw II Survive. *West Syde Gz*. Untouchable Records (5555), 1995.

Real G.B.Z. *Real G.B.Z*. Terrible T Records (TST104), 1994.

Rebirth Brass Band (as "Rebirth Jazz Band"). *Here to Stay!* Arhoolie Records (1092), 1984.

———. *Feel Like Funkin' It Up*. Rounder Records (2093), 1989.

———. *Hot Venom*. Mardi Gras Records (MG 1053), 2001.

Recon. *Makin Moves*. South Coast Music Group (SS-0011), 1999.

Ricky B. *B for Bounce*. Mobo Records (MOBO 1), 1994.

———. "City Streets (Hey Pocky Way)." Mobo Records (MOBO 00), 1995.

———. *Ricky B*. Mobo Entertainment (MOBO-19), 1995.

Rockers Revenge. "My '9' and My Beeper." Big "T's" Records (KMT-1), 1989.

Rockshee. *Rockshee's My Name*. Alliv Records (AR4405), 1992.

Ruthless Juveniles. *Hard as tha' F**k*. Mobo Records (MOBO6), 1992.

———. *Hard as tha' F**k II*. Mobo Records (MOBO20), 1995.

R.Y.P. "Straighten It Out." TTH Marketing Co. (AVL94175), 1994.

S.A.C. Mafia. *Socca Ballin'*. Untouchable Records (1003), 1998.

The SD's. "Watch the Clock." J.B.'s Records (173), n.d. (between 1980 and 1984).

Sess 4-5. *Nuthin But Fire.* Nuthin But Fire Records, 2004.

Short T. & Daddy Yo. "Both Sides of the Story." Flip Side Records (STDY1124), 1994.

The Showboys. "Drag Rap." Profile Records (PRO-7111), 1986.

Silkk the Shocker (as "Silkk"). *The Shocker.* No Limit Records (P2 50591), 1996.

———. *Charge It 2 da Game.* No Limit Records (P2 50716), 1998.

———. *Made Man.* No Limit Records (P2 50003), 1999.

———. *My World, My Way.* No Limit Records (P2 23221), 2001.

———. *Based on a True Story.* Koch Records (KOC-CD-5758), 2004.

Silky Slim. "Sister Sister." Profile Records (PRO-7377), 1992.

——— (as "Silky"). *Bouncing in a 6 Tray.* Big Boy Records (BB0007), 1994.

Sissy Nobby. *What Is It?* Money Rules Records, 2002.

———. "Lay Me Down." Mixpak (MIX003), 2010.

Skull Dugrey. *Hoodlum fo' Life.* No Limit Records (P2 50543), 1996.

Slugga. *The Rookie of the Year.* King's Entertainment, 2004.

Slugged Up Niggas. "Slugged Up Killa." Parkway Pumpin Records, 1994.

Smoke 1 Click. *Ruff Rugid & Raw.* Smoke 1 Records (SMK18767), 1996.

Snoop Dogg. *Da Game Is to Be Sold, Not to Be Told.* No Limit Records (P2 50000), 1998.

Soulja Slim (as "Magnolia Slim"). *Soulja fa Lyfe.* Parkway Pumpin Records (PKY 2010), 1994.

——— (as "Magnolia Slim"). *Dark Side.* Hype Enough Records (HYPE 102), 1995.

———. *Give It 2 'Em Raw.* No Limit Records (P2 53547), 1998.

———. *The Streets Made Me.* No Limit South (NLS2001), 2001.

South Coast Shorty. *The Hot Girl.* South Coast Music Group (SCMG-0005), 1997.

Sporty T. "Sporty Talk-n-Sporty 93." Big Boy Records (BB0001), 1993.

———. *Big Balla: Jackin' for Bounce '94.* Big Boy Records (BB0006), 1994.

———. *It's All Good.* Big Boy Records (BB0015), 1995.

———. *Street Soldier.* Big Boy Records (BBR-0028), 1997.

Stag. "That's the Way of the World." Lamina Records (LR3001), 1992.

———. "Dance the Way You Like Making Love" / "Pop That Booty." Lamina Records (LR5001), 1992.

Stop Inc. "Second Line." JB's Records (2602), n.d.

Tec-9. *Straight from tha Ramp!!* Cash Money Records (TEC99504), 1995.

———. *Ready 4 War.* Take Fo' Records (TFP-1601-2), 2000.

Tim Smooth. *I Gotsta' Have It.* Yo! Records (YO-1235), 1991.

———. *Straight Up Driven 'Em.* Rap-A-Lot Records (P2 53891), 1994.

———. *Da Franchise Player.* Mobo Records (MOBO 0027), 1998.

———. *Let It Be Written.* Camped Out Records (COR-0001), 1999.

Too Loaded Records Presents The South Coast Compilation: Str-8-Ballin. 2 Loaded Records (TLR-9702), 1997.

Too Short. "I Ain't Trippin'." (Jive 1232-1-JD), 1988.

Tre-8. *Fright Night.* Smoke 1 Records (SMK18700), 1995.

———. *I Fadem All.* Smoke 1 Records (SOR-0001), 1996.

———. *Nuttin but Drama.* Smoke 1 Records / South Coast Music Group (SCMG0008), 1998.

———. *Armageddon.* Smoke 1 Records (13853-0003-2), 1999.

TRU. (as "The Real Untouchables"). "Christmas in the Ghetto." No Limit Records (NLR 1225), 1992.

———. *Who's da Killer?* No Limit Records (NLR187), 1993.

———. "Living That Life" / "I'm Bout It, Bout It." No Limit Records (DPRO 50914), 1995.

———. *True.* No Limit Records (P1 53983), 1995.

———. *Tru 2 da Game.* No Limit Records (P2 50660), 1997.

———. *Da Crime Family.* No Limit Records (P2 50010), 1999.

———. *The Truth.* Koch Records (KOC-CD-5790), 2005.

———. *Understanding the Criminal Mind.* No Limit Records (NLR 1006), 1992.

U.N.L.V. *6th & Baronne.* Cash Money Records (CSH-6000), 1993.

———. *Straight Out tha Gutta.* Cash Money Records (CSH-0003), 1994.

———. *Mac Melph Calio.* Cash Money Records (CSH-0187), 1995.

———. *Uptown 4 Life.* Cash Money Records (CMR-9609), 1996.

———. *Greatest Hits with New Songs.* Cash Money Records (CMR-9615), 1997.

———. *The Return of U.N.L.V.: Trend Setters.* Blazin South Records, 2001.

———. *Keep It Gutta.* B Real Entertainment, 2003.

Urban Blues Vol. 2: New Orleans Bounce. Imperial Records (LM-94004), 1970.

Vockah Redu and Tha Cru. *Can't Be Stopped.* C2K Entertainment (C2K001), 2000.

Weebie. *Show the World.* Mobo Records (MOBO 0031), 1999.

West Bank Coalition. *West Bank Coalition.* Emoja/Psychopathic Records (PSY00783), 1993.

Wet Boys. *Get Wet.* Sporty Records/White Label/Me & Mine Entertainment (MXM-9004-2), 2000.

Da Wild Boyz. *Time for da Real.* Go Get Em Records (72435-25042-1-3), 2000.

Wild Gyrlz Reprezentin. *Female Maffia.* No Mursy Records, 1998.

Xcel N Choice. *Xcel N Choice.* Pack Records (DRPC9315), 1993.

Index

Page numbers in italics refer to illustrations.

Matt Miller was born in St. Louis, Missouri, in 1969, and spent most of his childhood in Charlotte, North Carolina. He moved to Atlanta in 1988 to attend college at Emory University, where he majored in Spanish. After several years working as a cataloger at the Woodruff Library, he earned a PhD in American studies at Emory's Institute of Liberal Arts. He has published articles on New Orleans rap and on southern rap in general, focused around the idea of the "Dirty South." He codirected the documentary film *Ya Heard Me* (2008), a full-length portrait of New Orleans's rap scene and its history. A longtime musician and collector of recordings, he continues to be involved in a variety of bands and other music-related projects. He currently lives in Atlanta with his wife and two daughters and teaches at Emory University.